THE POLITICS OF IMMIGRATION IN WESTERN EUROPE

Edited by
MARTIN BALDWIN-EDWARDS
and
MARTIN A. SCHAIN

FRANK CASS

First published 1994 in Great Britain by
FRANK CASS & CO. LTD
Newbury House, 890–900 Eastern Avenue
Newbury Park, Ilford, Essex IG2 7HH

and in the United States of America by
FRANK CASS
c/o International Specialized Book Services, Inc.,
5804 N.E. Hassalo Street,
Portland, Oregon 97213–3644

British Library Cataloguing in Publication Data
Politics of Immigration in Western
Europe. – (Journal of West European
Politics, ISSN 0140–2382)
I. Baldwin-Edwards, Martin II. Schain,
Martin A. III. Series
325.4

ISBN 0–7146–4593–1 (hardback)

ISBN 0–7146–4137–5 (paperback)

Library of Congress Cataloging-in-Publication Data
The politics of immigration in Western Europe / edited by Martin
Baldwin-Edwards and Martin A. Schain.
p. cm.
"First appeared in a special issue on 'The Politics of immigration
in Western Europe' of West European politics, vol. 17, no. 2 (April
1994)" – T.p. verso.
Includes bibliographical references.
ISBN 0-7146-4593-1 (cloth) – ISBN 0-7146-4137-5 (paper)
1. Europe – Emigration and immigration – Government policy.
I. Baldwin-Edwards, Martin, 1956– II. Schain, Martin A., 1940–
JV7590.P66 1994
325′.24 – dc20 94–11485
CIP

This group of studies first appeared in a Special Issue on 'The Politics of Immigration in Western Europe' of *West European Politics*, Vol. 17, No. 2 (April 1994), published by Frank Cass & Co. Ltd.

Typeset by Florencetype Ltd, Kewstoke, Avon
Printed in Great Britain by Redwood Books, Trowbridge, Wiltshire

Contents

For Harry Schain, an American son
of European immigrants;
and in memory of Valerie Burman,
a long-suffering and dedicated mother.

ACKNOWLEDGEMENTS

The Editors would like to thank Ms Jennifer Bell of New York University for her substantial editorial assistance, as well as the scholars who reviewed (anonymously) the articles for this volume.

The Politics of Immigration: Introduction

MARTIN BALDWIN-EDWARDS and MARTIN A. SCHAIN

Immigration has emerged as a powerful political issue throughout all of Western Europe during the past decade. Hardly a day passes without some new revelation of an act of violence, an electoral change, the emergence of a new political party or association, or the debate of some policy initiative in a major European country. Indeed, in ways that were wholly unexpected just a few years ago, every aspect of political life has been touched by the issue of immigration. In every country in Western Europe, new movements have emerged, anti-immigrant political parties have gained electoral strength and have altered the balance of political forces. This new balance has influenced policy changes as governments have attempted to deal with challenges that threaten understandings and agreements which have existed for decades. The emergence of the issue of immigration has influenced the way in which European governments perceive and deal with such diverse problems as economic growth and change, social policy, security, and the political construction of Europe.

This Special Issue of *West European Politics* is devoted to an analysis of how immigration has emerged as a political issue, how the politics of immigration have been constructed, and what have been the consequences of this construction for politics in Western Europe. As we can see from the articles in this Special Issue, what has been termed the issue of immigration in fact involves far more than the flow of migrants legally entering Western Europe. It also involves asylum-seekers, residents without papers and the numerous foreigners and people of foreign origin who have been resident in Western Europe for many years and (in some countries) for several generations. The word 'immigration' has often been applied to ethnic relations in what is becoming a *de facto* multi-cultural Europe. Mass publics perceive a vast increase in the presence of immigrants and the cross-border flow of migrants during the past five years. In fact, whatever the political validity of the perception, the reality is far more complex.

TABLE 1

PERCENTAGE OF FOREIGN POPULATION IN SELECTED OECD COUNTRIES

	1980	1982	1984	1986	1988	1990
AUSTRIA	3.7	4.0	3.6	3.6	3.9	5.3
BELGIUM	9.0	9.0	9.1	8.6	8.8	9.1
FRANCE		6.8				6.4
GERMANY	7.2	7.6	7.1	7.4	7.3	8.2
ITALY	0.5	0.6	0.7	0.8	1.1	1.4
NETHERLS.	3.7	3.8	3.9	3.9	4.2	4.6
U.K.			2.8	3.2	3.2	3.3

Source: SOPEMI, *Trends in International Migration* (Paris: OECD, 1992), p. 131.

TRENDS IN EUROPEAN IMMIGRATION

Legal immigration into Western Europe has been low if steady since the oil crisis of the 1970s, when most countries restricted immigration from non-European Community countries. During the decade of the 1980s, the percentage of foreign legal residents in Western Europe increased slightly (see Table 1), with the largest proportionate increases in Norway, the Netherlands, Switzerland and Austria. In absolute terms, the foreign population increased most in Germany and actually declined in France. However, these figures must be read in the context of the low rate of naturalisation in Germany and the relatively high rate in France.

The legally present foreign population of Italy increased threefold during the 1980s, but remained under 800,000. Perhaps more important, for the first time in modern history, Italy, along with other southern European countries, in the past decade has become a country of net immigration rather than of emigration. Despite these changes, the overall distribution of foreigners across Europe has remained largely unchanged, with the vast majority located in Germany and France, followed by the UK, Switzerland and Belgium.

Starting in the late 1980s, new flows of migrants have occurred.[1] These include increases in both family reunion and guestworkers; flows

TABLE 2

ASYLUM SEEKERS INTO SELECTED OECD COUNTRIES (THOUSANDS)

	1980	1982	1984	1986	1988	1990	1991
AUSTRIA	9.3	6.3	7.2	8.6	15.8	22.8	27.3
BELGIUM	2.7	3.1	3.7	7.6	4.5	13.0	15.2
FRANCE	18.8	22.5	21.6	26.2	34.3	54.7	50.0
GERMANY	107.8	37.2	35.3	99.7	103.1	193.1	256.1
ITALY			4.6	6.5	1.4	4.7	27.0
NETHRLDS.	1.3	1.2	2.6	5.9	7.5	21.2	21.6
U.K.	9.9	4.2	3.9	4.8	5.7	30.0	57.7

Source: SOPEMI, *Trends in International Migration* (Paris: OECD, 1992), p. 132.

from Eastern Europe, mainly affecting Germany and Austria; largely illegal migration, mostly originating from Africa, into the southern European countries; and a marked increase in the number of asylum-seekers.

Asylum-seekers

The number of asylum seekers increased dramatically in the late 1980s (see Table 2). The largest increase in absolute numbers was in newly unified Germany, although proportionately short-term influxes were greater in Belgium and the UK. Even before unification, more asylum-seekers were entering Germany than the rest of the European Community. With the collapse of communist regimes in the Soviet Union and Eastern Europe, and with the expansion of the war in former Yugoslavia, the number of asylum-seekers grew rapidly in every country in Western Europe. This was particularly true in Germany, but only in Germany and Sweden did the number continue to increase through 1992. In France, the number of asylum-seekers declined after 1989, in Spain after 1990, and in the UK, Italy and Austria after 1991.

The decrease in the number of asylum-seekers is generally a result of legal and administrative changes that have made it more difficult for kers actually to enter countries in Western Europe and also gee status. These changes include, at the national level, such carrier or airline sanctions; strict visa requirements; penal- undocumented asylum-seekers; the invention of so-called nal zones in airports, circumventing both constitutional requirements and international legal obligations; the notion of 'safe countries' of first asylum, generally defined as those countries signatory to the 1951 Geneva Convention and 1967 Protocol; the concept of 'safe countries of origin', denying access to asylum procedures; and accelerated procedures, which deny a full hearing for the applicant.[2]

At the transnational level, both the Schengen Treaty and the Dublin Convention incorporate many of these devices, as well as addressing the issue of multiple refugee applications. Indeed, it is clear that the evolution of these institutions is intrinsically bound up with the desire of national governments not only to keep away asylum-seekers but also to evade judicial control.[3]

The US Committee for Refugees reports recognition rates in 1992 that range from about 28 per cent for France to 6.5 per cent for Spain to 4.5 per cent for Italy and Germany, to 3.2 per cent for the UK. In all cases these rates have been declining.[4] However, the trend across Europe has been to award proportionately more of certain inferior categories of recognition – humanitarian status, category B, or 'exceptional leave to remain' in the UK. These non-Convention statuses confer considerably fewer rights than full refugee status.

Illegal Immigrants

Illegal immigration has been widespread throughout Western Europe in the postwar period, yet it is only recently that unanimous condemnation of the phenomenon has been voiced, in the context of increased immigratory pressures. Nevertheless, illegal labour forms a significant part of almost all industrialised economies; it can be argued[5] that entire sectors of economies would not exist without illegal workers. This is most true in the case of less developed southern Europe; but generally, there is a political tension between the economic benefits of 'free market' illegal labour and liberal democratic norms.

Illegal migrants gain admission by many different routes, and also for different reasons, making it difficult to characterise and to estimate. It has been suggested that more than 75 per cent of refused asylum-seekers remain illegally;[6] other commentators point to 'overstayers' (students and tourists) as a significant proportion of illegal residents;[7] clearly, weak immigration controls combined with a large informal economy and geographical proximity to North Africa make southern Europe

TABLE 3

ESTIMATE OF ILLEGALLY PRESENT NON-NATIONALS IN 1991

	ILLEGAL MIGRANTS [persons who did not enter as asylum-seekers	ILLEGAL REFUGEES [refused asylum-seekers whose presence is not tolerated]
France	200,000	
Germany	350,000	300,000
Italy	600,000	
Spain	300,000	
Switzerland	100,000	
Other	400,000	350,000
TOTAL	1,950,000	650,000

Source: W.R. Böhning, 'Integration and Immigration Pressures in Western Europe', *International Labour Review* 130 (4), 1991, p. 450.

a prime location for illegal migration.[8] Perhaps one generalisation is valid, though: that restrictions on legal immigration have had the inevitable consequence of promoting illegal migration.

Estimates of the extent of illegal immigrants in Western Europe are difficult to obtain or verify. The ILO estimated for 1991 that there were 2,600,000 illegal residents representing some 14 per cent of the total foreign population (see Table 3). The countries most affected seem to be Germany, with 650,000 and Italy with 600,000.

Policy responses to the phenomenon are two-pronged.[9] Regularisation programmes provide a legal amnesty for illegals, satisfying certain conditions such as entry before a specified date, good health, regular employment, a valid passport, *inter alia*. Deportation programmes and penalties for employers constitute the other policy response; also, more efficient policing of borders in Spain and Italy appears to have had some impact on illegal immigration. Italy, France, the UK, Belgium, the

Netherlands, Austria, Spain and Sweden have all enacted various regularisation programmes in the period 1971–91; Germany has resisted, on the grounds that it would encourage illegal migration.[10]

PUBLIC PERCEPTIONS

In general, mass publics have been less than receptive to changing patterns of immigration. According to the latest Eurobarometer survey on attitudes towards immigration,[11] a majority of respondents (52 per cent) across the European Community feel that there are too many non-EC immigrants. This shows little change from both 1991 and 1992 surveys; however, individual countries exhibit more complicated trends. In countries in which immigration has been high since the Second World War (West Germany, France, Belgium and the UK), this trend has been evident for the past two decades. Opposition to the presence of Third World immigrants has been spreading more recently even to countries in which immigration is low but increasing, such as Greece, Italy and the former East Germany.

On the other hand, none of the particular differences of immigrants (nationality, race or religion) seems to disturb more than a relatively small minority of mass publics in EC countries. More than 80 per cent of Europeans find these characteristics 'not disturbing', with no change over the past three years. Asylum-seekers are accepted throughout the EC, but with restrictions. Only a quarter of those surveyed are prepared to accept them without restrictions.

What is most evident from these cross-survey data is that there is little consistent relationship cross-nationally between proportions of immigrant stocks and patterns of attitudes towards immigrants. The feeling that there are too many immigrants is strong even in many countries with small immigrant populations (with the notable exception of Ireland). Expressed tolerance for differences of nationality, race and religion is strongest in some countries with few immigrants (Ireland, Spain and Portugal), but is also strong in Italy where immigration has been growing, and in Britain and Germany, where the proportion of immigrant stock is relatively high. The intolerant minority is strongest in France and Greece (but below 30 per cent), the former with a large proportion of immigrants, the latter with an unknown proportion.

Despite the legal fact of 'Citizenship of the Union', the level of acceptance of other EC nationalities without restriction was only 35 per cent, and the pattern corresponded to that of acceptance of asylum-seekers: a rough correspondence between stronger acceptance among countries which have been traditional exporters of labour (with the exception of Greece) and weaker support among countries which are traditional importers of labour (with the exception of Denmark).

However, if we are looking for the sources of mass attitudes, an examination of the political process, rather than of demographic structure, may be more fruitful. For example, popular perception of the origins of resident foreigners is constructed by the political dialogue in Western Europe.[12] Throughout the decade of the 1980s, the French seemed to believe that most immigrants were from North Africa. In fact North Africans have never comprised a majority, and until the end of the decade they were outnumbered by Portuguese. Similarly, the immigrant problem in Germany is often seen in terms of the presence of Turks, but only a third of the foreign residents are from Turkey, and their proportion has not increased during the past decade. Finally, the largest single group of foreigners in Britain has always been the Irish, although the resident Pakistanis are generally perceived as the focus of anti-immigrant attention.

THE 'CRISIS OF IMMIGRATION'

What then is the 'crisis of immigration'? Despite the dire predictions in the press in 1989–90, the 'invasion' of Western Europe has not taken place, in part because of much tighter restrictions of border controls and their enforcement, in part because the predictions themselves were highly inflammatory. Thus, the 'crisis of immigration' is less a crisis of cross-border flows than it is a political crisis of élite and mass reaction to foreign-born people, only some of whom have arrived in recent years.

It is our view that although immigration is frequently seen as a problem with which policy-makers and mass publics are unhappily confronted, changing immigration patterns can also be understood as a process, or rather a network of processes. The first process is that of the push/pull of migration, the process that impels migrants to leave their native countries and migrate to Europe. While much of the 'push' is related to larger trends in Europe and in the world, the articles in this volume demonstrate that a great deal of the 'pull' is under the control of policy-makers.

The recent debate involves the construction of policies that would limit the pull, by creating obstacles to migration, whatever the cause. These obstacles include *inter alia* tighter border controls, increased visa requirements, employer sanctions, greater use of deportations, redefining the criteria for asylum, accelerated procedures, and co-ordination of national policies. There also exists a sub-debate, conducted largely within international organisations such as the International Labour

Organisation, the European Parliament and the European Commission. This stresses the inevitability of migratory pressure from the less developed world, not least in the context of massive population growth in North Africa and serious economic disparities in the world economy. This particular focus advocates development aid in various forms as a means of reducing the 'push' factors:[13] its principal disadvantage lies in its cost and the need for the industrialised world explicitly to address the structural nature of poverty and exploitation within the capitalist system itself. Thus it has little appeal to mainstream party politics.

The second process is that of incorporation or integration, a process which has had implications for a whole range of policy areas, but one that has also had an impact on the structure and relations among political institutions. In this process, immigrants are not only the objects of policy, but have become political actors who have had an impact on the process itself. Increasingly the politics of immigration involves conflicts between different visions and models of integration – conflicts that challenge long-accepted models of national identity and the nature of national integration.

The dynamics of both processes have been influenced by larger trends in Europe: some of these are historically rooted whilst others have emerged more recently.

The Process of Migration

Until the early 1970s, the process of migration developed in the context of the Cold War which prevented migration across the East-West division; a chronic labour shortage in Britain, France and FRG; a relatively poor periphery of Western Europe, particularly in Ireland, Spain, Portugal, Southern Italy, Greece, Yugoslavia and Turkey; and an expanding population along the southern shore of the Mediterranean. The rapid economic expansion of the countries of the European Community attracted workers from the more impoverished periphery, as well as from the former colonies of the major European countries. Italy was able to draw on labour from her own rural south, and for a time continued to export labour to other countries in Europe and as far as the United States, Argentina and Australia.

In this context, each labour-importing country developed its own policies and programmes both to attract and to mobilise necessary labour. Policies were constructed to attract and import workers, and to direct them into areas and industries with the greatest need. Through a combination of state and private efforts, a great deal of immigrant labour was imported with little popular reaction, and with little impact on the political system. Until the 1970s, 'immigration' was not regarded as a political problem either by political élites or by mass publics (with the major exception of the UK) and there seemed to be a reasonable fit between the needs of labour-exporting countries and those in Europe that were importing labour.

All of this changed rapidly during the first half of the 1970s. The first oil shock, combined with the long term trend of the decline of smokestack industry in Western Europe, brought an end to state policies favourable to the importation of immigrant labour. The previous synchrony of the needs of labour exporters and importers changed to a conflict of interests, and policies were gradually put in place which closed the doors of Western Europe to most legal labour immigration. However, this did not mean that all immigration was halted, since (with some variation from country to country) limited family reunification was still permitted. As a result, by the 1980s, resident foreign labour had become resident foreign communities, and, in countries where naturalisation and citizenship laws facilitated movements towards citizenship, ethnic communities. By the end of the decade, the 'problem' could no longer be seen solely in terms of labour migration.

Nevertheless, several trends have fuelled a continuing preoccupation with the process of migration. Ineluctable migratory pressure has grown during the past decade throughout the world. The growing income gap, as well as high rates of population growth in Third World countries, has encouraged migration towards the developed world. The communications revolution has resulted in a broad awareness of opportunities in Western Europe, and relatively easy, fast transportation has increased access. The force of these trends has been accentuated by war, the breakdown of order and the oppression and expulsion of ethnic minorities in the Third World. By the late 1980s, migration pressures were further fuelled by the end of the Cold War and the breakdown of order in the former Soviet empire.[14]

Thus migration push has intensified, and has challenged the ability of countries in Western Europe to control their frontiers. Immigration continues not only because it is physically difficult to stop (in fact statistics indicate that when states have acted to reduce the flow, these efforts have been moderately successful) but because it is difficult to halt for legal and political reasons; that is, cross-border migration flows have challenged treaty and legal obligations, as well as some of the fundamental understandings of the political process.[15] The level of legal immigration continues to be related to current economic needs, but also to a network of international agreements that limit state sovereignty, as well as to a network of rights which have been applied universally by legal authorities.[16]

The French continue to admit over 50,000 seasonal workers each year (about a third the level of the early 1970s), most of whom find employment in the agricultural sector. However, attempts by France and Germany to limit family reunification have been struck down by administrative and constitutional courts as a violation of international agreements – in effect making it impossible completely to suspend legal immigration. In addition, the courts have consistently affirmed a network of rights of resident immigrants, and have limited the ability of governments to prevent asylum-seekers from entering the country.

In August 1993 the French Constitutional Council challenged a core presumption of the Dublin and Schengen accords by ruling that legislation which would prevent asylum-seekers from entering the country was a violation both of the Geneva accords on refugees, as well as the French Constitution (specifically the Rights of Man). In total, 8 of the 51 articles of the new immigration law were censured: these covered family reunion, administrative detention, 'banishment' orders, and the new French form of a 'primary purpose' rule. (The latter applies to the UK, in that marriage to a national does not give an automatic right of residence.) The French provision addresses 'marriages of convenience' by proposing that a mayor should have the right to suspend the ceremony.

Two rulings by the German Constitutional Court in September 1993 attacked another core presumption of Dublin and Schengen, by refusing to consider Greece a 'safe third country' for asylum-seekers and authorising their applications to be made in Germany. Despite the fact that Greece is a signatory to the European Convention on Human Rights, and also of course to Dublin and Schengen, the Court considered that human rights provisions in these two cases could not be guaranteed in Greece.

The policy process is no longer confined to the narrow arena of ministerial and administrative interaction. As a result of the recent decision of the French Constitutional Council, for example, the French government decided in October 1993 to amend the Constitution. This decision has mobilised public opinion on both sides of the issue, but also has divided all of the major political parties, including the opposition Socialists.[17] In various ways, decision-makers now operate in an environment of heightened public awareness mobilised by social movements and political parties ranging from those on the anti-immigrant new Right to those who support immigrants on the civil rights Left.

The regulation of cross-border migration is therefore a political process which encompasses a partial international regime at the European Union level and a network of bilateral and multilateral accords which have limited state sovereignty, combined with national processes which differ from country to country. It is through this complex political process that a convergence of policy has been developing in recent years, since it has become clear that no single country in Western Europe is capable of regulating migration flows without influencing those in other countries. By focusing on this process, we accentuate the political choices that are being made in Western Europe with regard to migration flows, as well as the political and legal constraints that have defined these choices. In this context, the push-pull forces of migration that have been developing in the last few years are a condition of policy-making, but are not determinants of specific policy choices.

The Process of Incorporation/Integration

Like the process of migration, there has been considerable change in the process of policy-making on incorporation and integration. Since the 1970s the policy environment has changed, the institutions involved in the process have changed, the arena of decision-making within which the process has taken place has expanded, and, as a result, the dynamics of the process are different now from what they were 20 years ago. Perhaps most striking, the range of issues which are now touched by questions of integration has grown in ways that were hardly anticipated even a decade ago.

In most countries in Western Europe, the demographic heritage in the 1990s is record-high levels of foreign-born residents (Table 1). Although, immigration flows have generally levelled off, the high proportion of foreign-born residents is a result of the cumulative impact of high immigration flows over a long time, combined with low indigenous birth rates throughout Western Europe.

Until recently, policies related to the incorporation and integration of resident immigrants have varied considerably from country to country within Western Europe, and have followed the norms of national traditions. Different conceptions of citizenship and nationality have emerged out of different histories, and can be represented by four 'ideal types':[18]

(1) *The Imperial Model*: this facilitates the integration of different peoples in multi-ethnic empires, for example, the Ottoman and British Empires, whilst simultaneously expressing the dominance of one national group.
(2) *The Folk or Ethnic Model*: this is a structural expression of an ethnically homogenous society, with common descent, language and culture. This model typifies a closed society, which excludes immigrants from citizenship and social membership. *Ius sangui-*

nis (citizenship by parental nationality) is the norm; naturalisation is difficult. (Germany is the closest example.)

(3) *The Republican Model*: the nation is defined as a political community, with a constitution, laws and citizenship. Immigrants can be 'assimilated' into the society, provided that they accept the political rules and national culture. *Ius soli* (citizenship by birthplace) is the norm; naturalisation is moderately easy. (France is a clear example.)

(4) *The Multicultural Model*: this is a fairly new model, which essentially is a modified Republican model. The political community is based on a constitution, laws and citizenship; in admitting immigrants to the society, adherence to the political rules is required but recognition is made of cultural and ethnic differences. Again, *ius soli* is normal, and the naturalisation process is straightforward. (Australia, Canada and arguably Sweden are the best examples: but varying influences can be seen in the Netherlands, USA and the UK.)

Across Europe, there have existed different versions of these patterns over time. The change was nowhere more marked than in the UK, where citizenship of the British Empire existed until 1962; the subsequent shift away from this model was accompanied by limited moves to a multicultural model. For those countries without colonial histories or a republican approach, a guest worker policy could be viewed purely as an economic process. Thus the folk model, with its restrictive *ius sanguinis* tradition, offers no process of integration or assimilation of immigrants. By contrast, the republican model in France allows *ius soli*, thereby granting second generation citizenship.

By the 1970s the pressures of high levels of foreign-born populations had combined with institutional changes to diminish the effectiveness of existing systems of incorporation/integration. In France, the Communist Party and the trade unions could no longer effectively integrate immigrant workers through their weakened organisational networks, and the French school system proved to be a weak instrument of cultural and economic integration.[19] In Germany, the 'guest worker' approach specifically excluded the possibility of full integration, but such an approach was increasingly conflicting with the reality of the long-term residence of the 'guests'. For Britain, the concept of Empire citizenship was increasingly coming into conflict with the assumption that only limited numbers would use this privilege.

Existing systems of integration/incorporation were also weakend by changing migration patterns. Earlier patterns of immigration tended to be linked to incorporation, since workers were directed towards those industries where their employment was required. Later family immigration has put pressure on institutions, particularly housing and schools, that were not orientated towards the integration of numerous non-European immigrants.

On the one hand, as a result of growing disagreement among political élites within national communities about policies of integration, the process of decision-making became increasingly conflictual at the national level. On the other, the changing institutional arrangements within Western Europe meant that claims by immigrants to rights within countries could be made beyond the traditional institutions of the nation-state.[20] In this context, the place of immigrant groups in both the national communities in Western Europe and the European Union is a political issue that is far from settled on either level. Even if 'zero cross-border immigration' could be effected, the issues of integration would remain.

The political actors engaged in the process of policy-making on integration are far more numerous than they were two decades ago. They now include the structures of a changing European Union, several well-established, anti-immigrant political parties, as well as a complex network of organised groups that claim to speak for immigrant communities in most European countries.[21]

The policies which have emerged from this more complex process combine a certain broad convergence of approach with a more intense nationalism. While European countries have collaborated in common efforts to close the gates of Europe to cross-border immigration, naturalisation processes have been eased in Belgium, the Netherlands, and most recently in Germany; while the new French government passed legislation in 1993 that made acquiring citizenship and naturalisation somewhat more difficult. Most West European governments have also put into effect legislation that establishes not only rights for resident immigrants but also programmes (especially in housing and education) to aid their integration. At the same time, violence against immigrant communities has increased throughout Western Europe, and anti-immigrant political parties have mobilised significant electoral support.

The presence of high proportions of foreigners throughout Western Europe, and their emergence as political actors in the 1980s with their own ideas of how they fit into the national community, has contributed to the emergence of larger questions of national identity in a changing European world. Yet the disagreement among leaders of leading political parties about how to approach these questions, and their growing inability to mobilise the electorate, has provided political space both to the new parties of the anti-immigrant Right as well as to immigrant actors themselves. The reassertion of nationalist identities by the new Right has, perhaps, focused public attention on the questions about these identities in a more complex European world.

CHANGES AND QUESTIONS

The articles in this volume all deal with the two political processes outlined here in various ways. They also deal with questions that emerge out of these processes. Miles and Kay show, in their historical examination of Britain, that there is little determinism in any particular set of migration pressures: political, economic and social factors all play a significant role. In this light, we might ask why has there been a growing convergence in policies on migration and integration? Has it been the movement towards European unification analysed by Butt Philip, or the kind of international learning implied by Crowley and Weil? Both perspectives argue against the force of historical cultural heritage in policy formation. Indeed, in Wischenbart's article, the formulation of immigration legislation in Austria has meant a wholesale re-working of the cultural heritage of the Austro-Hungarian Empire, a model of governance that seems more relevant in the new Europe than it was in the Europe at the turn of the century.

Both Faist and Schnapper deal with different aspects of the rapid expansion of the decision-making arena on immigration in recent years. In effect, both imply that the definition of issues is a key element in expanding the network of participants. Schnapper argues that the question of immigration is central in Europe today because it has been transformed from a labour market problem to one of national identity. As in the United States at the turn of the century (and perhaps once again in the 1990s), questions of national identity tend to mobilise both popular sentiment and a broad range of interests. For Faist, the development of 'social citizenship' in Germany has been a means of incorporation without citizenship, but also has expanded the political opportunities for immigrants themselves. Of course, such an approach also links immigration questions to a broad range of other social and economic policies.

Veugelers' analysis raises other issues about expansion. Focusing on political parties and elections, his article argues that party competition is a key driving force behind the expansion of conflict and the linkage of immigration to larger issues. De Wenden implies that through their positive political action, immigrant groups in France have also contributed to the expansion of political conflict and the linkage of immigration to a broad range of political issues. These analyses are not mutually exclusive, and they present us with the building blocks of a larger model within which we can begin to systematise the relationship between immigration and European politics in the 1990s.

Finally, several of the articles in this volume raise questions about the effectiveness of the state in implementing policies, especially policies that would limit immigration and promote integration. Miller, Butt Philip and Bauböck and Çinar all deal with this question in a somewhat different way. Miller, in his analysis of the enforcement of employer sanctions, notes considerable success and effectiveness in controlling illegal labour. Butt Philip shows that European co-operation has emerged not simply from the process of European unification, but also through a reluctant recognition of policy limitations at the national level. State effectiveness in the integration process is much less clear, both because of variable criteria of effectiveness and because the process is inextricably entwined with the outcome. Bauböck and Çinar sketch the still significantly divergent approaches to citizenship and nationality, whilst themselves propounding the need for a weakening of the traditional exclusive ties between citizen and state. In a world in which national frontiers are no longer easily defended by armed force and economic sovereignty, it is hardly surprising that citizenship and national identity, the last bastions of the ideology of the nation-state, should be deeply-felt political issues. Although international co-operation and the role of the European Union are still minimal in this area, the articles in this volume all deal with a more complex world than the nation-state can hope to encompass.

NOTES

1. See John Salt, 'Current and future international migration trends affecting Europe', in *People on the move: new migration flows in Europe* (Strasbourg: Council of Europe Press, 1992); also M. Baldwin-Edwards, 'Immigration after 1992', *Policy & Politics* 19/3 (1991), pp.199–211.
2. For the most detailed discussion of these and other asylum issues, see Danièle Joly, C. Nettleton and H. Poulton, *Refugees: asylum in Europe?* (London: Minority Rights Group, 1992).
3. See David O'Keeffe, 'The Schengen Convention: a suitable model for European integration?', *Yearbook of European Law*, Vol. 11 (1991), pp.185–219.
4. See US Committee for Refugees, *World Refugee Summary, 1993* (Washington, DC: 1993).
5. See, e.g., the discussion in Sarah Collinson, *Europe and International Migration* (London: Pinter, 1993), pp.13–19.
6. See W.R. Böhning, 'Integration and Immigration Pressures in Western Europe', *International Labour Review* 130/4 (1991).
7. See, e.g., Collinson (note 5), pp.61–2; Salt (note 1), p.62.
8. Baldwin-Edwards (note 1).

9. M. Baldwin-Edwards, 'Immigration and migrants in the Europe of the 1990s', *European Access* 3 (1992), p. 15.
10. See Stephen Castles and Mark Miller, *The Age of Migration* (London: Macmillan, 1993), pp.90–6.
11. Commission of the European Communities, *Eurobarometer 39*, June 1993. Survey conducted in spring 1993.
12. An important analysis of immigrants as *both* economic and political actors can be found in Aristide Zolberg, 'International Migrations in Political Perspective', in Mary M. Kritz, Charles B. Keely and Silvano M. Tomasi (eds.), *Global Trends in Migration: Theory and Research on International Population Movements* (NY: Center for Migration Studies, 1981).
13. See, e.g., Böhning (note 6).
14. For an interesting discussion of the issues surrounding the evolution of European immigration policies, see Anthony Fielding, 'Migrations, institutions and politics: the evolution of European migration policies', in Russell King (ed.), *Mass Migration in Europe* (London: Belhaven Press, 1993).
15. On the issue of demography and destiny, see Demetrios G. Papademetriou, 'At the Precipice? Some Thoughts About Where Europe is With Regard to Migration, How It Got There, and What It Might Do About It', Paper prepared for a conference on 'The Dimensions of International Migration in Europe', sponsored by the Centre for Strategic and Int'l Studies, Taormina, Italy, April 1993.
16. This argument is developed most fully by James F. Hollifield in *Immigrants, Markets and States* (Cambridge: Harvard UP, 1992).
17. *Le Monde*, 21 Oct. 1993.
18. See Castles and Miller (note 10), pp.35–41.
19. In fact, the Communist Party was far less interested in acting as a force of integration in the 1980s. In many ways the school system operated on the basis of conflicting directives about its integrative mission. See Martin A. Schain, 'Immigrants and Politics in France', in John S. Ambler, *The French Socialist Experiment* (Philadelphia: ISHI, 1985).
20. A process analysed by Yasemin Soysal, in *Limits of Citizenship in the Contemporary Nation-State System* (Chicago: Univ. of Chicago Press, forthcoming).
21. For an analysis of nationalist and post-nationalist strategies of citizenship, see Miriam Feldblum, 'New Citizenship Strategies in Postwar Europe: Nationalist and Post-Nationalist', a paper prepared for presentation at the Meetings of the American Political Science Assoc., Washington, DC, Sept. 1993.

The Politics of Immigration to Britain: East–West Migrations in the Twentieth Century

ROBERT MILES and DIANA KAY

This analysis places recent interest in East/West migration in a historical perspective. It argues that East/West migration to Britain is not a new phenomenon: Russian Jews arrived at the turn of the twentieth century and members of the Polish Armed Forces and Displaced Persons in the mid-to late 1940s. Official responses to these refugee movements varied as did the ideological representations of the incomers. In particular, prevailing political and economic considerations as well as 'race-thinking' informed official responses. Current British policy towards refugees from former Yugoslavia reinforces the argument that refugee status is socially determined, rather than inherent in a particular set of circumstances.

Over the past 20 years, the focus of social science research on the politics of migration to Britain has been on responses to the entry and subsequent settlement of British subjects of colonial origin. The source of these colonial migrants (from the periphery of the world economy, specifically the Caribbean and the Indian subcontinent) has meant that migration has usually been interpreted as a dimension of a North–South relationship. While other migrations have been, numerically and economically, almost as important (e.g., the uninterrupted migration from Ireland to Britain), this colonial migration has generated a specific political discourse and set of meanings which have led to the hegemonic view that an immigrant is, by definition, a 'black' person.

Political developments in Europe since 1989 (notably the disintegration of the former Soviet bloc and the unification of Germany) have stimulated new migration flows within the 'unified' Europe. Given the emphasis on North–South migration, these East–West movements (real and speculated) appear to be historically novel: commentators often refer to the current migrations as new in a way which exhibits a remarkable amnesia. This interpretation is challenged by embracing a longer-term historical perspective: these recent intra-European migrations are a recurrence of previous patterns of (especially refugee) migration within Europe.

In the case of Britain, one can cite, for example, the arrival of Russian Jews in the late nineteenth and early twentieth centuries, the movement of Spanish republican and German Jewish refugees in the 1930s, and the migration of ex-members of the Polish Armed Forces and the recruitment of East European workers from refugee camps after 1945. In this study, we will connect recent East–West migrations with earlier East–West migrations, and analyse the politics of immigration to which they gave rise.

IMMIGRATION AND THE RUSSIAN JEWS: 1880–1905

Between 1880 and 1905 over 120,000 Russian Jews arrived in Britain.[1] Many migrants were refugees, victims of the repressive policies towards Jews and other minority groups within the Russian Empire. Yet considerable population growth amongst the Russian Jews, and restrictions on residence and trade, meant that there were related economic pressures behind the movement.[2]

Before 1905, entering Britain presented few legal obstacles. The absence of immigration controls meant that when ships carrying Russian Jews docked at British ports, their 'alien' passengers disembarked freely. However, this movement of Russian Polish Jews was to be the last unregulated immigration to Britain. With the 1905 Aliens Act, the British state abandoned the ninteenth century liberal democratic beliefs in the automatic right of asylum and in the free movement of peoples.[3] Henceforth, the state acquired the power to exclude 'undesirable and destitute' (a definition that had a class as much as a racist dimension[3]) aliens from entering the country. From 1905 'immigrant ships' (defined as those carrying 20 or more alien passengers) had to berth at specific ports so that immigration officials could control entry. In addition, enforcement was partly transferred to the shipping masters, who were subject to fines should those rejected or awaiting the outcome of an appeal escape.

To explain why an immigrant presence – and that of Russian Polish Jews in particular – became a sufficiently major political issue to lead to the passage of the first modern legislation to control immigration, we need to examine both the wider national and international context in which the migrants arrived as well as the localised setting into which they were inserted. Concerning the national context, the late nineteenth century witnessed a decline in Britain's economic prosperity. Economic preoccupations led to a questioning of the merits of continuing a free trade policy: the issue of state intervention, restriction and protection was placed on the political agenda. The protectionist camp (supported largely by Conservative politicians) pressed for restrictions on the entry of people as well as goods on the grounds that Britain was importing 'unfair competition' in the form of impoverished immigrants whose assumed willingness to work for low wages undercut and displaced British workers. Consequently, immigration restriction became linked to the wider case for protectionism.

The arrival of the Russian Jews exacerbated ongoing tensions in the labour and housing markets. Concerning the former, immigrants became concentrated in a few trades (e.g., garment making, furniture construction) which were characterised by workshop settings, extensive division of labour, seasonality, and long hours of work: conditions known popularly as the 'sweating system'.[5] Many of these trades were undergoing structural change and the resulting uncertainty was shared by British workers in these sectors. Yet the latter often identified the immigrants as the cause of any misfortunes (low wages, or unemployment) rather than joint victims, and trade union hostility to the Russian Jews was expressed in debates at the the annual Trade Union Congresses in 1892, 1894 and 1895.

In addition, the pattern of immigrant settlement exacerbated tensions in the housing market. The Russian Jews were residentially concentrated in certain towns and cities, and within these, within certain neighbourhoods. Opposition to their presence was particularly virulent in the East End of London, where there was a pre-existing housing shortage[6] and where the Russian Jews came to be seen as responsible for pushing up rents and intensifying overcrowding.

These localised tensions combined with the national preoccupations to transform 'the alien' into a problematic presence. More specifically, the 'alien' became synonymous with the 'Jew' and the 'alien question' synonymous with the 'Jewish question': economic and political opposition to the migration embraced anti-Semitic strands. The themes of wage cutting and displacement were given specific content and force by pre-existing stereotypes of the Jew as willing to work for anything. Additionally, opposition was expressed to the cultural presence of Jews. The economic and residential concentration of Jews strengthened perceptions of them as members of an alien culture which was both incompatible and inferior to British ways. In this way the opposition drew upon pre-existing stereotypes and images to politicise and racialise their presence: excluding the 'undesirable' meant not only the poor but also the 'racially inferior'. Although the period was marked by high emigration of British people, the view that the Russian Jewish immigrant could replace this loss in any comparable way was discounted by those who argued on racialised grounds.

Opposition to the Russian Jews was organised by pressure groups such as the British Brotherhood League and by backbench Conservative MPs in areas of high Jewish immigration. Soon the Jewish presence became a national political issue and the consequences of the Russian Jewish migation formed the subject of official inquiries, notably the Royal Commission on Alien Immigration of 1903.

Arguments about the dangers posed by 'unassimilated minorities' and the threat of immigrants undercutting and displacing British workers were all repeated in the late 1940s and after, but with very different consequences and policy implications. Although the response to the Russian Jews is partly differentiated from subsequent East–West migrations by its anti-Semitic component, it did form part of the collective memory of state responses and was referred to in the 1940s for the 'lessons' it provided. It is to this period that we now turn.

EAST–WEST MIGRATION IN THE POSTWAR PERIOD: 1945–1951

The second main East–West migration to Britain during the twentieth century occurred during the mid to late 1940s. Between 1939 and 1950, the number of aliens aged over 16 living in Britain almost doubled from 239,000 to 429,329.[7] Most of this additional alien population was made up of three separate streams of East Europeans.

The first stream was formed by Poles from the Polish Armed Forces. The Polish government and armed forces in exile had been permitted to enter Britain in 1940 after the fall of France and numbered some 30,500 persons. These were joined by the Polish II Army Corps (from the Italian Campaign) which was brought to Britain in 1946 and reunited with families and dependants who had been in camps in the Middle East and Africa. In 1949 the resident Polish population formed by the ex-armed forces and their dependants totalled 127,900 persons.[8]

The second migration was formed by over 80,000 Displaced Persons (DPs) of various East European origins (mainly Balts, Ukrainians, Poles and Yugoslavs). This group was specially selected under an official British government programme known as the European volunteer worker scheme and recruits were known collectively as European volunteer workers (EVWs).[9]

The third stream was formed by some 8,000 Ukrainian prisoners of war who were brought to Britain in 1947 at the instigation of the British War Office. These former members of the Halychyna Division had been held since the end of the war under British protection in Rimini, Italy.

As pressure from the Soviets for their return increased, the British War Office shipped them to Britain 'in total defiance of every single immigration regulation'.[10]

Although each migration had distinct features, a common underlying cause was the political division of Europe and the refugees' shared anti-communist politics which led them to resist repatriation to their homelands at the end of the war. The reasons for their admission to Britain require a longer explanation. British immigration legislation had been amended and extended since the 1905 Aliens Act, notably by the 1920 Aliens Order which strengthened the powers of the Home Secretary and restricted the access of aliens to the British labour market by introducing a work permit system.[11] Why then was the law not used to exclude these East Europeans?

Part of the explanation lies in domestic economic considerations. The *Economic Survey* of 1947 reported a need for a larger labour force than was currently available and for 'special measures' to increase it.[12] Among the measures introduced was the recruitment of foreign labour. The formation of the Polish Resettlement Corps in 1946 (which aimed to disband the Polish Armed Forces in Britain by placing them in civilian employment) was inspired partly by the contribution which Polish labour could make to critical labour shortages in agriculture and coal mining.[13] Likewise the recruitment of DPs was largely determined by labour demands in Britain.[14]

However, these economic considerations were supplemented by British foreign policy objectives and international pressures. The International Refugee Organisation (established in 1947) identified the resettlement of DPs in third countries as a major goal and pressed the British government (amongst others) to take its 'fair share' of non-repatriables.[15] The British government responded to these pressures by directing them along lines which furthered domestic economic interests (i.e., by selecting the healthy, young and fit DPs who could work as unskilled manual labour in 'essential industries'). Finally, in the context of the emerging Cold War, the East European refugees could be seen as a political asset. In the case of the Ukrainian Division, their possible contribution to British intelligence played a part in bringing them to Britain, even though they had participated in the murder and extermination of Jews.[16]

Hence, the mid- to late 1940s was a period in which immigration was identified by the government as being (although with qualifications, as will be seen later) in the 'national interest'. Economic and political considerations supported a more positive immigration policy than had hitherto been adopted and responses included, for the first time, an official scheme to recruit up to 100,000 aliens for selected British industries.

The break with the restrictionist thinking of the past was made explicit in parliamentary debates. One Labour MP argued that 'the Home Office has for many years. . . . shown a too nationalistic approach to immigration, and must now reckon with the dire necessity of taking into our population, and assimilating into our national life, hundreds of thousands of people of other nationalities and races'. Another argued that there was a need for 'a complete mental readjustment on the part of the people of this country towards the immigration of a large body of foreigners'.[17]

Yet East European labour refugees were not considered by the government to be the ideal solution to problems of labour supply. At the inaugural meeting of the Cabinet Foreign Labour Committee, the Home Secretary argued for a temporary addition of foreign labour and made plain his preference for workers from Western Europe 'whose traditions and social background were more nearly equal to our own'.[18] However, most other west European countries were also experiencing labour shortages, and the main 'surplus population' was formed by prospective settlers from the more 'unequal' and 'dissimilar' eastern Europe.

The British government responded to the gap between ideal and reality by attempting to confine the recruitment of DPs within the framework of a temporary labour migration scheme. Selection policies were biased towards the single, young and healthy, and recruits were landed in Britain initially for one year, even though the political impossibility of a mass return to DP camps in Germany was acknowledged privately. As individual work permits were time-consuming to administer, the Home Secretary used his powers to vary the Aliens Order of 1920 by landing the EVWs *en bloc* as a pool of labour upon which industry could draw as needs determined.

Although the immigration of DPs and the settlement of Poles in Britain was largely determined by labour demand, restrictionist thinking which had predominated since 1905 was not completely jettisoned. Official concern that the DPs once in Britain should not subsequently become an 'economic burden' by drawing public assistance or leak away from the essential work to which they had been assigned, influenced the terms of recruitment. Hence, the EVW scheme built in employment controls which limited recruits' freedom on the labour market.

Moreover, the government had to address the perception of alien labour as representing cheap competition if it was to win the support of British labour for the scheme.[19] Unlike the earlier migration of Russian

Jews, the Poles and DPs were being brought into a more organised work setting and into a national situation where trade unions had more say in decision-making. The government gained the consent of the trade union leadership by guaranteeing 'safeguards' intended to prevent foreign labour from undercutting or displacing indigenous workers. In addition, some details governing the employment of Poles and DPs were left to industry-level negotiations between employers and the workforce.

Although short-term economic interests dominated policy-making, the social and political repercussions of an increased East European presence were not neglected. There was official awareness that political developments in central and eastern Europe made permanent settlement a likely outcome of the EVW scheme. Consequently, there was official concern to ensure that those being brought in were of good human 'stock'. In the main Parliamentary debate on Displaced Persons, speakers from both government and opposition portrayed the DPs in positive racialised terms. They were variously described as 'ideal emigrants', as representing 'vigorous new blood' and as 'first-class people' who 'would be of great benefit to our stock' and whose 'love of freedom was so intense' as to constitute 'the spirit and the stuff of which we can make Britons'.[20]

Subsequently, DPs became internally differentiated along a North–South divide. The most favourable judgements were reserved for the Balts from the 'North' who were regarded as being eminently 'assimilable'. Their strong family organisation, their capacity for hard work, and their familiarity with a more advanced industrial culture were all quoted approvingly by British government officials who visited the DP camps.[21] By contrast, DPs from south-east Europe were often referred to as 'simple peasant types', unversed in the ways of a complex industrial culture and more 'racially distinct', forming part of an ill-defined but inferior 'Slav race'.[22] Consequently, there was a racialised bias towards the recruitment of Balts, but as their numbers proved insufficient to meet economic needs, eligibility was extended to other national groups of DPs.

As a State-sponsored migration, the government assumed responsibility for securing the acceptance of the DPs by the British population. Mention has already been made of the employment safeguards. In addition the government addressed anticipated tensions over accommodation by housing the volunteer workers in disused wartime hostels. Nevertheless, conflicts did arise over the Poles' and EVWs' entitlements to skilled work, food rations and the health services. In addition, the Fascist sympathies of a proportion of the Poles and EVWs were the subject of acrimonious discussion amongst British trade unionists. When adverse press publicity threatened to hinder the placing of Poles and EVWs in work, the government responded with a publication setting out the reasons behind the migration and attempting to dispel popular misconceptions.[23] The government relied on a humanitarian discourse by appealing to the British public to extend its 'traditional hospitality' to those whom it described as 'unfortunate victims of war'. Although a limited response, this did represent an official attempt to 'educate public opinion' and tackle 'prejudice'.

However, these limited official measures did not address the central contradiction which lay at the heart of the EVW scheme. Recruiting what was officially regarded as 'foreign labour' from amongst a refugee population led to policy tensions. As potential settlers, the DPs themselves raised questions about their rights to family reunification, to citizenship and to freedom on the labour market. Government policy was pulled between the need to incorporate Poles and EVWs into the 'British way of life' whilst at the same time officially restricting their freedoms, particularly in the labour market. In addition, although endorsing the policy goal of 'assimilation' with its related emphasis on 'dispersal' and 'mixing', the employment and accommodation policies pursued concentrated the EVWs in a few industries and in predominantly separate hostels. This led one government representative to argue that official policies were themselves encouraging 'racial and national separatism'.[24]

A further inconsistency exposed by the EVW scheme concerns the differential State response towards this Eastern European migration and that towards the incipient migration of colonial British subjects from the Caribbean. Although the late 1940s was a period in which the politics of immigration became positively linked to the 'national interest', the British government clearly pursued a selective immigration policy. The postwar Labour government resolved that Jewish DPs were not eligible for recruitment under the EVW scheme and rejected a proposal to set up an official recruitment scheme for colonial migrants from the Caribbean.[25]

In sum, unlike the earlier movement of Russian Poles at the turn of the nineteenth century, the migration of East European DPs in the 1940s was highly controlled. A quota was set on the numbers to be recruited, and the terms and conditions of their entry were explicit. And political controls by central and East European governments over the exit of their nationals meant that the British government was not faced with the prospect of an open-ended commitment. The carefully selected DPs, together with the Poles from the armed forces, were regarded as making a significant contribution to economic reconstruction and as 'lovers of the free world' a valuable political statement about, if not an active contribution to, Cold War politics and ideology. Throughout the 1950s, the terms 'refugee' and 'anti-communist' were often used interchangeably, and East European refugees shaped the institutions and influenced the discourse about refugees.[26]

THE RETURN OF EAST–WEST MIGRATION: 1988–1992

During the early 1990s, the British political debate about immigration has once again encompassed the potential for migration from central and eastern Europe[27] and for refugee migrations into Europe.[28] This renewed focus on East–West migration is interpreted using a discourse constituted around the immigrations that occurred between the early 1950s and the mid-1980s. As previously noted, from the moment that the first British subjects arrived in Britain from the Caribbean in the late 1940s, the State defined their presence as problematic.[29] Their legal status as British subjects was marginalised by describing them as 'coloured immigrants' whose arrival created a 'race relations' problem in Britain. This was repeated following the arrival of British subjects from the Indian subcontinent during the 1950s.

The British state faced two difficulties in seeking to control and then stop these migrations. First, during the 1950s, most of the migrants were welcomed (often reluctantly) by employers facing labour shortages. Second, as British subjects, they had the right to enter and settle in the UK. This right was not affected by immigration legislation passed earlier in the century because it applied exclusively to aliens. Hence, any attempt to limit or prohibit their entry (while simultaneously permitting the continued entry of other British subjects resident in Canada and Australasia who were more favourably conceived as 'kith and kin') was open to the charge of being racist. The story of the way in which successive governments transformed immigration and nationality law between 1962 and 1982 to realise this racist project is well known.[30]

The legislation was justified with the claim that 'strict immigration control' is necessary to ensure 'good race relations'. Simultaneously, the State removed most restrictions on the entry of millions of citizens of member states of the European Community and guaranteed the right of entry of millions of citizens of foreign states who have a parent or grandparent born in Britain. In reality, immigration control is 'strict' only for certain categories of people: in common sense terms, the people recognised as 'immigrants' are 'black' people (for only they cause 'race relations' problems), and therefore it is their entry into

Britain that is deemed to require strict regulation. Thus, with the (important) exception of citizens of member states of the EC, the system of 'strict immigration control' created during the 1960s and 1970s had no implications for people defined in British law as *aliens*. Neither did it have implications for people who sought entry to Britain on the basis of a claim for political asylum.

The consequences of the politics of immigration since the early 1950s have begun to be transcended by a 'new' situation, although it can only be considered 'new' if the history of earlier East–West migrations to Britain is ignored. Since the mid-1980s, given the logic of racialised control, the limits of the legislation passed between 1962 and 1982 and of its legitimating rationale have become increasingly evident. The first sign of change occurred when the government cast doubt on the legitimacy of many of the migrants claiming refugee status: in 1986 the government spotlighted the arrival of Tamils seeking asylum in the UK following the outbreak of civil war in Sri Lanka.[31] Thereafter, it became increasingly common for government ministers to reproduce the 'old' idea of immigration as a problem by the 'new' claim that many of these refugees were 'bogus', that they were 'really' economic migrants in disguise.

The effectiveness of this discourse was strengthened by the fact that a large proportion of those seeking asylum in the UK had a 'Third World' origin. In the period 1989–91, of the 78,210 applications for asylum, more than half (41,980) were by people from Africa (mainly from Ethiopia, Somalia, Uganda and Zaire). A further 19,800 applications were made by people originating from Asia, most of whom were from the Indian sub-continent.[32] These African and Asian refugees were included in the conception that equated 'immigrant' with 'black person'. This characterisation 'reduced' those seeking asylum to the same status as the 'coloured' immigrants from the Caribbean and Indian subcontinent, whose entry had been largely stopped by 'strict immigration control'. The implication was that 'unscrupulous coloured people' would stop at nothing to subvert 'our' rational and civilised systems of control, thereby necessitating yet more 'strict controls'.

But not all asylum seekers are 'black'. Included in the total number of those seeking asylum in 1989–91 were 8,395 people from Europe and the Americas, a large proportion of whom were Kurds fleeing from Turkey.[32] Moreover, following the declaration of independence from Yugoslavia by Croatia and Slovenia in June 1991, the number of asylum seekers from this part of Europe has increased but only small numbers have been admitted to Britain. Given the geography of Europe, the majority of refugees fleeing from the former territory of Yugoslavia have moved into Hungary, Austria, Germany and Switzerland.[34] In response to requests that other European nation states 'share the burden', the British government has argued that the refugees should remain as close as possible to their former homes in order to facilitate their return when the conflict ceases.[35] Clearly, it is not just asylum seekers from Africa and Asia that the State is seeking to exclude from Britain.

This is indicative of the evolution of a new politics of immigration in Britain which is shaped by the changing international context. There are several dimensions to this. From the early 1970s, the number of refugees seeking to flee to Western Europe and North America increased,[36] and, as a result, the 'refugee problem' was globalised during the 1980s.[37] In a capitalist world economy connected by mass media, electronic transmission and Boeing 747s, it became increasingly possible for refugees (not to mention any others prompted to migrate) at the periphery to know of, and travel to, its centre. In Europe, this has coincided with the (uneven) economic and political integration of its constituent nation states, a process that has necessitated collective decision-making on matters of collective interest.

The increasing mobility of people has been defined as one of these matters and, since the mid-1980s, member states of the EC have been seeking a common refugee policy as part of a common migration policy which includes the free movement of citizens of member states within the EC.[38] Given the intention of most member states to remove border controls between each other's territory in order to facilitate the free movement of their citizens, there is a possibility that non-citizens resident in EC member states (i.e., Third Country nationals) will appropriate this same right for themselves. In sum, and for example, Germany's 'immigration problem' is therefore also Britain's 'immigration problem': within the European Union, the 'problem' of immigration is now a transnational, European issue.

And that 'immigration problem' also has a European character and origin. Since the mid-1980s, an increasing proportion of those seeking asylum in the EC originate from elsewhere on the continent of Europe: the number of asylum seekers in Western Europe originating from Eastern Europe rose from 29,065 in 1984 to 115,662 in 1988. The number has increased further since 1988, the immediate cause being the collapse of communist political regimes.[39] The conflict in ex-Yugoslavia has generated the greatest number of refugees so far, although most of those displaced remain within the borders of the former 'nation state'.[40] In addition, there has been considerable speculation about a flood of 'economic migrants' from east to west as a result of the mass unemployment that results from the introduction of 'free' capitalist relations of production in east and central Europe.[41]

In sum, British state policy on immigration is now shaped by its participation in the evolution of European Union policy while immigration legislation and procedures in each member state are becoming increasingly alike. Nevertheless, the situation in each EU member state continues to exhibit certain specificities which refract different legal arrangements and immigration histories, as well as distinct 'national interests'. This is evident in Britain in the content and official rationale for the *Asylum and Immigration Appeals Bill*, published and debated in 1992. Its effects should be assessed in relation to the *Carriers Liability Act* and to visa policy concerning aliens.[42]

The Bill enshrines in UK law the 1951 United Nations Convention on the Status of Refugees, primarily in order to use the Convention's narrow, individualised definition of refugees[43] to legitimate the government's restrictive intentions. It provides for asylum seekers to be fingerprinted and removes the obligation of local authorities to provide housing to asylum seekers. In circumstances where refusal is mandatory, those refused asylum will have no right to appeal against the decision, while others refused asylum will have the right to appeal to a special adjudicator, in some cases within 48 hours of the decision. Those people with limited leave to enter the UK, but who are refused asylum, can be deported.

More generally, the Bill removes the right of appeal of all (non-EC) visitors and people seeking to study in the UK against a refusal of a visa to enter the UK. Hence, by combining in the same legislation measures concerning the rights of those seeking asylum in the UK with measures relating to the rights of (non-EC) foreigners who are seeking to enter the UK for personal or educational reasons, the Bill 'reduces' rhetorically the status of refugee to that of any other immigrant.

The Conservative government's rationale for the Bill expresses the main themes of the contemporary politics of immigration in Britain: it embodies old and new motifs. The Home Secretary's speech, which opened the Second Reading of the Bill on 2 November 1992,[44] restated two shibboleths. The first is that the UK has a long and 'honourable' tradition of offering asylum to those individuals fleeing 'individual persecution'.[45] The second is that 'good race relations' depend on 'strict immigration control'. Why, then, is 'strict immigration control' considered to be in need of reinforcement?

The Home Secretary[46] envisaged a potential for large movements of people from Eastern Europe, as well as from Africa and Asia, into Western Europe. In the light of already 'terrible pressures' on employment, housing and the social services in 'this already crowded country', he claimed that it is 'common sense' that the government cannot allow the entry of anyone fleeing from a 'poverty-stricken country' or from 'a country in part of whose territory there is civil war or political strife'. He asserted that, during the late 1980s many of those seeking to escape such conditions 'discovered' that they could by-pass 'strict immigration control' by claiming political asylum. Hence, legislation is necessary to ensure that 'bogus applicants' are discovered at the earliest moment. If this is done, the tendency for 'bogus applicants' to become, in effect, permanent settlers because of the time taken to expose them will be reversed, and this will make it easier to deal with 'genuine claimants'. Thus, yet more 'strict immigration control' will allow a separation of the 'bogus' and the 'genuine' refugee, and thereby 'civilised values' will be sustained.

These claims were echoed and supplemented in the subsequent debate. Conservative MPs referred to an 'entitlement' to 'maintain the way of life which people already living in this country want' and to 'tolerance' being 'under strain' as a result of 'overloading' the 'social system'. These are old arguments. Yet there were also references to dangers of the reappearance of fascism in Germany as a result of a 'vast influx' of East Europeans and to the need to 'find alternative shelter for potential refugees close to their own homes'. These reflect the recent Europeanisation of the 'immigration problem', although the latter also indicates the extent to which the EU constitutes an arena within which national states seek to pursue a national politics of immigration.

CONCLUSION

At the beginning of the twentieth century, the British state responded to a 'flood' of immigrants arriving from the east with legislation. Nearly a hundred years later, there are anxious glances in the same direction, seeking the first signs of another, and greater 'flood', although on this occasion there are similarly anxious glances in other directions too. If the British state is participating in the building of a 'Fortress Europe', it is a fortress which is thought to need walls facing east as well as south. What can we conclude from this survey of British immigration politics conducted from the perspective of East–West population movements?

First, claims by government ministers that humanitarian concerns determine their response to the migration of refugees cannot be sustained. It is clear that labour market considerations play a central role in the State's reaction. During the late 1940s the 'unfortunate victims of war' originating from eastern and central Europe (or rather the young, fit and healthy 'victims') were identified not only as useful units of labour but also as 'good stock' and 'lovers of freedom' who would make 'good citizens'. Resources were found to bring them to Britain and 'our own people' were subjected to a propaganda campaign to neutralise their 'prejudice'. Some 50 years later, in the context of a major economic depression and mass unemployment, another group of 'victims of war' from eastern Europe are, for the British state, just another section of the international unwanted who should stay where they are, or at least as close as possible to the war. On this occasion, the propaganda has been intended to ensure that the 'tolerance' of 'our own people' is not 'strained': the maintenance of 'our civilised values' has depended upon depicting the majority of refugees as cheats.

Political considerations are also important. The admission to Britain of Ukrainian prisoners of war in 1947 was determined mainly by foreign policy and security interests. Yet, when there are only largely humanitarian reasons to admit refugees, as in the case of refugees fleeing the war in what was Yugoslavia, we witness a refusal on the part of the British state to play any significant role in making available a place of asylum. The social and legal status of refugee is socially determined rather than inherent in a particular set of circumstances, and so perceived political interests play a major role in attributing the status and in acting in accordance with it.

Second, the evolution of the law and practice of immigration control in Britain is as much a response to the migration of other Europeans as to the migration of 'black' people from the Caribbean, Indian subcontinent and Africa.[47] The history of modern immigration control begins with the response of the British state to an East-West migration of people fleeing persecution, and the principles established in the 1905 Aliens Act were then refined and elaborated in response to security and social concerns (including concerns about 'racial pollution') before and after the First World War. Significantly, the principles of the 1922 *Carriers Liability Act* have a precedent in the Aliens Act of 1905 which required the active participation of ships' captains to enforce the system of control.

Third, East European migrants have been racialised, although in different ways, in the course of the political debate about the legitimacy of their presence or attempt to enter Britain. For many of those anxious to control or halt the arrival of Russian Jews, the Jews were signified as both alien and as a distinct and unassimilable 'race'. A hundred years later, such an explicit biological racism is not articulated by State representatives, but nevertheless the common sense 'logic' that 'good race relations' depends on 'strict immigration control' suggests that alien status is still an expression of a difference of 'race'. The continuous centrality of 'race' thinking to the politics of immigration control is further confirmed by the racialisation of the EVWs in the late 1940s, although on this occasion with a different ideological content and intention. The migrants (or rather, a large proportion of them) were legitimated as 'good stock': given the economic role to which they were being assigned, they were 'just like us'.

NOTES

1. L.P. Gartner, *The Jewish Immigrant in England 1870–1914* (London: Simon Publications, 1973), p.30.
2. Ibid., p.21.
3. B. Porter, *The Refugee Question in Mid-Victorian Politics* (Cambridge: CUP, 1979), p.218; B. Gainer, *The Alien Invasion: The Origins of the Aliens Act of 1905* (London: Simon Publications, 1972).
4. R. Miles, *Racism After 'Race Relations'* (London: Routledge, 1993).
5. Gartner (note 1), p.63.
6. Ibid., p.147.
7. *Parliamentary Debates (Commons)*, Vol. 483, col. 140, 1 Feb. 1951.
8. J. Zubryzcki, *Polish Immigrants in Britain: A Study of Adjustment* (The Hague: Martinus Nijhoff, 1956), p.62.
9. J.A. Tannahill, *European Volunteer Workers in Britain* (Manchester: Manchester UP, 1958); D. Kay and R. Miles, 'Refugees or Migrant Workers? The Case of the European Volunteer Workers', *Journal of Refugee Studies* 1/3–4 (1988), pp.214–36; D. Kay and R. Miles, *Refugees or Migrant Workers? European Volunteer Workers in Britain 1946–1941* (London: Routledge, 1992).
10. D. Cesarani, *Justice Delayed: How Britain became a Refuge for Nazi War Criminals*, (London: Heinemann, 1992), p.114.
11. P. Gordon, *Policing Immigration: Britain's Internal Controls* (London: Pluto Press, 1985), p.11; A. Dummett and A. Nicol, *Subjects, Citizens, Aliens and Others: Nationality and Immigration Law* (London: Weidenfeld, 1990), p.146.
12. *Economic Survey for 1947*, Cmd.7046, HMSO.
13. K. Sword, 'The Absorption of Poles into Civilian Employment in Britain, 1945–50' in A.C. Bramwell (ed.), *Refugees in the Age of Total War* (London: Unwin Hyman, 1988).
14. Kay and Miles (note 9).
15. K. Salomon, 'The Cold War Heritage: UNRRA and the IRO as Predecessors of UNHCR' in G. Rystad (ed.), *The Uprooted: Forced Migration as an International Problem in the Post-War Era* (Lund Norway: Lund UP, 1990); W. Jacobmeyer, 'The 'Displaced Persons' in West Germany' in Rystad.
16. Cesarani (note 10), p.133.
17. *Parliamentary Debates (Commons)*, Vol. 433, 14 Feb. 1947.
18. CAB134/301, Cabinet Foreign Labour Committee, 14 March 1946, Public Records Office (hereinafter PRO), Kew, London.
19. R. Miles and D. Kay, 'The TUC, Foreign Labour and the Labour Government, 1945–1951', *Immigrants and Minorities* 9/1, 1990, pp.85–108.
20. *Parliamentary Debates (Commons)*, Vol. 433, cols. 749–766.
21. LAB8/90, Draft Report on Recruitment of Baltic DPs for Hospitals, PRO, London.
22. LAB8/1385, undated memorandum on progress of Balt Cygnet, PRO, London.
23. Ministry of Labour and National Service, *Workers from Abroad*, (1948).
24. LAB10/652, *National Joint Advisory Council*, 26 April 1950, PRO, London.

25. Cesarani (note 10), pp.4–5; C. Harris, 'British Capitalism, Migration and Relative Surplus Population', *Migration* 1, (1987), pp.47–90.
26. G. Rystad, 'Victims of Oppression or Ideological Weapons? Aspects of US Refugee Policy in the Postwar Era' in Rystad (note 15); J. Cels, 'Responses of European States to *de facto* Refugees' in G. Loescher and L. Monahan (eds.), *Refugees and International Relations* (Oxford: Clarendon Press, 1990).
27. E.g., *The Economist*, 28 Nov. 1992; *Hommes & Migrations*, No. 1155, 1992.
28. E.g., D. Joly, C. Nettleton and H. Poulton, *Refugees: Asylum in Europe?* (London: Minority Rights Group, 1992).
29. S. Joshi and B. Carter, 'The Role of Labour in Creating a Racist Britain', *Race and Class* 25 (1984), pp.53–70.
30. R. Miles and A. Phizacklea, *White Man's Country: Racism in British Politics* (London: Pluto Press, 1984); R. Miles and J. Solomos, 'Migration and the State in Britain: an Historical overview' in C. Husbands (ed.), *'Race' in Britain: Continuity and Change* (London: Hutchinson, 1987).
31. Cels (note 26).
32. Joly *et al.* (note 28), p.29.
33. Ibid.
34. *The Independent*, 2 Dec. 1992.
35. Ibid., 19 Nov. 1992.
36. G. Loescher, 'Introduction: Refugee Issues in International Relations' in idem and Monahan (note 26), p.17.
37. J. Desbarats, 'Institutional and Policy Interactions among Countries and Refugee Flows' in M.M. Kritz, L.L. Lim and H. Zlotnick (eds.), *International Migration Systems: A Global Approach* (Oxford: Clarendon Press, 1992) p.279.
38. E.g., P. Gordon, *Fortress Europe? The Meaning of 1992* (London: Runnymede Trust, 1989); Joly *et al.* (note 28) R. Fernhout, '"Europe 1993" and Refugees', *Ethnic and Racial Studies* (in press).
39. Joly *et al.* (note 28), p.30.
40. *The Independent*, 2 Dec. 1992.
41. E.g., *The Economist*, 28 Nov. 1992; A. de Tinguy and C. Wihtol de Wenden, 'L'Est Entre en Jeu', *Hommes & Migrations*, No.1155, 1992, pp.6–13; F.W. Carter, R.A. French and J. Salt, 'International Migration Between East and West in Europe', *Ethnic and Racial Studies* (in press).
42. Joly *et al.* (note 28), pp.121–8; Fernhout (note 38).
43. Joly *et al.* (note 28), pp.11–21; A. Zolberg, A. Sergio and S. Astri, *Escape from Violence: Conflict and the Refugee Crisis in the Developing World* (NY: OUP, 1989), pp.21–7.
44. *Weekly Hansard*, No. 1598, cols. 21–113.
45. For a different evaluation of this tradition, see B. Wasserstein, *Britain and the Jews of Europe, 1939–1945* (Oxford: OUP, 1988).
46. *Weekly Hansard*, No. 1598, cols. 21–36, 2 Nov. 1992.
47. R. Miles, 'Who Belongs?: The Meanings of British Nationality and Immigration Law', *Journal of Law and Society* 18/2 (1991), pp.278–85.

Recent Immigration Politics in Italy: A Short Story

JOHN W.P. VEUGELERS

The short history of recent Italian immigration politics spans four phases: (1) until 1986, an incoherent policy with little control over flows; (2) increased mobilisation of public opinion, followed by the extension of foreign workers' rights and a flawed amnesty campaign; (3) renewed mobilisation of public opinion in 1989, and Italy's alignment with the Schengen group; (4) lower political salience since the events at Bari in 1991. The mobilisation of public opinion drives cycles of immigration policy-making activity, but legislative procedures structure influence within policy networks and thus indirectly condition policy content. The weakness of xenophobia, the dismantling of the Ministry for Italians Abroad and Immigration, and preoccupation with the crisis of Italy's postwar system have made immigration an unimportant political issue since 1991.

Italy is a country with a century-long experience of mass emigration, for which the arrival of hundreds of thousands of immigrants since the mid-1970s has raised entirely new political questions. While this article focuses on the cycles, content and effects of Italy's policy responses, associated processes are also examined, namely interparty and inter-ministerial dynamics, the fluctuating pressures of public opinion, and the roles of unions, voluntary associations, and immigrant groups.

Four analytical questions underpin this historical account. First, in order to address the question of influence in policy-making, an attempt has been made to identify sides in the making of specific pieces of immigration policy, and to examine whether policy outcomes reflect conflict or accommodation between forces. The second question concerns the direction of policy in terms of liberalisation versus restriction: does a policy change expand or contract the flow of foreigners, increase or decrease their rights? The third question pertains to the centralisation of immigration policy: how extended is the policy-making network, and do decision-making or implementation tend to fall to the same actors? Finally, to what extent do policies bring Italy into harmony with international conventions and agreements?[1]

FROM SENDER COUNTRY TO COUNTRY OF IMMIGRATION

Italy became a country of immigration later than other industrialised countries in Western Europe, partly because its postwar colonial ties were weaker than those of Britain, France, Belgium and the Netherlands. Yet, other countries which also lacked such ties – Switzerland and West Germany – became receiving countries before Italy. The major reasons for the delay in immigration to Italy were the greater pull of labour opportunities elsewhere, and the presence of a large domestic reserve of cheap labour. Until the 1970s, massive migration flowed from Italy's rural south and northeast to the industrial area between Genoa, Turin and Milan, as well as to France, Belgium, Switzerland, West Germany, Argentina, Australia and North America.[2]

TABLE 1

EMIGRATION AND RETURN MIGRATION OF ITALIAN NATIONALS, 1950–86

Period	Departures	Entries	Net Balance
1950–60	3,137,712	1,395,623	−1,742,089
1961–72	2,956,667	2,135,438	− 821,229
1973–86	1,247,284	1,324,083	+ 76,799

Source: Odo Barsotti and Laura Leccini, 'L'immigration des pays du Tiers-Monde en Italie', *Revue Européenne des Migrations Internationales* 5/3 (1989), Table 1.

As Table 1 suggests, the oil shock of 1973–74 marked a turning point in Italian immigration. Though return migration had long been high, after 1973 it exceeded emigration. Further, after the oil shock, Third World migration to Italy rose sharply as push conditions worsened in Africa and Asia while France, Switzerland, West Germany and Great Britain adopted more restrictive policies. By 1977 an estimated 300,000 to 400,000 aliens were in Italy, and their number continued to rise thereafter. The average annual increase in Italy's foreign population was 7.2 per cent between 1981 and 1985, and 16.7 per cent between 1986 and 1990.[3]

Unlike other industrialised societies in Western Europe, Italy became a country of immigration within a context of deindustrialisation and rising unemployment. Further, the country has an enormous underground economy and longstanding disparities in regional development. Thus, foreign workers were shut out of relatively well-paid, protected industrial jobs from the start. Instead, they found illegal work in small and medium-scale manufacturing, as well as jobs which Italians would not fill in the primary and tertiary sectors – in agriculture and fishing, in

TABLE 2

FOREIGN POPULATION IN ITALY, 1975–91

	1975	1980	1985	1990	1991
Foreigners, in thousands	186.4	298.7	423.0	781.1	896.8
% of total population	0.3	0.5	0.7	1.4	1.6

Sources: Continuous Reporting System on Migration/SOPEMI, *Trends in International Migration* (Paris: OECD, 1992), p. 131, Table 1; Italy, Ministry of the Interior (1987, 1992).

restaurants and garages, and as pedlars and domestics. Often, the legal or economic status of foreign workers has been precarious because they tend to be self-employed, non-unionised, hired seasonally, or exploited in the underground economy.[4]

IMMIGRATION POLICY TO 1986: GAPS AND CLANDESTINITY

Until late 1986, Italian policy toward the entry, residence and rights of aliens lacked comprehensiveness. By framing immigration primarily as a threat to public order, the state failed to regulate and co-ordinate other dimensions of the phenomenon including flows, employment, housing, education, training, health and family unification. Moreover, the sudden rise of immigration since the 1970s was met by a profusion of ministerial directives and amendments whose opaqueness, inconsistencies and lacunae encouraged administrative discretion and arbitrariness.[5]

Finally, the statutes contradicted the Italian Constitution of 1948, which recognises the right of asylum, equal civil and social rights for foreign residents, and the limitation of Italian sovereignty by broad international laws. In particular: (1) the core of the law on foreigners (which dated from 1931 and was designed to bar anti-Fascists) subjected non-nationals to special restrictions over entry, movement, residence and property ownership; (2) under legislation passed in 1948, foreigners could be expelled if unable to show their funds were both sufficient and legally obtained; (3) in March 1982 the Ministry of Labour instructed local authorities to stop issuing work permits to non-EC citizens; (4) while Italy was a signatory of the 1951 Geneva Convention on Refugees, it did not ratify the Bellagio Protocol and thus was exempt from taking refugees on the now outdated grounds that it was a country of emigration; (5) when Italy ratified ILO Convention 143 (1975) in April 1981 with the aim of defending the rights of Italians living and working abroad, it was endorsing principles not upheld at home, since the ILO Convention censures discrimination, defends freedom of movement, and recognises foreigners' equality in the areas of pay, job training and security, union and cultural rights, social security and family unification; (6) Italy's statutes failed to conform with the European Parliament's recommendation 990 of 1984.[6]

Italy's non-system of immigration regulation appears to have been harsh: in 1984 alone, 12,500 aliens were refused entry, a further 13,645 were expelled, and 26,684 others were either arrested or handed over to the authorities. Yet, foreigners without funds or steady legal employment could not regularise their status. A high level of clandestinity resulted, because restrictive laws coexisted with loose regulation and employers' readiness to break the law in hiring cheap, flexible labour. Though it is impossible to be precise about the extent of clandestine work, experts agree undocumented workers numbered in the hundreds of thousands by the early 1980s.[7]

Despite these problems, immigration politics emerged late in Italy. Public opinion was generally indifferent, and those involved in maintaining the system of clandestine work – foreigners, their employers in the underground economy, the state – kept silent about the situation. In any case, it was impossible to form a reliable picture of the new foreign presence because the state could not provide trustworthy statistics. Politicians and the general public could still believe that Italy was a stepping-stone for migrants, not a final destination. Immigrants also lacked a voice, for they had no voting rights and were not organised into autonomous associations or political groups. Finally, immigration remained a buried issue because there were no xenophobic political parties or movements exploiting it.

Attempts at immigration reform in the early 1980s were unsuccessful. Bill 694 of 1980 (*Norme integrative della disciplina vigente per il controllo degli stranieri*) made employment a condition of legal residence, and would have barred foreigners lacking a prepaid return travel ticket. While Bill 694 received Senate approval, it was withdrawn following criticism for its preoccupation with public order. The next important legislative proposal focused on the regularisation and control of migrant labour. Bill 1812 of 1982 (*Disciplina dell'occupazione in Italia di lavoratori subordinati stranieri extracomunitari*) was sponsored by Minister of Labour Di Giesi after consultation with the major unions, which at this point largely shared his ministry's blindness to questions of foreigners' rights and integration. The bill included measures to regularise undocumented workers, punish those who hired or trafficked in illegal workers, and regulate the entry and employment of foreign workers. Bill 1812 received the approval of a parliamentary committee (the *Commissione lavoro emigrazione del Senato*) but died when the Spadolini government fell in November 1982.[8]

PARLIAMENTARY COMMITTEES AND THE FIRST REGULARISATION CAMPAIGN

When France's *Front National* scored its breakthrough in the 1984 European elections, immigration still was not a public issue in Italy. However, in August 1985 Prime Minister Craxi linked recent terrorism in Italy to foreigners at the University of Perugia, and the mass media then indulged in a guessing-game concerning the 'true' number of immigrants in Italy. A terrorist attack on the Leonardo da Vinci International Airport near Rome in December 1985 reinforced public criticism of lax border controls and inadequate policing, though some also warned about the dangers of racism.[9]

The following year, Bill 1820 (which later became Law 943 of 1986) was presented in standing committees of the Senate and House of Representatives. Under the Italian system, a bill can pass without going before a plenary session of Parliament if the committees approve it. In this case, the committees' members belonged to parties in and out of government, including the Communist Party and the neo-fascist MSI (*Movimento sociale italiano-Destra nazionale*). The Communists worked in tandem with the Christian Democrats on Law 943. While the smaller parties usually pay less attention to international relations, both the Communists and the Christian Democrats had a few members whose activism in immigrant politics flowed out of their earlier involvement in emigration politics. These politicians also had close contact with the areas of Italian civil society which were most involved with immigrants – the labour movement and Catholic voluntary associations.

In discussions held in the parliamentary committees, the MSI's deputies (but not the MSI's senators) registered the only consistent dissent with the bill. However, in a backroom deal the neo-fascist deputies agreed to abstain rather than cast their dissenting votes. In return, the bill was reworded so the MSI-backed CISNAL union might have a place in the new advisory board on immigrant affairs.[10] A leading Christian Democratic sponsor of the bill, Franco Foschi, later thanked the MSI deputies 'who had chosen not to identify themselves with positions which had brought success to the far right in France'.[11] The bill was then passed with no votes against – and three MSI abstentions.

At this time, immigrants were not autonomous political actors. Their interests were mediated by the *Comitato per una legge giusta* organised by Aldo de Matteo of the *Associazioni Cristiane dei Lavoratori Italiani* (ACLI). The *Comitato per una legge giusta* performed three main functions: (1) expanding the pro-immigrant lobby beyond Catholic groups like the ACLI and Caritas (a charity long involved with Italy's immigrants) by bringing in unions and lay associations representing a range of ideological and partisan tendencies; (2) co-ordinating intensive lobbying of all the parties; (3) forming public opinion through meetings, articles and press conferences which explained that foreigners did not steal jobs from Italians. The mobilisation of public opinion turned out to be decisive, not only in forming a partisan consensus, but also in getting the law passed despite resistance from the Foreign Ministry and the Ministry of the Interior.

The making of Law 943 (1986) confirms that in Italy, as in France, Great Britain and former West Germany, positions on immigration tend to cross-cut established party cleavages.[12] This episode also confirms that interparty dynamics in Italian policy-making cannot be mechanically deduced from partisanship, the social bases of party support, or the structure of coalitions.[13] Instead, the making of Law 943 is a classic example of *trasversalità*: politicians' positions cross-cut partisan divisions, while log-rolling brings the opposition on side and thus perpetuates the Italian parties' colonisation of state and society.

The making of Law 943 also shows how the postwar Italian political system has been able to provide a modicum of efficacy, despite what Giuseppe Di Palma calls the system's low overall performance.[14] True, the bureaucracy is over-regulated, pervasive clientelism stifles change, and proportional representation creates unstable coalitions and frequent government turnover. Still, a good part of the system's limited performance is achieved in the multi-party parliamentary committees. Outside of their meetings, lobbyists for different interests seek to influence committee members. In the committees, partisan intransigence relaxes as politicians confer with civil servants, forge compromises, strike deals, distribute patronage – and enact the majority of Italy's laws.[15]

After more than a decade of rising immigration, administrative confusion and societal indifference, Law 943 of 1986 (*Norme in materia di collocamento e di trattamento dei lavoratori extracomunitari immigrati e contro le immigrazioni clandestine*) gave Italy the foundation for a more comprehensive and coherent immigration policy. The law applied specifically to employees from non-EC countries (*lavoratori subordinati extracomunitari*), their immediate families, employers and the relevant public agencies. Briefly, the Law had three main features: (1) foreign workers were given the same rights as Italian workers, in accordance with ILO Convention 143 (1975); (2) future admissions of aliens were tied to labour market needs; (3) irregularity or clandestinity were to be controlled by introducing an amnesty allowing the regularisation of undocumented workers, and by punishing those who hired or trafficked in undocumented workers.[16]

The amnesty administered under Law 943 was only a partial success. As may be seen from Table 3, the status of only about 105,000 foreigners (17 per cent of whom were women) was regularised, less than half the estimated total of clandestine workers.[17] Many factors hampered the campaign. The powerful Ministry of the Interior did not fully co-operate, and the regularisation process tested the efficiency of no less than three of Italy's bureaucracies: the local administrations (*comuni*) for documentation, local police headquarters (*questure*) for regularisation, and provincial labour offices for registration on the employment roll. Another problem was the lack of publicity surrounding the regularisation campaign, despite all the media attention lavished on 'the immigrant problem' after the terrorist attack at Leonardo da Vinci International Airport a few months earlier. Finally, while Law 943 punished employers who hired undocumented employees, documented foreign workers would earn the same as Italians. Many undocumented foreigners apparently chose not to regularise rather than price themselves out of the labour market. Others registered as unemployed while continuing to work illegally in their old underpaid jobs.[18]

Apart from these problems of implementation, Law 943 represented only a start because it did not lift Italy's geographic exemption from the Geneva Convention on Refugees. It also begged the issue of foreigners' political rights, such as the right to vote in local elections, and the linkage between immigration levels and employment policy was never institutionalised. Finally, Law 943 applied mainly to workers, and even then only to full-time employees (whether employed or formerly employed). It failed to address the status of students or seasonal, professional, part-time, co-operative or self-employed workers.

THE 'MARTELLI LAW' AND THE SECOND REGULARISATION CAMPAIGN

In December 1988 Premier Ciriaco De Mita charged Rosa Russo Jervolino (a Christian Democrat and the Minister for Social Affairs) with the preparation of a new immigration bill. Though anti-racist groups had organised since 1987, and the mass media were now paying more attention to 'the immigrant problem', the predominant public attitude toward immigration remained one of surprise rather than hostility or concern.[19] The unions were now lobbying on behalf of

TABLE 3

REGULARISATIONS AND NON-EC RESIDENTS IN ITALY, 1986–90

	Regularised under:		Resident on
	Law 943 (1986)	Law 39 (1990)	31 Dec. 1990
Morocco	19,283	50,538	77,971
Tunisia	8,919	29,918	41,234
Algeria	671	2,132	4,041
Libya	169	176	2,604
Egypt	5,261	7,180	19,814
Ethiopia	2,392	1,512	11,946
Somalia	1,208	4,344	9,443
Senegal	7,531	16,643	25,107
Ghana	3,296	6,600	11,443
Nigeria	1,104	3,776	6,855
Cape Verde	682	530	4,991
Mauritius	1,218	2,799	5,367
Philippines	9,538	13,351	34,328
China	4,498	9,747	18,665
Sri Lanka	9,494	4,527	11,454
India	1,241	2,339	11,282
Pakistan	958	3,137	6,497
Bangladesh	385	3,444	4,883
Brazil	905	2,867	14,293
Argentina	900	2,518	12,893
Colombia	474	960	5,524
Dominican Republic	530	1,685	4,415
Peru	632	1,976	5,253
Chile	813	787	4,248
Venezuela	216	387	5,046
Yugoslavia	6,386	12,226	29,790
Poland	466	5,539	16,966
Hungary	72	424	4,147
Romania	180	686	7,494
USSR	24	334	6,447
Turkey	774	1,576	4,695
Iran	2,900	2,601	14,630
Lebanon	467	1,592	5,802
Jordan	473	999	5,703
Other Developing Countries	5,807	9,348	62,171
Other Countries	5,445	6,839	117,689
Total	105,312	216,037	635,131

Source: Continuous Reporting System on Migration/SOPEMI, *Annual Report-1990* (Paris: OECD, 1991), p.22, Table 8.

immigrants, but their efforts were fragmented by the number of ministries involved in immigration affairs.

Minister Russo Jervolino lacked influence, however. While Social Affairs is a weak ministry without an independent budget, other ministries involved in immigration affairs had large budgets, more senior ministers, and different agendas. The Ministry of the Interior was directly involved in the Trevi agreement on international crime and terrorism, and played up immigration as a threat to public safety. The Foreign Ministry, which was responsible for border controls rather than the integration of immigrants into Italian society, also played down immigration reform, for it did not want to compromise negotiations over agricultural trade, fishing rights and natural gas with the Maghreb countries which sent so many immigrants to Italy. And in the eyes of the parties, the subjects of immigration policy – Italy's foreigners – counted for little because they did not belong to the electorate. As in 1986, when public reaction to terrorism spurred new immigration legislation, more decisive government action awaited another sensational event.

Vice-Premier Claudio Martelli grabbed the responsibility for a new immigration bill when public opinion reacted strongly to the murder of an immigrant from South Africa, Jerry Essan Masslo, in August 1989. Martelli was a newcomer to immigration politics, and the party he represented, the Socialists, had no specialists in the area. However, public opinion was now mobilised and expectant, and as both Vice-Premier and the senior Socialist in the coalition government, Martelli had more influence over the parties and his fellow ministers than Russo Jervolino. Martelli was also to show strong political will, particularly when Minister of Labour Donat Cattin suddenly tried to relax the conditions under which foreign workers could register in provincial labour offices.

Whereas Law 943 (1986) was passed in committee, the Martelli Law followed a different legislative path. It began as a decree law (*decreto-legge*), a government emergency decree which expires within 60 days unless Parliament converts it into a law. As with Law 943 (1986), the mechanics of the legislative procedure affected participation in the key consultations as well as the new law's content.

According to press coverage at the time, the making of the decree law involved collective debate and negotiation. In fact, the decree was conditioned by the foreign policy concerns of top bureaucrats who wanted to show the EC that Italy was serious about controlling immigration. Before the government issued the decree law, a high-profile discussion carried by the mass media – mostly about goodwill and the importance of pluralism and racial tolerance – attracted intellectuals and representatives of parties, immigrant groups, associations and social movements. For the Socialists, the near consensus of public opinion on immigration signalled a chance to show national leadership while mending their party's image as a promoter of social solidarity.

Martelli engaged in a series of consultations which seemed to import into the policy process the openness and liberalism of the public discussion on immigration. The framing of the law was another matter, however. A group of civil servants from different ministries together convinced Martelli that a liberal policy toward North Africa would further alienate the EC, which saw Italy's borders as porous. Instead, the new law should simply harmonise Italy with the Schengen group.[20] The initial resistance of unions, Catholic voluntary associations, and the Christian Democrats weakened after they were persuaded that a more liberal policy might open the way for an Italian Le Pen.

In part, Decree Law 416 of 30 December 1989 simply codified previous ministerial directives.[21] Very briefly, it:

- ended Italy's exemption from the 1953 Geneva Convention on Refugees, and specified asylum-seekers' legal rights;
- broadened residence categories, and gave nationals from non-EC countries the right to enter Italy for reasons of tourism, education, health or work (whether self-employed or as employee);
- provided for entry visas 'where prescribed';[22]
- asked ministries to co-ordinate and systematise immigration flows and the socio-cultural integration of non-EC migrants, given conditions in the labour market, universities and social services;
- clarified expulsion procedures, and gave aliens legal means of contesting expulsion orders;
- announced a second amnesty campaign.[23]

A decree law clears the first hurdle once it receives government approval. However, legislation by decree '. . . cuts both ways. It gives the government special powers of initiative and enforcement, but the need for immediate conversion by Parliament, and the risk that a filibustering minority can block it, also advise against controversial provisions.'[24] Two of the established parties used the second step in the legislative process as an opportunity to test the political payoff from xenophobia. The MSI and the *Partito repubblicano italiano* (PRI) threatened passage of the new law by tabling over 60 restrictive amendments in Parliament.[25]

It may be recalled that the co-operation of the neo-fascist MSI allowed passage of the 1986 immigration law. While anti-immigrant hostility has breathed new life into far right parties elsewhere in Western Europe, racism has never been central to the MSI's ideology. When the Martelli Law was under discussion, the MSI's main problems were the blockage of its electoral support at about 6 per cent, and the fact that the end of the Cold War was turning the party's traditional *raison d'être*, anti-communism, into an historical relic. MSI leader

Gianfranco Fini tested xenophobia before and during discussion of the Martelli Law, but then backed off. Neither he nor his short-time successor, Pino Rauti, have since pursued the anti-immigrant strategy of their counterparts elsewhere in Europe. Immigration remains a controversial and potentially divisive issue within the MSI, so its leaders must weigh the potential gains from xenophobia against risks to the party's unity and image.[26]

More serious was the hostile position of Giorgio La Malfa, leader of the PRI. While the PRI attracts even less electoral support than the MSI, the party enjoyed greater political leverage because it belonged to the government coalition. Playing on fears of crime and social turmoil, the PRI pressed for more restrictive legislation, and championed the Florentine shopkeepers who organised and attacked foreigners while the Martelli Law was before the House early in 1990. La Malfa's gamble does not appear to have paid off electorally, for in the April 1990 administrative elections his party lost support.[27] Nonetheless, by stalling and threatening to create a governmental crisis, La Malfa extracted concessions before 90 per cent of the House approved the new law on 28 February 1990.[28] All but one of the 13 original articles of the Martelli decree were amended by Law 39 (1990):

- many of the Parliament's modifications were isolated, concerning matters such as refugee status, educational and professional equivalencies, and residence, study, and work permits;
- the border police received wide powers of discretion in granting entry to asylum-seekers;
- annual budgets were now specified, including:
  - 20 billion lire annually to the Ministry of the Interior for processing refugee applications
  - 30 billion lire annually to fund local immigrant and refugee support and information centres
  - 19 billion lire in 1990, 29 billion lire in 1991 and 1992 respectively, for added policing
- staffing allocations were also specified:
  - 300 new social workers, sociologists and psychologists to be hired by the Ministry of Labour
  - 1,000 new police positions

Comparison of the decree and the subsequent law reveal the parties' particular prejudices toward foreigners. For example, Parliament changed Article 7.2 to read:

> Those aliens who breach entry and residence laws shall also be

> expelled from the national territory, as shall those who are directly or indirectly responsible, in Italy or abroad, for serious infractions of currency, customs, or other Italian fiscal laws, or of laws protecting the artistic heritage, *or concerning labour trafficking as well as living by the avails of prostitution or the crime of statutory rape and other sexual offences.*[29]

In sum, when the parties converted the Martelli decree into law, they shifted the emphasis toward public order and gave significant discretionary, budgetary and staffing means to the ministry which had carried so much administrative weight in past immigration policy – the Ministry of the Interior.

As Table 3 shows, more than twice as many aliens were regularised under Law 39 (1990) than in the 1986 campaign. The second campaign was better publicised via radio and television, and 500,000 copies of the Law were translated into eight languages and distributed to foreigners. The second regularisation campaign was also better funded and staffed, the help of voluntary associations was officially encouraged, and authorities were instructed to accept any of a wide variety of documents as acceptable identification. Nonetheless, discrepancies in bureaucratic procedures and efficiency reproduced the north–south split in the country's development, and the Ministry of Labour's attempts to help foreign workers to register led to a minor clash with the Ministry of the Interior.[30]

FORGETTING THE DEBACLE AT BARI

While the Martelli Law was being made to gain control over Third World immigration, the Second World was falling apart. By the time Vice-Premier Martelli signed the Schengen agreement in November 1990, Italy was receiving increasing numbers of immigrants from Eastern Europe. Already in July 1990 some 4,000 Albanian asylum seekers had landed at Brindisi, and in February 1991 another handful of Albanian soldiers and civilians asked for asylum. The following month, at a time Italy was barring foreign workers, a further 21,300 Albanians were allowed into the country. While the government was divided over what to do next, the administration was incapable of meeting the new arrivals' basic needs in food, shelter and medical care. Eventually, the government decided to grant work permits to all of the Albanians, then to relocate them across Italy.[31]

On 7–8 August 1991 another 15,000 or more Albanians landed at the port of Bari. This time the government stood firm by repatriating most of the new arrivals, restricting maritime landings, and pledging $70 million in aid to Albania. While the events at Bari received wide mass-media coverage in Italy and abroad, the ensuing public polemic was brief. La Malfa tried to exploit the events at Bari by blaming them on the so-called Martelli Law, but public opinion dropped the issue once the Albanians were gone. Indeed, since Bari both politicians and the general public seem to have decided that Italy's future policy toward Second and Third World immigration lies in the hands of the Schengen group, if not the EU.[32]

Indifference on the part of the government and top politicians underlies the history of the short-lived Ministry for Italians Abroad and Immigration. Instituted by government decree in April 1991, the ministry's responsibilities included the planning of immigration flows and the co-ordination, direction and promotion of initiatives in the areas of employment, information, statistics and legislation. The government appointed Margherita Boniver of the Socialist Party as the new minister, but without portfolio, which meant the new ministry had no budget of its own. Further, its authority in immigration matters could not infringe upon the competencies of other ministries.[33]

Without a strong minister, lacking its own budget and staff, the Ministry for Italians Abroad and Immigration could not wrest the leadership on immigration policy from other ministries. The responsibility for dealing with the crisis at Bari reverted to Minister of the Interior Vincenzo Scotti rather than Boniver, and most of her ministry's budget for 1992 was allocated to deal with the Yugoslavian refugee crisis. Nor did the Ministry for Italians Abroad and Immigration receive added authority under the citizenship law enacted in February 1992. Instead, citizenship remained primarily a responsibility of the Ministry of the Interior, along with the Foreign Ministry and the Ministry of Justice.[34]

The Ministry for Italians Abroad and Immigration was dropped not much more than a year after its birth, when the new Amato government was formed in June 1992. On the face of it, the ministry's demise did not reflect a lesser preoccupation with immigration on the part of the new government. That commitment was weak under previous governments. Morover, the Boniver ministry was not the only one eliminated – other ministries disappeared too, and in this light the Ministry for Italians Abroad and Immigration was simply one of the casualties in Premier Amato's fight against the Italian spoils system known as *lottitazione*.

Yet, the Boniver ministry could hardly have been corrupt or clientelistic, for it had few resources to tempt anyone. Instead, it was axed precisely because none of the parties had a material interest in its survival. Further, the ministry disappeared before being absorbed into another ministry, the first time this has ever happened. For immigrant groups and their allies, the Ministry for Italians Abroad and Immigration seemed both a policy co-ordinator and counterweight to the large ministries. Without it, the representation of immigrants' interests once again became fragmented and overstretched by the task of addressing different ministries. Meanwhile, the powerful Ministry of the Interior continues to carry the most weight in immigration policy.

The established political parties have been largely silent on immigration since the events at Bari. Immigration was not a partisan issue in the general elections of April 1992, and neither the MSI nor the PRI have systematically pursued the xenophobic positions that tempted them when the Martelli Law was in the making. The new northern Leagues, whose ideology tends to put Third World immigrants and southern Italians into the same stigmatised social category, are currently the most xenophobic parties. Yet, even if anti-immigrant hostility unifies part of the Leagues' subculture, it has yet to become a consistent theme in leaders' public statements. All this could easily change, given the Leagues' ongoing growth, increasing voter dealignment, and the continued erosion of the Left and Catholic subcultures.[35]

Italy's immigrants have yet to organise into a coherent political force. They do not vote, and they lack both economic influence and autonomy from unions and Catholic associations. Existing immigrant associations display an absence of strong leadership and are fragmented along regional and ethnic lines. When Vice-Premier Martelli consulted with immigrant representatives in 1989–90, they seemed unacquainted with the political issues, out of touch with their communities, and unable to present concrete demands. The Catholic associations have long lobbied on behalf of foreigners, and continue to do so, but this does not help the immigrants' organisational autonomy. And while the biggest trade unions worked hard to recruit foreign workers between 1986 and 1990, like the Catholic associations they will not put independent resources at the disposal of immigrant groups. Moreover, in lobbying and collective bargaining the unions tend to neglect foreigners' special needs in the areas of housing, language, and social and health services.

While the press continues to follow the more sensational aspects of immigration, including skinhead attacks on foreigners, and the Leagues continue to test xenophobia, now there is the sense that Italy is no longer the soft underbelly of the European Union. It sent the Albanians packing while the whole world watched, and attention has shifted to Germany as it deals with its own refugees, guest workers and neo-nazis: Italy should just wait and see what is done about immigration at the EU level, then follow. If Italy's postwar political system were still in place, the next cycle of immigration policy-making would await another sensational event capable of capturing public opinion.

However, since 1992 Italy has experienced a political crisis without parallel in the rest of Western Europe, and this crisis has pushed immigration off the political agenda. The social and political inclusion of foreigners is not a priority in a country burdened with a new wave of terrorist bombings, the privatisation of its largest firms, constitutional and electoral reform, the defence of its embattled currency, huge budgetary and public sector debts, one fight against the Mafia and another against a corrupt public contracting system, business scandals, and the continued disintegration of its established political parties.

The new political system which is expected to emerge from the crisis ought to be characterised by new structures of policy-making and interparty competition. Accordingly, the patterns identified in the present study may belong to a dying way of doing politics. If the present crisis does indeed bring on the transformation of the political system, future research will have to trace out the implications of such change, not just for Italy's immigration politics, but for its policy-making and interparty dynamics as a whole.

NOTES

Research funded by the Social Sciences and Humanities Research Council of Canada, and Princeton University's Council on Regional Studies and Center of International Studies (MacArthur Foundation Fund). Thanks also to Guido Bolaffi, Roberto Chiarini, Stephen Hellman, Richard Katz, Roberto Magni, Gianfausto Rosoli, Nadia Urbinati, Mark VanLandingham, the Centro Studi Emigrazione, and the Canadian Academic Centre in Rome. An earlier version of this article was presented at the 1992 Meetings of the American Political Science Association in Chicago.

1. This article draws on interviews the author conducted in 1992 with Italian politicians, civil servants and trade union officials. All have participated in immigration politics, and their statements were cross-checked. Interviewees were assured of confidentiality, so they are not cited as sources.
2. Antonio Golini, 'L'Italia nel sistema delle migrazioni internazionali', *Studi Emigrazione* 25/91–92 (Sept.–Dec. 1988), pp.544–65; Umberto Melotti, 'L'immigrazione straniera in Italia', G. Cocchi (ed.), *Stranieri in Italia* (Bologna: Misure/Materiali di Ricerca dell'Istituto Cattaneo, 1990), pp.31–43.
3. Continuous reporting system on migration/SOPEMI, *Annual Report – 1980* (Paris: OECD, 1981), pp.113–14; idem, *Trends in International Migration* (Paris: OECD, 1992), p.17, Graph 2.
4. Marina Capparucci, 'Fasi di accumulazione e flussi migratori: Italia e Terzo Mondo', *Studi Emigrazione* 25/91–92 (Sept.–Dec. 1988), pp.570–80.
5. Between 1963 and 1985 no fewer than two dozen ministerial directives (*circolari ministeriali*) and amendments were issued for residence matters alone, mostly by the Ministry of Labour. *Dossier Europa Emigrazione* 11/7–8 (July–Aug. 1986), pp.46–7.
6. Gianfausto Rosoli, 'Problemi e prospettive degli interventi legislativi sull'immigrazione in Italia', *Studi Emigrazione* 23/82–83 (June–Sept. 1986), pp. 476–91; Jacqueline

Costa-Lascoux, 'L'Europe des politiques migratoires: France, Italie, Pays-Bas, RFA', *Revue Européenne des Migrations Internationales* 5/2 (1989), pp.167–73; Piero Calabrò, 'I non-diritti dei clandestini e degli irregolari, i nuovi diritti degli stranieri con la legge n.39/90', *Da clandestino a cittadino: Riflessioni e proposte sulla condizione dell'immigrato in Italia* (Rome: Ital-Uil, 1990), pp.9–13.

7. Gianfausto Rosoli, 'Aspetti giuridici dell'emigrazione straniera in Italia', *Dossier Europa Emigrazione* 10/9 (Sept. 1985), pp.10–11. According to an undersecretary from the Ministry of Labour, up to 1.4 million non-EC workers were in Italy in 1986; see Italy, *Senato della Repubblica*, 9th Legislature, 529th sitting, 11 Dec. 1986, p.14.
8. M. Laura Vannicelli, 'Immigrati: il disegno di legge n.1812 del ministro Di Giesi', *Dossier Europa Emigrazione* 7/4 April 1982), pp.11–12.
9. On media coverage of immigration in 1985, see Gianmario Maffioletti, 'Fatti di parole', *Dossier Europa Emigrazione* 11/2 (Feb. 1986), pp.9–11.
10. *Gazzetta Ufficiale della Repubblica Italiana*, 12 Jan. 1987, Article 2.2(b).
11. Italy, *Camera dei Deputati*, 9th Legislature, 13th Commission, 7 Mar. 1986, p.17.
12. Herbert Kitschelt, 'Left-Libertarians and Right Authoritarians: Is the New Right a Response to the New Left in European Politics?', paper presented at the Conference on the Radical Right in Western Europe, Univ. of Minnesota, Minneapolis, USA, 7–9 Nov. 1991, p.23, n.51.
13. Most Italian studies of public policy focus on parties or jurisprudence. Determining whether the parties' role in making Law 943 was typical requires a different understanding of public policy. See Gloria Regonini 'Le politiche sociali in Italia: metodi di analisi', *Rivista Italiana di Scienza Politica* 15/3 (Dec. 1985), pp.335–77; Gianfranco Pasquino, *Istituzioni, partiti, lobbies* (Rome: Laterza, 1988); Maurizio Ferrera, 'Italian political science and public policies: A late but promising encounter', *European Journal of Political Research* 21 (1992), pp.469–81.
14. Giuseppe Di Palma, *Surviving Without Governing* (Berkeley and Los Angeles: Univ. of California Press, 1977), pp.5–7, 194–8.
15. 'During the first five legislatures (1948–72) over 75 per cent of all laws were passed at committee stage.' Paul Ginsborg, *A History of Contemporary Italy: Society and Politics 1943–1988* (Harmondsworth: Penguin, 1990), p.488, n.30.
16. *Gazzetta Ufficiale della Repubblica Italiana*, 12 Jan. 1987.
17. Continuous reporting system on migration/SOPEMI, *Annual Report – 1989* (Paris: OECD, 1990), p.94, Table 3.
18. Continuous reporting system, on migration/SOPEMI, *Annual Report – 1988* (Paris: OECD, 1989), p.32; Raimondo Cagiano de Azevedo and Leonardo Musumeci, 'The new immigration in Italy', Roberto Leonardi and Piergiorgio Corbetta (eds.), *Italian Politics: A Review*, Vol.3 (London: Pinter, 1989), p.75.
19. Luigi Manconi, 'Razzismo interno, razzismo esterno e strategia del chi c'è c'è', Laura Balbo and Luigi Manconi (eds.), *I razzismi possibili* (Milan: Feltrinelli, 1990), p.46.
20. Roberto Magni, 'Dal lavoro alla persona. La riforma degli attuali meccanismi delle leggi di immigrazione', *Studi Emigrazione* 30/109 (Mar. 1993), p.128.
21. Bruno Nascimbene, 'Lo straniero in Italia: profili giuridici alla luce della l.n.39/90', *Studi Emigrazione* 27/101 (March 1991), p.120.
22. In order to be admitted to the Schengen group, Italy had to require visas from nationals of Turkey, Morocco, Algeria, Tunisia and Libya. Jacqueline Costa-Lascoux, 'L'espace Schengen', *Revue Européenne des Migrations Internationales* 7/2 (1991), p.166.
23. *Gazzetta Ufficiale della Republica Italiana*, 30 Dec. 1989, pp.26–30 ('Norme urgenti in materia di asilo politico, di ingresso e soggiorno dei cittadini extracomunitari e di regolarizzazione dei cittadini extracomunitari ed apolidi già presenti nel territorio dello Stato').
24. Di Palma, (note 14), p.192.
25. Dwayne Woods, 'La questione dell'immigrazione in Italia', Stephen Hellman and Gianfranco Pasquino (eds.), *Politica in Italia* (Bologna: Il Mulino, 1992), pp.279–80.
26. Piero Ignazi, *Il polo escluso. Profilo del Movimento Sociale Italiano* (Bologna: Il

Mulino, 1989); Manconi (note 19), pp.52–4; Roberto Chiarini, 'Le Mouvement social italien et la question des immigrés', paper presented at the Joint Sessions of the European Consortium for Political Research, Bochum, Germany, April 1991. For an example of contrasting positions within the MSI, compare the interviews with Alessandra Mussolini and MSI deputy Teodoro Buontempo in *Panorama*, 22 Nov. 1992, pp.74–5.

27. Laura Balbo and Luigi Manconi (eds.), *I razzismi reali* (Milan: Feltrinelli, 1992), pp.99–102.
28. *Corriere della Sera*, 23 Dec. 1989, p.11.
29. *Gazzetta Ufficiale della Repubblica Italiana*, 28 Feb. 1990 (parliamentary modifications to the decree law emphasised by the author).
30. Massimo Saraz, 'La legge 39/90. L'osservatorio sulla sua attuazione', Presidenza del Consiglio dei Ministri, *Atti della Conferenza Nazionale dell'Immigrazione* (Rome: Editalia, 1991), pp.388–9; Marina Forti, 'Inclusi, esclusi, semi-esclusi', Balbo and Manconi (note 19), pp.105–22.
31. Of this group, 9,000 found work, 8,500 registered as unemployed, another 645 were granted political asylum, and 1,143 were later repatriated. Continuous reporting system on migration/SOPEMI, *Trends in International Migration* (Paris: OECD, 1992), p.66.
32. Ibid.; Woods (note 25), pp.280–1; Balbo and Manconi (note 27), pp.26–9.
33. *Gazzetta Ufficiale della Repubblica Italiana*, 22 April 1991.
34. *Gazzetta Ufficiale della Repubblica Italiana*, 15 Feb. 1992. The new citizenship law retained the primacy of the *jus sanguinis* principle, but the conditions for naturalisation by *jus soli* were relaxed somewhat: a non-EC citizen might acquire Italian nationality after 10 years of legal residence.
35. Vittorio Moioli, *I nuovi razzismi: Miserie e fortune della 'Lega Lombarda'* (Rome: Edizioni Associate, 1990); Renato Mannheimer (ed.), *La Lega Lombarda* (Milan: Feltrinelli, 1991); Dwayne Woods, 'The Centre No Longer Holds: The Rise of Regional Leagues in Italian Politics', *West European Politics* 15/2 (April 1992), pp.56–76.

How to Define a Foreigner? The Symbolic Politics of Immigration in German Partisan Discourse, 1978–1992

THOMAS FAIST

This article tries to answer two questions. First, how did Germany, a de facto *country of immigration, manage to espouse a counterfactual ideology in the 1980s and early 1990s? Second, what have been the political consequences of upholding a political discourse that denied the reality of immigration? In a polity that officially denies migration and the development of a multiethnic society, issues such as immigration regulation and the settlement of the regulation of labour migrants' immigration have not been directly addressed in partisan discourse. An ethno-cultural conception of citizenship has facilitated a politics of exclusion of 'guestworkers' from voting rights, but inclusion of ethnic Germans, and a redefinition of asylum as labour migration. This has reinforced the symbolic uses of politics by Christian Democratic and populist parties and politicians: immigration, asylum and the multiethnic polity have come to be meta-issues that can be referred to as causes of manifold problems in a context of rising unemployment and a 'crisis of the welfare state'. Moreover, the main alternative to the dominant partisan discourse – 'multiculturalism' – has remained a mirror image of an ethno-cultural conception of membership by advocating a similar one-dimensional positive image of cultural autonomy of ethnic groups in multiethnic states, excluding issues of socio-economic and political participation.*

THE PARADOX OF DE FACTO IMMIGRATION AND THE IDEOLOGY OF A NON-IMMIGRATION COUNTRY

Between 1945 and 1989 net immigration into the old Federal Republic of Germany amounted to more than 18 million people. During the same period about 16 million immigrated into the United States, one of the classical countries of immigration. If we take the proportion of immigrants as a percentage of the total population, it is higher in Germany than in the United States.[1] In the German case, immigrants include expellees and refugees from Eastern Europe (ethnic Germans) and migrant labour from the Mediterranean ('guestworkers'); in the American case all those immigrants are counted who entered legally. Thus, it is remarkable that the government of the Federal Republic has clung to the idea that Germany is not a country of immigration. There has been no public discourse on immigration regulation. Instead of immigration, conflicts over the constitutional right to political asylum have occupied centre stage. Thus, we are left to explain a political paradox: How did a *de facto* country of immigration manage to espouse a counterfactual ideology in the 1980s and early 1990s? More specifically, what have been the politics of *de facto* immigration? And what have been the political consequences of upholding a political discourse that denied the reality of immigration?

In a polity that officially denies the reality of immigration, issues that arise from the settlement of guestworkers, for example, citizenship rights, and immigration regulation have not been directly addressed. Instead, immigration has figured prominently in the politics concerning unemployment and cutbacks in the welfare state. In this situation, political parties try to define the terms and images that serve above all tactical purposes in inter-party competition. Those political parties that are successful in defining issues have more chance of succeeding in the electoral arena. Political actors are not only or primarily interested in solving issues and problems that arise from policies: they also strive to originate events. Conflict between the major actors in the German political system, political parties, can be seen as a discourse in symbolic politics.[2] Symbolic politics uses substitutes to address substantive policy problems.

In Germany, as in all other West European countries, immigration has moved from 'low politics' to 'high politics', as immigration came to be a highly politicised issue during the 1980s. For German political parties, the symbolic politics of immigration and integration may have been attractive for at least two reasons. Symbolic politics that promoted the return of guestworkers to their countries of origin in the early 1980s offered a way to avoid discussions of membership and citizenship of settled migrant labour. And the inter-party conflicts that resulted in restrictions placed upon the right to political asylum in the early 1990s allowed political actors to bypass fundamental questions of immigration control and distributional conflicts in the welfare state.

First, immigration of guestworkers and ethnic Germans raises issues of political membership. Those political parties interested in incorporating ethnic Germans (CDU, *Christlich Demokratische Union* and CSU,

Christlich Soziale Union) tried to cast membership in cultural terms, engaging in the symbolic politics of the 'foreigners' problem' (*Ausländerproblem*). The CDU and CSU pursued policies that centred upon 'assimilation' of guestworkers to German society, or their 'return' to the sending countries. In 1983 the German government implemented a short-lived return policy. This policy effort was symbolic. Based on earlier French efforts it could be predicted that only few guestworkers would return to the country of origin after having settled in Germany. This 'assimilation' versus 'return' strategy also impeded efforts of the social democrats (SPD, *Sozialdemokratische Partei Deutschlands*), interested in including settled guestworkers into the electorate. Second, immigration raises issues of admission to the territory of the national state. In particular, problems of transnational border control became apparent after the fall of the 'Iron Curtain' and 'The Wall.' The rapid increase in the number of immigrants in the late 1980s and early 1990s – ethnic Germans and asylum seekers – called into question the ability of the federal government to control Germany's borders and regulate immigration (see Table 1). During the 1980s administrative efforts to greatly restrict the right to asylum had not substantially altered the number of refugees entering Germany. The high number of refugees may have even been in part an unintended consequence of *de facto* immigration policies. To apply for political asylum was for many migrants the only way of entering one of the richest countries in the world. Eventually, in 1992, the major political parties settled on a compromise to change the constitutional right to political asylum. Even though the latest changes in the constitution appear to have resulted in a decline of asylum seekers, other migratory flows could increase, for example unauthorised migration. Thus, although various policies have curbed the admission of particular groups, it is hard to see how, short of rigorous border control through police-state methods, Germany can substantially decrease the total number of immigrants, especially with respect to clandestine population movements.

Symbolic politics meant that immigration gained the status of a meta-issue.[3] Immigration and asylum could be referred to as a cause of manifold problems. For conservative parties and the emerging right-wing populist *Republikaner*, the symbolic politics of asylum was appealing because certain groups of immigrants and asylum seekers could easily be connected to a host of domestic issues. For example, distributional struggles over social goods during the periods of relatively high unemployment since the late 1970s, and after German unification in 1990, made it easier for politicians to refer to immigrants as competitors in the economic realm. Conservative and populist groups have also

TABLE 1

ADMISSION OF ASYLUM SEEKERS AND ETHNIC GERMANS, 1980–1992

	ASYLUM SEEKERS		AUSSIEDLER
Year	Number	Recognition Rate (per cent)	Number
1980	107,818	12.0	1968–1984:
1981	49,391	7.7	652,897
1982	37,423	6.8	
1983	19,737	13.7	
1984	35,278	26.6	
1985	73,832	29.2	38,968
1986	99,650	15.9	42,788
1987	57,379	9.4	78,523
1988	103,076	8.6	202,673
1989	121,318	5.0	377,055
1990	193,063	4.4	397,075
1991	256,112	6.9	221,995
1992	438,191	4.3	

Source: Statistisches Bundesamt 1992, p.91; and Bundesminister für Arbeit und Sozialordnung, 'Ausländer – Daten: Bevölkerung, Beschäftigung, Arbeitsmarkt' (1993), p.13.

emphasised the threat of immigrants to the alleged ethnic homogeneity of the German national state.

The symbolic uses of politics regarding immigration can be found in all West European countries. Since the late 1970s political discourse in Western welfare states has been full of references to immigrants as economic competitors and as unwilling to assimilate culturally. Also, the gradual restrictions placed upon immigration and political asylum have not been a peculiar feature of German policy. Indeed, the emergence of restrictive policies has been the hallmark of politics in all West European and North American nation-states since the early 1970s. Increased xenophobia has not been a peculiarly German phenomenon, either. For example, in 1991, more violent attacks against immigrants were recorded in Great Britain than in Germany.[4]

The specific nature of the German situation has been that the legally defined ethno-cultural understanding of citizenship has eased the symbolic use of immigration in political conflicts. The fiction of a country of non-immigration could only be upheld by a political discourse of symbolic politics that defined membership exclusively in ethno-cultural terms. The German polity at once demands that immigrants assimilate culturally and, at the same time, denies the opportunity for cultural assimilation and political participation through an ethnic understanding of membership. This understanding is codified in German citizenship law, the *Reichs- und Staatsangehörigkeitsgesetz* that dates back to 1913. This law is explicitly based upon an ethnic concept of membership that defines belonging to a polity in cultural terms, that is, language, customs, and ancestry. The ethno-cultural understanding of membership could be used to reinforce a discourse that portrayed certain groups of guestworkers and asylum seekers as causes of unemployment during economic recession and as welfare cheaters. These exclusionary efforts appealed to the ethnic solidarity of the native population.

Beginning with the writings of Friedrich Meinecke and Hans Kohn,[5] this ethno-cultural principle has been contrasted to a republican principle that grounds membership in a polity in political participation instead of cultural assimilation. In Europe, these writers claimed, France comes closest to this type. Yet, these two different versions of national identity – ethno-cultural versus republican, Eastern versus Western nationalism – can be found to varying degrees in all Western national states, and are not exclusively limited to either Eastern or Western versions of nationalism and citizenship. Whereas this earlier literature has referred to ethno-cultural and republican concepts of citizenship as real types that can be found in specific countries,[6] this analysis uses these notions as principles that guide empirical analysis. In Germany, the CDU and CSU have vigorously supported the ethno-cultural concept of citizenship, while the SPD has taken steps to advance the republican principle.

Three main groups of immigrants and asylum seekers have played different roles in the calculus of political party strategists (Table 2). First, a settled immigrant population, mainly guestworkers from southern and south eastern Europe, emerged in the course of the labour migrant recruitment and settlement, accompanied by family reunification.[7] Second, owing to the constitutionally guaranteed right to asylum, refugees from Eastern Europe and developing countries have applied for political asylum in the Federal Republic. Third, special provisions have brought refugees (*Flüchtlinge*) and expellees (*Vertriebene*) from Eastern Europe in the 1940s and 1950s to the Federal Republic. Based on legislation passed in the 1950s, large numbers of ethnic Germans (*Aussiedler*) could come to Germany in the late 1980s and early 1990s after the opening of borders in eastern Europe.

The first section deals with symbolic politics and the ethno-cultural understanding of membership and political citizenship. It is about conflicts over immigrants as bearers of political rights. In the second section, the analysis focuses on how immigration came to be a meta-issue in a period of economic recession and the 'crisis of the welfare state.' It discusses 'welfare chauvinism,' namely, the role of symbolic politics in

TABLE 2

THE POSITION OF DE FACTO IMMIGRANTS GROUPS AND ASYLUM-SEEKERS IN PARTISAN DISCOURSE

category	labor migrant	refugees (political asylum)	ethnic Germans
dominant label in public debate	"*Gastarbeiter*"	"*Asylant*"	"*Aussiedler*"; "*Vertriebener*" (expellee) "*Flüchtling*" (refugee)
period of main immigration	1960-1973	since late 1980s	1945-1953; 1988ff.
numbers (1992)	ca. 6.5 million 7.3% of the population	See Table 1	ca. one fourth of the population (old FRG)
claim to political rights	via a long and arduous process of naturalization	via a long and arduous process of naturalization	quasi-automatic
claim to social rights	permanent residents (secure legal status): similar to German citizens (exception: *extracommunitari* in labor markets)	asylum seekers: social assistance in kind; recognized asylees: similar to labor migrants	same claims as native citizens
key terms in the partisan debates	"integration" (SPD); "assimilation" or "return" (CDU/CSU)	"abuse" of the right to asylum; "abuse" of social rights and services	"return" to home country
period of politicization (meta-issue)	late 1970s/early 1980s; 1989ff.	late 1970s/early 1980s; 1989ff.	---------
use for political parties	potential electorate for SPD meta-issue for CDU/ CSU and *Republikaner*	-------------- meta-issue for CDU/ CSU and *Republikaner*	actual electorate for CDU/CSU

the debate over social rights of immigrants and asylum seekers. The third section analyses the consequences of symbolic politics for the general political discourse on immigration and examines the dominant alternative to the ethno-cultural concept of membership in German political discourse, multiculturalism.

SYMBOLIC POLITICS AND POLITICAL CITIZENSHIP: VOTING RIGHTS FOR GUESTWORKERS AND ETHNIC GERMANS

The symbolic politics of immigration prohibited a debate over political participation of immigrants in the German polity and emphasised cultural assimilation. Nevertheless, guestworkers and ethnic Germans have played important roles as potential electoral support groups for the CDU/CSU and the SPD. However, while the CDU/CSU successfully incorporated ethnic Germans as voters, the SPD failed to include settled guestworkers. Based on an ethnic understanding of membership in the German polity settled guestworkers were denied political rights, while the very same principle served to legitimate immigration of ethnic Germans from Eastern Europe.

Extrapolation from historical evidence and public opinion polls suggests that guestworkers would constitute a prime electoral clientele for the SPD. Blue collar workers have formed a classical support group of social democracy in Germany. In the 1980s up to 20 per cent of the blue-collar working class in major industrial areas were guestworkers (e.g., in the Ruhr metropolitan region). If settled foreigners had the right to vote in local elections, the magnitude of change would be considerable: in Frankfurt, the city with the highest proportion of immigrants in the Federal Republic (more than 20 per cent), voting rights for settled foreigners would increase the populace by more than 15 per cent.[8]

The major unanticipated effect of migrant worker policy has been the emergence of a multi-ethnic society in the Federal Republic during the last three and a half decades. In the late 1970s SPD politicians began publicly to emphasise policies to further integrate the guestworker population that had come to settle in Germany. *Gastarbeiter* recruitment policy was an active policy of the German federal state, carried out by the Federal Employment Agency. Until the mid-1970s policy-makers in federal government were able to cast labour migration in exclusively economic terms. When a substantial part of the guestworker population stayed on and did not return to the country of origin, and a second and third generation of foreigners grew up in Germany, incremental policy changes occurred. The originally dominant Ministry of Labour began to share responsibilities with the federal Ministry of Interior and its counterpart in the *Länder*.

At this time, the Kühn Memorandum (1979) proposed policies to address both socio-economic problems of settlement (e.g., integration of second-generation immigrants in schools and labour markets) and naturalisation, a move from *ius sanguinis* to *ius soli*. Heinz Kühn (SPD), a former prime minister of North Rhine-Westphalia and the first federal ombudsperson for foreigners' affairs, recommended active policies of anti-discrimination in the workplace, schools, housing and social services. Groups within the SPD suggested a 'right to settlement' (*Nieder-*

lassungsrecht), a policy suggestion that avoided any reference to citizenship.[9]

Many of the proposals of the Kühn Memorandum found their way into SPD campaign platforms in 1980. In particular, the SPD committed itself to grant local voting rights to settled immigrants. Nonetheless, the SPD was careful not to play into the hands of CDU/CSU campaigns that seized upon the issues of voting rights and asylum for campaign purposes. The CDU and CSU party leadership kept a low profile and accused the SPD/FDP government of not handling problems of asylum and foreign workers well. Less prominent CDU/CSU politicians went further to dramatise the issue, introducing terms such as 'overflooding', 'too many foreigners,' and 'abuse of asylum'. SPD Chancellor Helmut Schmidt took great care to avoid the issue of election rights for foreigners, fearing that this would advantage the CDU/CSU candidate for chancellor in 1980, Franz-Josef Strauss (CSU).[10]

In the late 1970s, when the settlement of guestworkers became more and more obvious, both the CDU and the CSU framed the integration of guestworkers as the 'foreigners' problem' (*Ausländerproblem*). The CDU and CSU emphasised the *Ausländerproblem* in their return to power on the federal level in 1982/83. In his first governmental declaration in autumn 1982, Chancellor Helmut Kohl (CDU) declared 'foreigners' policy' to be one out of the four most urgent issues to be addressed in his emergency programme. Speaking to steelworkers in Dortmund, Kohl declared that he intended to reduce the number of foreigners in Germany by about one million. Modelled on the French example, the new CDU/CSU-FDP government gave financial incentives for guestworkers to return to their countries of origin (1983–84). Few returned. Moreover, the government set up a commission to study the 'foreigners' problem.' Nothing happened. In his second governmental address in spring 1983, Kohl did not even mention the 'foreigners' problem.' The symbolic uses of this strategy were obvious: There was not much difference between the actual policies the Social Democratic/Liberal federal government (SPD and FDP) pursued until 1982, and those of the succeeding Christian Democratic/Liberal coalition government.[11]

While this symbolic use of politics may have paid off for the CDU in competing with the SPD for votes in the 1980 and 1983 elections, its success in addressing the challenge of right-wing populist parties turned out to be much more ambiguous. Conflicts over immigration were connected to structural changes in the postwar German party system. Three factions have been integrated within the CDU: the economic liberals have organised in the *Wirtschaftsausschüsse* (interests of entrepreneurs), Catholic and Protestant labour in the *Sozialausschüsse* (interests of unions and churches); and national-conservatives were well represented in the Bavarian CSU. For a long time this setup constituted the hallmark of the CDU/CSU as a 'catch all party' (in Otto Kirchheimer's phrase) that differed from other conservative parties in other European countries, for example the British Tories. Since 1983, national-conservatives have had other choices available, for example the *Republikaner*. The party was founded by two estranged members of the CSU.[12] The *Republikaner* has exploited the fact that CDU and CSU made promises to cut down on the number of foreigners (and 'assimilate' those remaining). Although the CDU and CSU had used the *Ausländerproblem* as a campaign issue before the emergence of the *Republikaner*, the rise of a right-wing competitor may have accelerated the symbolic uses of politics by the CDU and the CSU. After all, immigration was a prime rallying issue for the populist *Republikaner*.[13] Although the *Republikaner* did not succeed in entering the federal parliament in 1987 and 1989, they managed to surpass the crucial five per cent threshold in the 1989 European election and to enter the parliaments in several *Länder*. In the *Landtag* elections in Baden-Württemberg in 1991, the CDU, along with tabloids such as *Bild*, strongly exploited xenophobic tendencies. However, the CDU experienced heavy losses while the *Republikaner* entered the *Landtag*. Election analysts concluded that votes for right-wing parties came from voters who normally considered themselves followers of one of the big parties: the CDU/CSU (and the SPD).[13]

Although the conservative and right-wing parties have been most successful in defining the issues regarding immigration and integration, the SPD has been the most active party in incorporating guestworkers in the political realm.[15] The SPD has organised most immigrant members of all parties, especially Turkish workers.[16] Also, the Turkish Social Democrats co-operate with the SPD. Co-operation between Turkish organisations and German parties has flourished above all on the local level. Membership overlap between German parties and Turkish organisations also seems to be most widespread in social democratic organisations. In Berlin and in the Ruhr area, for example, many members of the *Türkische Sozialdemokraten* are also members of the SPD. This co-operation has become closer over time, because Turkish organisations have moved from an orientation towards the country of origin to the politics of interest articulation in the country of settlement.[17]

However, the SPD did not succeed in securing voting rights for foreign residents with unlimited residence permits. In 1989 the *Länder* of Hamburg, Bremen, and Schleswig-Holstein, all governed by a social democratic majority or plurality, introduced laws to grant voting rights in local elections to foreigners that had resided in the Federal Republic for more than five years. The CDU *Land* Baden-Württemberg and the CSU *Land* Bayern appealed to the Federal Constitutional Court. In order to prevent enfranchisement of guestworkers, the CDU used the argument that 'the people' (*das Volk*) is constituted by citizens. Arguing that guestworkers do not belong to the *Volk*, the CDU and CSU rejected proposals such as voting rights for settled migrants.[18] The Court revoked the regulations of the SPD states. The central argument of the court's majority opinion was that 'all state power derives from the people'. Since the constitution (Basic Law) does not include foreigners in the *Volk* (ethnos), the judges declared the *Länder* laws unconstitutional. Thus, ultimately, the court denied voting rights to permanent foreign residents because they do not belong to 'the people' (*das Volk*).[19]

While the CDU and CSU managed to exclude guestworkers from voting rights, these parties have also benefited from the quasi-automatic political integration of expellees and refugees in the 1940s and 1950s, and of ethnic Germans since the late 1980s. The CDU/CSU federal government reaffirmed frequently that ethnic Germans are not immigrants but returnees. Ethnic Germans have had an automatic right to enter the Federal Republic, analogous to the law of return in Israel and Japan. It has practically guaranteed access to German citizenship to all those refugees from Eastern Europe who can make some distant claim to German ancestry. Because they were automatically enfranchised, ethnic Germans could be easily incorporated into political parties. The CDU/CSU had a special interest in incorporating large numbers of ethnic Germans.[20] As election analyses have documented, the CDU/CSU was able to catch most of the votes of ethnic Germans, expellees, and refugees since the late 1940s.[21]

The CDU/CSU could justify the quasi-automatic admission of numerous ethnic Germans since the mid-1980s for various reasons. First of all, until 1989, the reception of ethnic Germans served as a reminder of the continuing communist threat to the Federal Republic of Germany during the Cold War. Unless the SPD wanted to be denounced as a communist junior partner, the party had to consent unconditionally to the policies of invitation for ethnic Germans.

Second, as long as ethnic Germans suffered the fate of expulsion, it could also be implicitly used as a reminder of the 'lost territories' in the East. It was only after the successful implementation of the *Ostpolitik* initiated by Chancellor Willy Brandt (SPD) that the CDU/CSU gradually started to soften its rhetoric on a Germany returning to the borders of 1937. It was not until 1991 that CDU-chancellor Helmut Kohl signed a treaty with Poland recognising the Oder-Neisse line as the border between Germany and Poland. Resistance to *Ostpolitik* in the CDU/CSU was also based on the fact that expellees and refugees had a powerful political lobby in the 1950s. Compared to guestworkers, they experienced swift political incorporation. Politically, refugee organisations (*Vertriebenenverbände*) have acted as pressure groups within the CDU and CSU.[22]

Third, the CDU and CSU have consistently pointed out that ethnic Germans are Germans as defined by the Basic Law. The category 'ethnic German' is a legal construct of the Cold War,[23] based upon the citizenship law of 1913. According to the current thinking, ethnic Germans should be allowed to enjoy the same constitutional rights and duties as all other Germans, for instance, admission and mobility in the Federal Republic. Ethnic Germans deserve special help because they are compatriots who had to suffer tremendously under the harsh effects of World War II. They adhered to the German language and culture in adverse circumstances. In short, the powerful principle of ethnic solidarity is paramount in justifying a special status for ethnic Germans. Immigration policies toward ethnic Germans are based on Article 116 of the Basic Law. According to this article, specified by the Federal Law on Expellees and Refugees (1953), Germans are all those who either hold German citizenship or who are German refugees and expellees who migrated to the German Reich (in the borders of 1937) until the end of World War II. Since 1949 successive federal governments based their policies on the assumption that all ethnic Germans in the communist 'Eastern bloc' have been subjected to 'pressure of expulsion'. The Law on Expellees and Refugees has constituted a foil for numerous administrative orders that enlarged the group of ethnic Germans eligible for return to those citizens of East European countries who were born after 1945 and could show some proof of German ancestry. The refugee policies of the Federal Republic's have contributed to a reinvigoration of a feeling of German ethnic identity among citizens of German descent in Eastern European countries.

In sum, while political inclusion of guestworkers has been contested, political incorporation of ethnic Germans has remained almost undisputed. Underlying the conflict over voting rights for guestworkers and the unquestioned incorporation of ethnic Germans has been a debate over the definition of the ethno-cultural concept of citizenship. The CDU and CSU used the symbolic politics of 'return' or 'assimilation' of guestworkers to circumvent questions of political citizenship. To justify exclusion of guestworkers and inclusion of ethnic Germans, the CDU and CSU were able to draw upon German citizenship law. The SPD failed to advance the principle of 'no taxation without representation' to promote the political rights of settled migrants.

SYMBOLIC POLITICS AND SOCIAL CITIZENSHIP: 'WELFARE CHAUVINISM' AND THE DEBATE OVER ASYLUM

The ethno-cultural concept of citizenship and the symbolic politics of immigration have reinforced each other. In particular, the political debate over asylum turned into a substitute debate on two issues, on rights and membership in the welfare state, and the regulation of immigration without really addressing immigration as an issue. The question raised by conservative and right-wing parties was also to what extent asylum seekers and certain groups of immigrants have a claim to social rights. Thus, the symbolic politics of asylum included the politics of 'welfare chauvinism', the unwillingness of natives to share welfare state benefits with certain immigrant groups and asylum seekers who are perceived as 'intruders'. Above all the CDU, CSU, and the *Republikaner* focused on political asylum as a meta-issue in the context of high unemployment rates among the native population and alleged welfare fraud by asylum-seekers. By contrast, the SPD unsuccessfully tried to separate the issues of immigration and integration, on the one hand, and political asylum, on the other. In order to separate immigration and asylum, the SPD proposed explicit immigration laws.

Asylum-seekers from developing countries, those granted asylum (*Asylberechtigte*), and certain groups of immigrants could be framed as being 'different' in crucial realms. These groups were perceived to be culturally different. Cultural difference was equated with a rejection of assimilation on the part of immigrants and asylum seekers. Even before the number of asylum-seekers drastically increased in the latter part of the 1980s, it was elevated to a key issue in electoral campaigns by the CDU and CSU in the late 1970s. At that time the negative term *Asylant* entered political debates and since then has been applied to unwanted refugees, particularly those from developing countries.

The tactical use of the asylum question in inter-party conflicts is obvious in a phrase coined by CDU general secretary Volker Rühe: 'Every additional *Asylant* is a *SPD-Asylant*'.[24] The Christian parties introduced key terms into political debate, such as 'over-foreignisation', 'flood of asylum-seekers', 'limits of endurance' and 'the boat is full'. Former interior minister of Bavaria, Edmund Stoiber (CSU) even spoke of 'racialised society' (*durchrasste Gesellschaft*). The expression brought back memories of racial categories used during the Nazi regime. The head of the CDU parliamentary group in the Bundestag, Alfred Dregger, introduced the term 'flooding' in parliamentary debates in the mid-1980s. 'Flooding' in this context alludes to the Muslim threat to Europe in past centuries. The continuity of the juxtaposition of 'Islamic' (oriental) versus 'Christian' (occidental) culture in symbolic politics has been striking. For example, Turkish immigrants are thought to be unwilling to 'assimilate' because they belong to Islam, a perception aided by the Islamic fundamentalism that gained influence in Turkish and North African immigrant communities in Europe during the 1970s. When the inter-party debate on migration turned again from guest-workers to asylum seekers in the late 1980s, the same dichotomy was being seized upon, although most asylum seekers from Asia and Africa were not Muslims. Alluding to the infiltration of Muslim values, Edmund Stoiber entitled one of his contributions to the daily newspaper *Die Welt*: 'And German judges turn over the leaves of the Qu'ran'.[25] The important distinction here is European versus Non-European; a distinction that has increased in importance due to the opening of borders in Eastern Europe and European integration within the European Union ('Fortress Europe').

Thus, the flow of asylum seekers was portrayed as one of 'economic refugees' from developing countries (*Armutsflüchtlinge*) although most refugees actually were citizens of east European countries, such as the former Yugoslavia, fleeing war-torn and devastated regions (Table 3). In short, portraying immigration and asylum as a cultural problem and equating non-European cultures with Islam allowed party politicians from the CDU, CSU and the *Republikaner* to conflate two groups of immigrants, guestworkers from Turkey and asylum seekers from developing countries.

The language that accompanied German unification may have spurred the discourse of cultural difference. Among other things, it raised the issue of a collective identity as national identity. In the aftermath of German unification a rhetoric of national and ethnic identity, 'we' versus 'them', has resurged and may also have affected the perception of immigrants and asylum seekers as competitors for scarce goods such as jobs, housing and social services. Insofar as 'welfare chauvinism' and violence against foreigners is concerned, we are left with a paradox that points toward the crucial role of immigration and asylum as a meta-issue: in East Germany xenophobia exists without foreigners. The unification of Germany connected two states with different histories of immigration after World War II. The Federal Republic had a much higher percentage of immigrants (8 per cent) than the German Democratic Republic (1 per cent).

TABLE 3

ASYLUM SEEKERS AND ETHNIC GERMANS – COUNTRIES OF ORIGIN

ASYLUM SEEKERS (1992)			ETHNIC GERMANS (1991)	
Country	Number	Percentage	Country	Number
former Yugoslavia	122,666	28.0	Poland	40,129
Romania	103,787	23.7	former USSR	147,320
Bulgaria	31,540	7.2	Romania	32,178
Turkey	28,327	6.5	Hungary	952
Vietnam	12,258	2.8	CSSR	927
CIS	10,833	2.5	Yugoslavia	450
Nigeria	10,486	2.4	Other	39
Zaire	8,305	1.9		
Algeria	7,669	1.7	Total	221,995
Ghana	6,994	1.6		
Afghanistan	6,351	1		
Total	438,191	100.0		

Note: The figures do not measure substantial numbers of guestworkers' and asylum-seekers' out-migration during these years. The number of refugees applying for political asylum fluctuated between 4,000 and 9,000 in the mid-1970s.

Source: Statistisches Bundesamt 1992, p.91; and Bundesminister für Arbeit und Sozialordnung, 'Ausländer – Daten: Bevölkerung, Beschäftigung, Arbeitsmarkt' (1993), p.13.

Openly racist statements have been rare. This tendency has been visible above all among the *Republikaner*. They are more moderate in tone than their model, the French Front National and their German predecessors in the late 1960s, the NPD. The *Republikaner* have been so international as to borrow key terms such as 'difference' from the French New Right, whose ideologists (e.g., Alain Benoist) are indebted to German writers such as Moeller van den Bruck and Carl Schmitt. The symbolic politics of difference does not rest upon ideologies of racial superiority that connect physical and mental characteristics. In the language of the New Right, 'culture' and not 'nature' serves as the key distinction between 'civilisations'. Behaviour is thought to be based upon cultural differences. Although they are by no means identical, the late twentieth century rhetoric of difference did fit in easily with ethno-cultural concepts of membership to justify exclusion of 'intruders' from scarce goods.

The campaign rhetoric of the CDU, CSU, and the *Republikaner* suggested that asylum-seekers and selected groups of guestworkers could be held responsible for causing politico-economic problems such as unemployment and cutbacks in social services. Frequently, politicians of the *Republikaner*, such as party chairman Franz Schönhuber, have criticised policies that integrate guestworkers into the German welfare state as attempts to deprive German citizens of deserved social provision and give it instead to unworthy welfare cheaters, among them guestworkers and asylum seekers. Asylum seekers offered an even easier target than settled guestworkers because the former group has not yet contributed to social insurance schemes, such as health, unemployment, and pension funds. Rather, asylum seekers receive non-contributory benefits, that is, social assistance in kind.

In this way the symbolic politics of cultural difference has been inextricably connected to the politicisation of welfare state politics. Both asylum seekers and ethnic Germans are newcomers who have not contributed to social insurance funds.[26] Based on the ethnic definition of citizenship, ethnic Germans are treated *as if* they had paid into these insurance schemes. Asylum seekers only have claims to social assistance benefits in kind. Social assistance benefits in kind for asylum-seekers were further decreased in the early 1990s. One of the justifications used was that asylum-seekers increasingly were abusing their rights by making multiple applications for social assistance. Thus, the abuse of welfare services insinuated the alleged 'abuse' of the right to asylum and vice versa.

These allegations strengthened the distinctions made between 'economic' and 'political' refugees, a widespread dichotomy in the political discourse of all Western welfare states. The conclusion drawn by CDU and CSU politicians was that only the latter group had a legitimate claim to asylum.[27] Low recognition rates of asylum seekers in the first instance (below ten per cent) were taken as an indicator that most asylum seekers were 'economic refugees' who came to compete with Germans for jobs, housing and social services. It is striking that recognition rates further decreased in the early 1980s and have since then dropped again in the late 1980s, two periods in which the symbolic politics of asylum were prevalent (Table 1).[28]

The rhetoric of deterrence toward asylum-seekers and the welcoming of ethnic Germans accompanied the policy debate on asylum. The numbers of ethnic Germans were curbed by non-publicised bureaucratic means. The increasing numbers of ethnic Germans seeking shelter in the Federal Republic led to the new, more restrictive Law to Adapt Integration (1990) and the Ethnic German Reception Law (1991). For example, according to the new laws and regulations, application for acceptance has to be made before leaving the home area in eastern Europe. Thus, the Federal Office on *Aussiedler* Affairs has effectively implemented a *de facto* quota system.

The issue of political asylum, however, took centre stage in inter-party conflicts in 1991–92, rivalled only by the follow-up problems of German unification. Until 1993 asylum seekers came to Germany by asking for political asylum under Article 16 (II, 2) of the constitution: 'Every politically persecuted individual has a right to asylum.' Germany was unique in that it granted an individual claim to asylum for all those who are politically persecuted. Thus, the constitution obliged the Federal Republic to receive all those individuals who could show that they had been persecuted by state authorities on grounds of political belief, race, religion or membership in a certain social or ethnic groups in the country of origin. In short, German Basic Law gave individuals a claim to asylum. By contrast, the Geneva Convention grounds asylum in the prerogative of sovereign states.

After a protracted debate, the major political parties reached a compromise on the asylum issue (in December 1992; changes went into effect in July 1993). It was agreed that Article 16 should be replaced by a new Article 16a. Among other restrictions, all asylum-seekers now can be turned back at the border who enter the Federal Republic from neighbouring 'safe countries' (e.g., Austria, the Czech Republic and Poland); who come from countries declared to be 'free of persecution' (including Romania and Ghana, i.e., countries where many asylum-seekers came from in recent years, see Table 3); and those asylum-seekers whose application was already denied in other countries of the European Community. Effectively, the constitutional amendment implies that refugees who access Germany via land can be turned back without having the opportunity to enter the regular asylum process. One of the main attractions for politicians of all parties of supporting the changes of Article 16 was that the amendment promised immediate reductions in the number of asylum-seekers.[29]

While the conservative and populist parties heavily emphasised the fact that asylum seekers are both culturally different, that they are economic competitors, and that many abuse the social assistance granted by the German welfare state, the SPD wavered on the asylum issue, experienced lengthy internal conflicts, and finally accepted the position of the CDU and CSU. Originally, however, SPD politicians defended the right to asylum as a humanitarian obligation of the Federal Republic to politically persecuted individuals. The SPD faced a dilemma. On the one hand, the SPD followed an integrationist strategy for those migrants already in the country. On the other hand, the SPD was interested in controlling the flow of new immigrants to avoid undercutting wages and a potential downgrading of working and living conditions of native and settled migrant workers. The symbolic politics of immigration successfully portrayed political asylum as unlimited 'open border' policy with harmful consequences for the native population. During the recruitment of guestworkers in the 1960s, unions and the SPD had partly diffused the perception of immigrants as economic competitors undercutting wages by insisting that they received the same rights and duties as German workers in the workplace. Moreover, the economic climate in the 1960s was still one of expansion and growth, in which many German workers may have experienced upward occupational mobility; this was perhaps even facilitated by a massive influx of guestworkers who came to occupy unskilled and, increasingly, semi-skilled blue collar positions. In the 1980s, however, a growing number of SPD voters perceived guestworkers as a threat to job security, and asylum-seekers as competitors for scarce housing and social benefits.[30]

Since the absence of channels other than asylum for potential migrants had contributed to the overburdening of the asylum process, the SPD tried to solve the dilemma in proposing an immigration law that controlled the admission of non-refugees. However, the continued immigration of ethnic Germans already constituted a substantial annual intake of newcomers and thus partly foreclosed options for establishing other immigration channels. In this situation, the SPD leadership chose to give priority to populist trends within its (potential) electorate. It tried to satisfy those groups that were considered potential voters of the CDU.

MULTICULTURALISM: A MIRROR IMAGE OF ETHNO-CULTURALISM

One of the major alternative views to an ethnic understanding of membership has been the German version of multiculturalism. The debate on multiculturalism has surfaced in all West European and North American polities that have been faced with the incorporation of immigrants. Yet, it is no coincidence that the major alternative to an ethnic understanding of membership also carries the label 'cultural.' In Germany, the term did not refer to the political and economic realms of integration. Rather, it denoted the sphere of cultural assimilation and did not transcend cultural 'difference' or similarity as the main criterion of integration. Overall, proponents of multiculturalism primarily espoused a rather naive vision of non-conflictual ethnic relations.[31] Multiculturalism emphasised the cultural autonomy of ethnic groups over 'assimilation.' Intellectually, this position simply mirrored the ethno-cultural understanding of membership in a polity. It substituted a mono-cultural *völkisch* understanding with a similarly one-dimensional multicultural concept of membership. It is one-dimensional because it completely ignores the complex set of issues raised by politics in multiethnic polities. For example, there has been no debate on the extent of rights for minorities in the political and economic realms, such as, in the workplace and the housing market. In other European countries, like France, the United Kingdom, the Netherlands and Sweden the debate on multiculturalism has progressed beyond one-dimensional cultural concepts, due to policies that have recognised the reality of immigration and integration.

The term multiculturalism has also been used in a rather inconsistent way by all those who have rejected the 'assimilation' versus 'return' rhetoric of the conservative-liberal federal government.[32] In Germany, the term first circulated in church, union, and social democratic circles in the late 1970s. During the 1980s the term gradually spread within the community of experts on foreigners' issues, especially those who dealt with social and labour market policy, but also social workers, and teachers. Although the term 'multiculturalism' has been debated within political parties, it has never become an issue in inter-party debate. Nonetheless, there were attempts to frame political issues by using the term. Those CDU politicians who aimed to appeal to voters of the 'centre,' or who argued that metropolitan areas needed migrants as workers in order to compensate for demographic decline among the German population, were the main adherents of multiculturalism within the CDU (e.g., the former general secretary Heiner Geissler and the mayor of Stuttgart, Manfred Rommel).

Also, groups within the SPD and the Green Party were adherents of multiculturalism. For example, the Greens did not only reject an ethnocultural understanding of citizenship.[33] Sections within the Green Party took the high moral ground of seeing Germany as a haven for the world's refugees in an international state system with increasingly restrictive immigration and asylum laws. They even went beyond the constitutionally guaranteed right to asylum. The position could be considered more a matter of political confession than an actual policy proposal. The underlying argument was that the concept of persecution for reasons of race, religion, nationality, social group or political opinion no longer captured the needs of today's refugees in all cases. Therefore, Article 16 should be expanded to include all those who fled because of gender, sexual orientation, (civil) war, the death penalty, and other threats to life and political convictions. The normative justification vindicated a principled commitment to address the causes of flight and asylum on a global scale. The specific arguments made pertain to the German historical legacy and a general responsibility towards the peoples of the developing countries. Yet, this position has been plagued by a rather straightforward 'open border' policy. Possible political and economic consequences of a rigorous 'open border' policy have not been addressed.

CONCLUSION: TOWARDS A RECOGNITION OF IMMIGRATION

The successful use of symbolic politics in upholding the fiction of a non-immigration country has had various consequences for the political discourse on the politics of immigration and integration. First, immigration regulation did not develop as a legitimate policy objective. Instead, discussions focused on political asylum. Most of the arguments used by political parties in the debate over the constitutional issue of asylum – uneasily settling between the poles of 'not a country of immigration' and 'open borders' – did not move the public discussion to questions that form the cornerstones of any immigration policy, namely. admission and selection of immigrants. Immigration is not a legitimate policy objective that could be operationalised in laws and regulations of immigration. Indeed, the opening of the eastern borders has also spurred a new guestworker system, albeit on a smaller scale, *Werkvertrags-Arbeitnehmer*.[34] It is a reprise of the guestworker policies of the 1960s.

Second, the symbolic uses of politics helped to construct migration as a meta-issue: by not recognising the reality of immigration, it could be successfully used as a factor explaining the deleterious effects of economic crisis and policy failures. Ultimately, immigration as a meta-issue means that the reference to immigration as a root cause of policy failures, socio-economic and political problems has gained currency to such an extent that it can be used to legitimate changes in the constitution without having to draw upon and present substantive policy solutions.

Third, it is no coincidence that alternative concepts to the prevailing public German discourse of ethno-culturalism, that is, various versions of multiculturalism, have simply mirrored the ethnic-cultural understanding of membership in the German polity by advocating a similarly one-dimensional positive image of cultural autonomy in multi-ethnic states and excluding issues of social and political citizenship. Yet, as the discussion on voting rights and asylum showed, the ethno-cultural concept has not gone unchallenged. The position taken by the advocates of voting rights for immigrants corresponds to intellectual positions of an 'open republic' or an 'unfinished republic' that grounds citizenship in a republican tradition.[35] 'Republican' in this context means that membership in a polity is not a derivative of culture and heritage. Instead, active participation in political and economic life form the basis of membership and citizenship rights and duties.

To ground citizenship rights and membership in a polity in political participation and not in cultural assimilation could be a promising way to challenge the dominant ethno-cultural concept of membership and its use in symbolic politics. To the extent that the symbolic uses of politics have framed immigration as a meta-issue, it will prove exceedingly difficult to introduce politically viable alternative agendas. An ethno-cultural resurgence in all Western welfare states since the late 1970s suggests that immigration is a meta-issue common to all developed welfare states. Yet, to root membership in political participation would probably weaken the dominance of ethno-cultural concepts in German political discourse. An important implication could be that the very concept of membership would be less likely to reinforce the use of immigration as a meta-issue. In other words, the political discourse could move from the now dominant question of 'How to define a foreigner?' to 'How to define a citizen?'

NOTES

The author would like to thank Jens Borchert, Grete Brochmann, Kim Geiger and Dita Vogel for helpful comments on an earlier draft of this article.

1. Calculations based upon Statistisches Bundesamt, *Statistisches Jahrbuch für die Bundesrepublik Deutschland* (Wiesbaden: Steiner, various years), and Jeffrey S. Passel and Barry Edmonston, *Immigration and Race: Recent Trends in Immigration to the United States* (Washington, DC: Urban Institute, 1992).
2. Murray Edelman, *The Symbolic Uses of Politics* (Urbana: Univ. of Illinois Press, 1964).
3. Harold D. Laswell, *Power and Personality* (NY: Harper & Row, 1948).
4. Dietrich Thränhardt, 'The Political Uses of Xenophobia in England, France, and Germany' (Paper presented at the ECPR Joint Session of Workshops. Leiden/ Holland, April 1993).
5. Friedrich Meinecke, *Cosmopolitanism and the National State* (Princeton: Princeton UP, 1970; orig. 1909); and Hans Kohn, *The Idea of Nationalism. A Study of Its Origin and Background* (NY: Collier, 1967; orig. 1944)
6. See, e.g., William Rogers Brubaker, *The Politics of Citizenship in France and Germany* (Cambridge, MA.: Harvard UP, 1992).
7. Two groups with different legal status have to be distinguished: labour migrants from EC countries and those from non-EC countries. The former group faces few restrictions in regard to labour market access while the latter's legal status is clearly inferior. E.g., EC-nationals have the same labour market status as German citizens while *extracommunitari* get work permits only for jobs for which no German citizens and EC-citizens are available. In 1991 workers from EC-countries comprised about 510,000 workers, those from non-EC (Turkey and former Yugoslavia) countries about twice as many, about 1,200,000 – more than half of them from Turkey (Statistisches Bundesamt 1992, p.125).
8. Claudia Koch-Arzberger, 'Wahlverhalten von Ausländern – Chance oder Gefährdung

der Demokratie', in Karl Starzacher *et al.* (eds.), *Protestwähler und Wahlverweigerer. Krise der Demokratie?* (Köln: Bund Verlag, 1992), pp.113–30.

9. However, in a political climate, in which the asylum issue played an important role in electoral campaigns (1980), the proposals in regard to political rights were not implemented. Nevertheless, some of the changes brought about by the new 'Foreigners' Law' (1990) finally eased the process of naturalisation for the 'second' generation although the principle of *ius sanguinis* was not removed. The new law gives a claim to naturalisation to all those who have lived in Germany for 15 years. Young foreigners between 16 and 23 years of age can be naturalised if they have attended four years of school in Germany. The number of naturalisations increased by a factor of four from 34,913 (1985) to 141,630 (1991).
10. Dietrich Thränhardt, 'Politische Inversion. Wie und warum Regierungen das Gegenteil dessen erreichen, was sie versprochen haben', *Politische Vierteljahresschrift* 2/4 (1984), pp.440–61.
11. Karl-Heinz Meier-Braun, *Integration oder Rückkehr? Zur Ausländerpolitik der Länder, insbesondere Baden-Württemberg* (Mainz: Grünewald, 1988).
12. See Claus Leggewie, *Die Republikaner* (Berlin: Rotbuch Verlag, 1989).
13. Eike Hennig et al., *Die Republikaner im Schatten Deutschlands. Zur Organisation der mentalen Provinz* (Frankfurt: Suhrkamp, 1989), pp.32–9.
14. Dieter Roth, 'Die Republikaner. Schneller Aufstieg und tiefer Fall einer Protestpartei am rechten Rand', *Aus Politik und Zeitgeschichte*, B 37–38/90 (1990).
15. An important pressure group within the SPD, unions, have supported the SPD in these demands. The integrationist strategy is most obvious at the firm level, where immigrants have participated in economic democracy. They have the right to vote in works council elections and can become members of these councils. See Peter Kühne *et al.*, *'Wir sind nicht nur zum Arbeiten hier . . . ' Ausländische Arbeiterinnen und Arbeiter in Betrieb und Gewerkschaft* (Hamburg: VSA, 1988).
16. Estimates of foreigners in the SPD range widely from 6,000 to 50,000. In the CDU foreigners constitute 0.5 per cent (N = 3,689) (EC-citizens) and 0.1 per cent (N = 419) (*extracommunitari*). The CSU does not allow foreigners to become party members (Section 3 of the party constitution). (Source: Written correspondence with party HQ).
17. Ertekin Özcan, *Türkische Immigrantenorganisationen in der Bundesrepublik Deutschland* (Berlin: Hitit, 1989), pp.337–49
18. These parties also blocked attempts to ease the process of naturalisation. For party documents on immigration and integration, see Bernhard Blanke (ed.), *Zuwanderung und Asyl in der Konkurrenzgesellschaft* (Opladen: Leske + Budrich, 1993), pp.339–72.
19. In essence, this conflict is a reprise of the debates on the German citizenship law in 1913, when SPD members of the *Reichstag* argued that economically active foreign residents should have suffrage.
20. About a quarter of the West German population in 1989 was made up of refugees and expellees, including not only ethnic Germans but also citizens from the former GDR. About 13 million came between end of World War II and 1960. Closed borders ensured that the numbers of ethnic Germans who were actually able to emigrate remained quite small, on an average about 35,000 annually. But with the dissolution of communist regimes in Eastern Europe, the numbers grew dramatically.
21. Helga Grebing, *Flüchtlinge und Parteien in Niedersachsen. Eine Untersuchung der politischen Meinungs- und Willensbildungsprozesse während der ersten Nachkriegszeit 1945–1952/3* (Hannover: Verlag Hahnsche Buchhandlung, 1989).
22. Dietrich Strothmann, ' "Schlesien bleibt unser": Vertriebenenpolitiker und das Rad der Geschichte', in Wolfgang Benz (ed.), *Die Vertreibung der Deutschen aus dem Osten. Ursachen, Ereignisse, Folgen* (Frankfurt: Fischer, 1985), pp.209–18.
23. Karl Otto (ed.), *Westwärts – Heimwärts? Aussiedlerpolitik zwischen 'Deutschtümelei' und 'Verfassungsauftrag'* (Bielefeld: AJZ, 1990), pp.11–68.
24. Letter of Rühe to all CDU party branches in 1992, quoted in Thränhardt (note 4).

25. *Die Welt*, 17 Jan. 1989, p.17.
26. E.g., many laws in education and social services are not dependent upon citizenship status. Foreigners who have unlimited residence permits are not significantly disadvantaged *vis-à-vis* Germans with regard to social rights. See Hubert Heinelt, 'Immigration and the Welfare State . . . in Germany', *German Politics* 2/1 (April 1993), pp.78–96.
27. See also Klaus J. Bade (ed.), *Deutsche im Ausland. Fremde in Deutschland. Migration in Geschichte und Gegenwart* (München: C.H. Beck, 1992), pp.411–22.
28. On the politics and policies of asylum, see Ursula Münch, *Asylpolitik in der Bundesrepublik Deutschland. Entwicklung und Alternativen* (Opladen: Leske + Budrich, 1992).
29. In Europe, most asylum seekers during the 1980s have come to the Federal Republic; only Switzerland and Sweden have received similar levels of refugees on a per capita basis.
30. Roth (note 14).
31. For a critique, see Thomas Schmid: 'Multikulturelle Gesellschaft – großer linker Ringelpiez mit Anfassen'; *Die Neue Gesellschaft. Frankfurter Hefte* 6 (1989): pp.541–46. For a 'multiculturalist' approach that self-consciously discusses problems of multiethnic politics, see Daniel Cohn-Bendit, *Heimat Babylon. Das Wagnis der multikulturellen Demokratie* (Hamburg: Hoffmann und Campe, 1992), pp.283–348.
32. For an example, see Claus Leggewie, *Multi Kulti. Spielregeln für die Vielvölkerrepublik* (Berlin: Rotbuch Verlag, 1991).
32. The Greens have consistently brought up the issue of political citizenship and voting rights for foreigners. Their bill of settlement went further than SPD proposals. E.g., the party has suggested a claim to naturalisation after five years of residence in Germany. See Die Grünen, *Argumente: Die Multikulturelle Gesellschaft* (Bonn, 1990), pp.72–84.
34. Since the mid-1980s labour migrants have been recruited from Eastern European countries. The guestworkers of the 1960s and 1970s have thus been followed by contract labourers from Eastern Europe (*Werkvertrags-Arbeitnehmer*). Contracts were agreed upon with Poland, Hungary and the former Yugoslavia and the Czech Republic. About 30,000 contract labourers a month were employed in the early 1990s. See Amtliche Nachrichten der Bundesanstalt für Arbeit, *Ausländische Arbeitnehmer*, No.5 (Nürnberg: BfA, 1992), p.719.
35. Lutz Hoffmann, *Die unvollendete Republik. Zwischen Einwanderungsland und deutschem Nationalstaat* (Köln: Papyrossa Verlag, 1990); and Dieter Oberndörfer, *Die offene Republik. Zur Zukunft Deutschlands und Europas* (Freiburg: Herder, 1989).

National Identity and Immigration in Austria – Historical Framework and Political Dispute

RÜDIGER WISCHENBART

In 1992 several pieces of legislation concerning the rights and legal status of asylum-seekers and foreigners were passed by the Austrian Federal Parliament. The new regulations indicate on two different levels a far-reaching change in Austria's national self-understanding. On the one hand, in a redefinition of the country's national identity, the changes aim at a much closer political integration within the larger Western European context. On the other, Austria is revising some basic elements of her forgotten national identity by looking back at the almost forgotten remains of the multinational Austro-Hungarian Empire at the turn of the century. These changes also indicate the influence of the Far Right over the policy agenda and the political process, influence that extends well beyond its limited electoral appeal.

IMMIGRATION AND HISTORICAL TRADITION

In 1992 several pieces of legislation concerning the rights and the legal status of asylum seekers and of foreigners were passed by the Austrian Federal Parliament. The implementation of a more restrictive policy can be linked to the larger public debate on the limits of the country's capability to cope with recent streams of immigration, which had been triggered by political and social change after the fall of the 'Iron Curtain' in 1989. The new regulations, in fact, indicate on two different levels a far-reaching change in Austria's national self-understanding in their redefinition of a key issue connected tightly with the country's national identity.

On the one hand, the changes aim at a much closer political integration within the larger Western European context. This European entity extends beyond the European Union, Switzerland and Austria, roughly including, from the former socialist bloc Poland, the Czech Republic, Hungary, Slovenia as well as perhaps Slovakia, united in the role of a 'cordon sanitaire' facing the East. On the other Austria is forced to revise some basic elements of her national identity by looking back at the almost forgotten remains of the multinational composition of the Austro-Hungarian Empire as it existed around the turn of the century.

Austria is not yet a member of the European Union (EU), although she applied for membership in early 1989. Nevertheless, several aspects of the new regulations on foreigners fit into a much larger puzzle of restrictive regulations, through which the EU and several of its neighbours in Central Europe are trying to limit access for migrants from the large belt of poverty beyond their eastern and southeastern borders. France changed its law on foreigners and on immigration almost immediately after the general elections in May 1993 produced a solid conservative majority in parliament. In Germany, a profound debate on the question of asylum seekers, which all major political actors were forced to confront throughout 1992 and 1993, led to a change of the Federal Constitution in 1993. Simultaneously, Germany started to negotiate bilateral agreements with Poland and with the Czech Republic for close and pragmatic co-operation on the control of migratory movements. The new regulation in Austria was explicitly designed to fit into the general Western European context.

In 1993 the idea of an emerging 'European fortress' set up against immigration became popular in European newspapers to sum up all sorts of complex actions and reactions focused on the issue of 'foreigners'.

Yet far-reaching change had also become an issue in Austrian domestic politics after several decades of relative calm as a small, politically neutral state on the borderline between East and West which was largely ethnically homogeneous. In the early 1990s Austria suddenly is once again confronted with national politics which recall confrontations, much earlier in this century, when comparable streams of migration from different origins and nationalities moved across her borders from east to west and from south to north.

Without admitting it openly, Austria quickly became preoccupied with the resurfacing of some patterns of identity politics that have their origins in the turn of the century. The success of a national populist party as well as the logistic reactions by the coalition government of social democrats and conservatives have one focus in common: the refusal to admit the emergence of a multi-ethnic society resulting from general societal change on the peripheries of the continent.

The question now is how internal and external, past and present factors are intertwined in the current process.

THE END OF THE COLD WAR AND THE RISE OF THE EXTREME RIGHT

After the fall of the 'Iron Curtain' as a clearly defined borderline for Western Europe in 1989, which at that time included the EC and several neutral countries such as Austria, the changes ahead turned out to be a much rougher ride into an unforeseeable future. Not only Austria's traditional and comfortable role as a stable mediator between parts of Eastern Europe and the Balkans and the West was exposed to revision.

The wealth gap between the West – including Austria – and the former socialist countries, growing difficulties in the transition from a socialist to a market economy, increasing political unrest and very soon even the very existence of entire neighbouring states in limbo, were all factors which produced growing numbers of people all over eastern and south-eastern Europe who were looking for ways to migrate in search of better prospects. By virtue of geographical location as well as a framework of historical bonds, Austria found herself as the chosen haven many were suddenly heading for. But nobody – as elsewhere in Europe – was prepared for such a rush. In Austria, where the basis of national identity had already been shattered several times since the demise of the old Habsburg empire and, later in the century, with its self-immersion in Nazi Germany through the 'Anschluss' of 1938, once again historical change confronted the population with a highly ambivalent past.

When the 'Iron Curtain' came down in 1989 and thousands and thousands of Czechs and Slovaks, for the first time in decades, crossed the borders for a stroll in the streets of nearby Vienna, the old capital of the Austro-Hungarian Empire, newspapers headlines read:

> As in the Old Times: From Prague, Brno and Budapest to Vienna.[1]

Only three years later, the question of open borders with – according to successful populist politicians – too many 'foreigners' streaming into the country had become a front-page issue of quite another quality. Polls show convincing evidence that 'the problem of foreigners' is considered by a growing majority as one of the most important issues of politics.[2]

But even though today the 'problem of foreigners' and of immigration is automatically associated with the opening of the borders after the revolutions in Eastern Europe late in 1989, the debate was already well under way before this date. Since the late 1980s a public debate had been taking place on 'asylum-seekers' as well as on the growing number of immigrant workers, both originating mainly from socialist countries near Austria.

Regarded in sheer numbers and not within a larger political framework, neither development would seem of dramatic concern. By 1989 there were 15,790 claims for asylum with reference to the Geneva convention. It had roughly doubled compared to 6,724 in 1985, but it was far from crisis figures like 34,557, the number following the upheaval of Solidarnosc in Poland in 1981.

The figures for foreign labour recorded 167,381 'guestworkers', mostly Turkish (39,200) and Yugoslav (90,836), which Austria had been calling for, like Germany, since the early 1960s. Numbers in 1989 were still well below the peak of 226,801 'guestworkers' in 1973.

Nevertheless, public opinion seemed to shift following the end of the period of social and political modernisation and Austria's reshaping to fill the role of bridge between East and West, undertaken during the chancellorship of Bruno Kreisky in the 1970s and early 1980s. A certain political and societal consensus broke in 1986. At the convention of the Liberal (or Freedom) Party, the FPÖ, which had been in a coalition government with the Social Democrats, the SPÖ, since 1983, a young populist named Jörg Haider ousted the chairman of the liberals, vice-chancellor Norbert Steger.

Haider, a brilliant rhetorician and polemicist, introduced a loud and until then unheard style of populist attacks against the political establishment. He started to exploit popular anger and fears and succeeded within a relatively short time in leading the party from an average of 5 per cent of the vote in elections to up to 20 per cent. Within a party that is traditionally composed of a liberal and an antagonistic (formerly 'pro-Germanic-') 'national' wing, Haider stands for the latter. Nevertheless, he had started his career as a liberal.

Jörg Haider, born in 1950, used to run with the appeal of the young and modern challenger against representatives of what he calls the 'old parties', the conservatives and the social democrats. One may note that his rise coincides with the rise of the environmental movement, which won its first seats in the Federal Parliament in 1986.

By as early as spring 1989 Haider had confirmed the upward trend of his party by winning several regional elections, and he started to emphasise the issue of 'foreigners' which, at this time, had become a focus for very different types of right-wing opposition all over Western Europe. With great skill Haider responded with simple and often emotional formulas to diverse anxieties in different groups of the population. He reached namely those who are afraid to become losers in the process of modernisation, social change and other forms of political insecurity in the aftermath of 1989. Pinpointing the *alien* – the foreigners, the immigrants, the non-Austrians – as the major source of inconvenience and insecurity proved to be emotionally as well as politically a powerful and flexible tool in his pursuit of gaining power.

In autumn 1991 Haider was able to transform the electoral campaign for the city parliament in the capital of Vienna into a large debate on the issue of foreigners. On election day, most commentators were stunned when they saw that he had won 22.58 per cent of the vote, lowering the Social Democrats in their traditionally most powerful stronghold from 54.92 per cent (1987) to 47.69 per cent, and placing the conservatives, diminished from 28.40 per cent (1987), in a pitiful third place, with only 18.10 per cent.

With this victory in hand, Haider moved quickly and imposed on his party a more and more personalised rule. In the middle of the campaign for the presidency of the Republic, which would decide the successor to the contested Kurt Waldheim, Haider evicted several challengers within his own party and even attacked his own candidate to the elections, Heide Schmidt. Only months later he once again stunned his own entourage by suddenly opposing the government's wish to join the European Community, thereby provoking an eclat against the faction of pro-European liberals in his party. After several skirmishes, he came out as the winner and appeared to be even more irresistible to his followers.

The time seemed to be ripe to piece it all together in a single, comprehensive test. He chose again to place all his stakes on the 'problem of foreigners', the topic he had been so successful with.

The 'old parties' and their system were just overwhelmed by too many challenges. There was a full-scale war in former Yugoslavia, only a five-hour drive from the borders, with the European Community demonstrating its painstaking inability to keep the European house together. Then another neighbour, Czechoslovakia, began to fall apart. Old prejudices were revived aimed at those eastern and southern nations whose claim for nationhood and independence – according to popular belief – had caused the crumbling of the Habsburg's reign. Furthermore, economic challenges came from a partly recovering Czech Republic, from Poland and from Hungary who started to flood the domestic economy with cheap imports of cement and similar basic products, triggering instantly calls for protectionism. Forecasts spoke of the probability of a general recession ahead. And, last but not least, nationalist populist movements were visibly gaining momentum almost everywhere in Europe – which is of considerable importance in a country which under President Kurt Waldheim had for years been regularly accused of forming a cradle for authoritarianism and xenophobia. Now the populist and nationalist response was becoming more and more part of a European mainstream.

In October 1992 Haider presented the Federal government with nothing less than an ultimatum, calling for measures that would make his political outcries the official guideline for the government's policy. Otherwise, he promised to hold a nationwide *referendum* calling for, among other points:

- an amendment to the constitution declaring that Austria was 'not a country of immigration';
- an act requiring foreigners to carry an identification card to facilitate the struggle against the 'criminality of foreigners';
- a reinforcement of (military) border patrols against illegal immigration;
- further restrictions on the possibility of naturalisation (which is already, following *ius sanguinis* as in Germany, extremely prohibitive);
- more radical action against 'illegal profiteering';
- banning definitely all proposals of a right to vote for non-Austrians (as there had been campaigns for granting them the right to vote on local levels).[3]

The populist and nationalist outcry, unthinkable only half a decade before, was very much reminiscent of political disasters in Vienna's past, when it had not only been the capital of the multinational Habsburg empire, but also the place where one century ago xenophobia in the form of anti-Semitism had first become a modern mass movement. This had happened at a time when thousands and thousands of Jews from the East, along with Czechs, Hungarians and all other nationalities of central and south eastern Europe, were heading for the metropolis of Vienna.

VIENNA, IMMIGRATION AND THE CONSTRUCTION OF AUSTRIAN IDENTITY

'There is a wide gap between reality and self-assessment in Austria', wrote two of Austria's leading demographers, Heinz Faßmann and Rainer Münz, in a commentary on the question of immigration in June of 1991.[4] Their analyses are useful in attaining a better understanding of the ambiguities that arose out of the struggle around the referendum Haider called for and which had eventually taken place by the end of

January 1993. On the one hand, this referendum was supposed to define Austria as *not being a country of immigration*. On the other hand, Austria's very identity is traditionally based on concepts such as forming a 'bridge' between the West and the East,[5] being the product of an old and multifaceted fusion of Central European cultures and generating unity out of diversity. Moreover, its people are the product of different waves of mass migration, especially since the age of industrialisation and modernisation from the late nineteenth to the early twentieth century. All the glory of the Viennese 'Fin de Siècle' – whose value as an innovative culture of highest European virtues had been rediscovered only recently and instantly exploited by a huge tourist industry – was clearly the work of migrants from all parts of the late Austro-Hungarian Monarchy who converged on the capital and brought with them a vast and richly diverse array of impulses.[6]

In 1910, the year of her greatest expansion, Vienna had 2,031,421 inhabitants of which already only 48 per cent were born in the city (compared to 65.3 per cent today). Roughly one out of four Viennese was of Bohemian (thus mostly Czech) or Moravian descent. A total of 175,318 Jews (8.6 per cent) lived in Vienna, the vast majority of whom had arrived only recently from the eastern and south-eastern border regions of the monarchy (the single province of Galicia accounted for one out of three).[7] At the same time there was a massive exodus of people from these impoverished rural areas at the peripheries of Austria and Hungary heading for America. Between 1900 and 1910 approximately the same huge number of immigrants to the United States came from the Habsburg empire as from Italy, surpassing considerably the numbers of Germans or Russians. In 1914 the Imperial Counsel prepared a law to limit further emigration. However, World War I interrupted these considerations.

Given such a framework, one might expect certain similarities between the demographic features of Vienna and those of a centre of growth through migration like New York. In fact, reality shows quite opposite scenarios in the two places. First of all, with the exception of the Jewish quarters in the second district, the *Leopoldstadt*, Vienna never produced 'ethnic' neighbourhoods for longer than short periods of transition. And second, the city refused categorically to become what one might call today a *multicultural metropolis*. Instead it opted, for several reasons, for forced and nearly complete assimilation of its migrants within extremely short intervals – or blunt repulsion.

The most obvious example is the virtual disappearance of the Czech minority within little more than one generation. In 1900, 518,333 persons living in Vienna were born in Bohemia. Nevertheless, the census of

1910 mentions only 98,461 Czech or Slovak speakers. After the fall of the Empire and the founding of an independent 'CzechoSlovak Republic' a major remigration of approximately 140,000 to 150,000 individuals took place. Yet Vienna's census of 1923 showed another 81,353 (!) people speaking Czech or Slovak remaining in Vienna. Thus to the census figures of 1910 one has to add an estimated 150,000 *hidden* Czechs and Slovaks who for one reason or another declared themselves  'Germans' almost instantly after their arrival in Vienna. After World War II (and another, but minor wave of remigration thereafter) only a meagre 4,137 remained according to official data.[8]

Whereas Jewish migrants from Galicia and Bukovina were found in highly segregated areas of the city, Czechs and Slovaks were quickly dispersed across a large belt of rapidly expanding *proletarian* districts where they moved in as a cheap labour force. Most lived under miserable conditions, but the fact of migration from their home regions to the capital was such a *normal* biographical routine that very rarely one finds reflections and reasoning on their decisions to go to the capital. Soon they got a specific nickname in German as 'Ziegelböhm' which means 'Czechs working in the brickworks', particularly for the huge construction jobs done in the quickly expanding and modernising city. Yet when Victor Adler, the co-founder and intellectual leader of the Austrian Social Democrats, wrote in 1888 on their horrible working conditions, he portrayed in detail the system of exploitation, the bad salaries, the poor shelters. However, he did not mention the fact of their Czech nationality or the way they came to Vienna, for everybody knew it. It was just too obvious.[9]

Understandably, most of these early *guestworkers* expected to return home within a couple of years, but as a matter of fact, many stayed and founded families in Vienna. Whereas segregation did not happen in terms of an ethnic urban geography, socially it was a determining factor. The Viennese society lived in almost perfect endogamy. Those born in Vienna usually married only those who were also born in the city. Migrants from nearby regions intermarried at rates of more than 80 per cent and migrants from far away again followed the same pattern. This indicates the depth of the gap between the local population and the migrants, but it also reflects the desire of many Czechs and other *non-Germans* to remigrate back home some day.[10] It also exemplifies some of the closely-knit structures of a society that is hostile towards any agent of change.

In the meantime, Czechs were a politically very self-confident and socially well-organised ethnic minority with almost 400 associations of every type. Therefore, one could expect, they would resist even strong pressure for a given time. In fact, the massive waves of emigration back to their homeland, especially after the founding of the Czechoslovak Republic, only underline their strength. Yet for those remaining in Vienna, there was hardly an alternative to becoming a 'German'.

Probably the most powerful single factor in this process of rapid assimilation was the political response of the German-speaking majority in the city. Their policy combined three elements of suppression of ethnicity to great effect:

- the Viennese Czechs were *not* recognised as an ethnic minority;
- their schools were not officially recognised within the system of public education;
- whoever wanted to settle permanently had to swear an oath to uphold in the future 'with force and vigour the German character of Vienna'.

Karl Lueger, Vienna's legendary mayor from 1897 to 1910, put his conviction quite bluntly when he said: 'Vienna has to remain German, and the German character of Vienna must never be questioned.'[11]

Contemporary observers had no doubt about the difference in urbanisation in Vienna and in more advanced, western capitals: 'Concerning the mixture of its population, Vienna is singular among the populations of all European world cities', a handbook published in 1913 on 'Vienna in the Era of Emperor Franz Joseph I' informs us. 'Whereas in London, Paris or Berlin migration from the surroundings, in which foreigners from far away play no role, brings homogeneous elements to the population, Vienna is forced year after year to assimilate very large numbers of nationally and linguistically diverse elements.'[12]

The author omits that, within Central Europe, Vienna was by far not the only case of radical change of identities in the era of industrialisation. It was not even the most drastic.

In Budapest in 1870, after the rise of Hungarian power to oppose the emperor in Vienna, only 46 per cent of the urban population had declared Hungarian as their mother tongue. One out of five dwellers was German. Yet, in 1900, only three decades later, Budapest had become Hungarian to the extent of 78.88 per cent!

The rapid growth of Budapest's industrial areas at the turn of the century was fuelled largely by Slovak migrants from the northern regions of the country. Urbanisation and industrialisation along with the forceful accompaniment of nationalistic agitation were very effective tools in the process of transforming ethnic and cultural minorities into integral parts of the culturally and nationally dominant majority.

Even among workers, where 'non-Hungarians' accounted for considerably higher percentages than in the average population the unions had their part in transforming ethnical Slovaks, Poles or Serbs into Hungarians. For example, they published minutes and resolutions only in Hungarian.[13] Budapest functioned, exactly like Vienna, as a huge generator of homogenisation on behalf of the majority and against ethnic diversity. Migration was meant to produce members of the majority no matter what the origin of the migrants was.

As early as 1891, when Hungarian nationalistic propaganda was reaching one of its peaks, a demographer in Budapest felt the necessity to try to explain certain *surprises* implied by his data. Taking the results of the 1891 census, he wrote:

> Those however who studied the ethnography of Hungary thoroughly are compelled to admit that present day Hungary is not the result of Asian formations but a European product, a nation that came into being as the mixture of diverse peoples.[14]

What we observe is a pattern that was widespread all over Central and south-eastern Europe. In many of these regions there was a consistent difference in ethnicity between rural and urban populations. Even more, as a result of diverse historical developments, the links between the *village* and the *city* were much looser than in the earlier modernised and centralised states of Western Europe. Therefore, in the peripheries of the east and southeast, industrialisation and societal modernisation in the late nineteenth century provoked not only the usual rural-urban migration. It also enforced ethnic homogenisation, with those national groups which took over the political command in the more *modern* capitals imposing their *nationality* on the arriving migrants or even on formerly dominant ethnic groups. Only thereafter, for example, did Prague become overwhelmingly Czech, Budapest Hungarian, Maribor Slovenian. Thus politically there was no room for an idea like 'multiculturalism' or for ethnic diversity as a value. Only intellectuals, especially writers, mentioned the enormous cultural loss, and even they admitted how difficult (which meant always *impoverished* and *straining*) life was before migration, modernisation and homogenisation.

To quote only one voice, the Nobel-prize winning author Elias Canetti, who was born in 1905 in Ruse, on the Bulgarian border, and who had started his literary career in Vienna, wrote: 'The existence of different languages is the most mysterious fact in the world', and referring to the biblical story of the confusion of languages in Babel, he adds: 'God's act is the most devilish ever committed.'[15] If we believe Elias Canetti, diversity can be a terrible threat to those who have to cope with it on a day-to-day basis.

THE EMERGENCE OF AN AUSTRIAN IDENTITY

After World War I and after the dismantling of the Turkish and the Austrian multinational empires, which had, nevertheless, provided a certain *umbrella* over all this diversity and change, the successor states founded their newly won identities on the principle of nationalism. This implied automatically a notion of ethnic homogeneity, even though in most regions the facts and the historical heritage did not fit such an assumption. Under such circumstances, migrants being aliens or *foreigners* had at least to become ethnically invisible, for example by declaring themselves 'Germans' in Vienna or 'Hungarians' in Budapest.

When, in November 1918, a new republic was proclaimed in Vienna, the founding fathers called it '*Deutschösterreich*', which is 'German-Austria'.[16] At this time only around half of the Viennese population was born in the city, and nearly 30 per cent were born 'abroad', mostly in what had become the successor states.

During the short and politically shaky period of the First Republic (from 1918 to Austria's 'Anschluss' with Nazi Germany in 1938), the large debate on the state's 'national' identity was centred around two suggestions. A majority – even long before the rise of Nazism in Germany – saw a future only within the borders of a greater Germany. Among certain conservatives and, with only slight conceptual divergences, among communists the idea of an 'Austrian nation' took shape, but was abandoned in the violent clashes that soon brought down the whole body of the republic.

It was only after World War II, and after Austria as a mere component of the Third Reich had formally ceased to exist for seven years, that the founding fathers of the Second Republic rediscovered the notion of an Austrian nation and instantly made it the very ideological basis of their state. In the ruins of Vienna and after the annihilation of the Jewish population – which, alone, had upheld its distinct 'ethnic' districts in the Leopoldstadt – Austria as a state *and* as a nation were (re-) born. Of course, this nation considered itself as a largely ethnically homogeneous society, which, as a matter of fact, corresponded now to reality, as the annihilation or forced assimilation was nearly completed. In the postwar period the percentage of Austrians who considered their country a 'nation' was steadily growing. In 1956 only 49 per cent of the Austrian population saw Austria as a nation (whereas 46 per cent rejected such an assumption). In 1970, at the moment when Bruno Kreisky became chancellor, only 7 per cent produced a negative answer to the question of nationhood.[17]

Yet the country had not ceased by then to accept and assimilate large numbers of immigrants. Between 1945 and 1950 it accepted nearly 400,000 mostly German-speaking refugees who had been driven from Eastern Europe. After the Hungarian uprising of 1956, after the Prague Spring in 1968 and in the summer of *Solidarnosc* in Poland in 1981, significant numbers of refugees came to Austria. Nevertheless Austria considered herself only as a 'transit country' for those persecuted by communist regimes. But even as the majority indeed continued their journeys, to the USA, to Canada or Australia, considerable numbers stayed in the country.

Additionally, following the same pattern as Germany, Austria had encouraged the arrival of – mostly Yugoslav and Turkish – 'guest-workers' since the early 1960s, and in 1992 a total of 283,670 lived in Austria as *de facto* immigrants. The wars in the former Yugoslavia since 1991 have sent an estimated 67,000 refugees across the border. Proportional to Austria's population of 7.5 million, this exceeds even the number of war refugees that went to Germany. Thereafter, the Austrian government – in anticipation of growing popular resentment and a controversy with the European Community over the issue – closed this last Western European gateway to security. By doing so, Western Europe shifted the heavy burden of sheltering hundreds of thousands of war refugees to those buffer countries which have the weakest means to sustain them, namely Hungary, Croatia and Slovenia. Thus the question of the war refugees from Croatia and Bosnia became a first severe test for the functioning of the 'cordon sanitaire' which the peripheral countries were supposed to form in exchange for economic aid offered by the EC.

Altogether, since 1945, 680,000 persons (9 per cent of the total population) came as migrants and remained in Austria for permanent residence, 380,000 of whom have a mother tongue other than German.[18]

Despite these figures, the construction of an ethnically homogeneous Austrian nation that, from the beginning, was meant to bridge all sorts of ambiguities of the country's complex realities, could be upheld. Like any state with at least an implicit nationalistic self-assessment, Austria during a long period of internal and external stability was fairly well off.

NEW POLICIES AND OLD RESPONSES: THE IMPACT OF THE EXTREME RIGHT

Beginning in the second half of the 1980s, however, changes threatened this construction simultaneously in its orientation to the East as well as to the West. With European integration and, as the Waldheim scandal showed, with political isolationism becoming virtually impossible within the range of global networks of communication and interdependence, the concept of a national *island* had to be abandoned. And with the fall of the 'Iron Curtain' in 1989, also the other borderline, which everybody had considered 'unchangeable', suddenly disappeared.

The populist and, lately, the increasingly nationalistic course of Haider and his party is a response to this situation. Even those elements which some observers consider as being in contradiction with his former policy might be rather consistent in the long run.

For instance, in 1988 Haider suddenly attacked the wide consensus on the existence of an Austrian nation in a rhetorical fury, and came to a climax by calling it a 'monstrosity' ('*Missgeburt*').[19] Paradoxically, when he prepared the referendum against foreigners in 1992 his slogan was: 'Austria first!'

As the leader of a liberal party which at this time was still a member of the 'Liberal International' movement and which is sponsored considerably by entrepreneurial organisations, he had previously favoured the plans of the federal government to join the EC as soon as possible. In summer 1992 he suddenly became a fierce opponent of 'Brussel's bureaucracy' when, in the aftermath of the Maastricht treaties, opinion polls showed growing Euro-scepticism also among voters in Austria. These shifts allowed him to oppose the government on essential grounds of the 'interests of the nation'.

In autumn 1992 the Liberal Party leader started to campaign for his referendum on foreigners, and he did so despite the fact that at that very moment, a huge movement of humanitarian solidarity was extremely successful in the country collecting money for war refugees from the former Yugoslavia. Opinion polls showed in October 1992 that 48 per cent of the voters were *against* the referendum Haider proposed, and only 29 per cent approved of it. Yet at the same time, 76 per cent did not agree that Austria should accept 'more foreigners', and 66 per cent wanted to reject even refugees from war-torn Bosnia.[20] Apparently, giving money for humanitarian purposes could morally ease a fierce stand on political grounds.

It is exactly this kind of ambivalence that Haider exploits. He seizes popular emotions, and by formulating these issues in a polemic way as no other party involved in governing could do, he can force all others to respond. As soon as this happens, he has once again successfully taken the lead by defining the agenda.

As early as November 1992, for instance, Josef Cap, as a spokesman for the Social Democrats, declared that, of course, Austria was 'not a country of immigration'. A spokesman for the conservatives added that the legislation against foreigners Haider was campaigning for had already been introduced by the government itself. The weekly magazine *profil* concluded: 'Out of fear that the country might become divided, the coalition government anticipates Mr Haider's referendum'.[21]

The referendum itself was largely considered a defeat for Haider, as he had declared hastily during his campaign that he expected one million signatures. In fact only 417,278 voters (7.4 per cent) had undertaken the fairly complicated procedure of going to a voting office, identifying themselves (and thereby, especially in small communities, exposing themselves publicly) and signing. The return was clearly below Jörg Haider's support of up to 20 per cent of the voters. This was certainly partly a success of a loose and exceptional coalition of intellectuals, civil right groups, parts of the media, important representatives of the Catholic church and even the President of the Republic who rallied against what they termed the Liberal leader's 'playing with political fire'.

A map detailing the distribution of participation suggests several conclusions. On the one hand, there is almost no coincidence between the distribution of foreigners in different regions of the country and the number of signatures for the referendum. On the other hand, participation is above the national average in urban centres such as Vienna and Graz where the risk of being personally exposed as 'racist' or 'xenophobic' is fairly limited. Even more interesting is a clear and compact corridor in the centre of the country, running from upper Austria through the Alpine parts of Salzburg and Styria to Haider's political home-county of Carinthia, regions with virtually no foreigners or refugees at all. It is significant that these are rather closed regions, with populations which might be very threatened by growing competition within the EU. The participation is below average in rural areas with traditions of rural self-confidence, such as in Tyrol, and astonishingly in the fairly poor regions bordering Hungary and the (former) Czechoslovakia.[22]

In the week following the referendum, Haider said publicly that by now he would attack even more harshly those preparing Austria to join the European Community.

It might be quite similar groups of the population whom he considered his potential followers and hoped to attract when he attacked the 'monstrosity' of the Austrian nation and later called for 'Austria first' – those afraid of being among the losers as a result of societal change, modernisation, and the opening of borders or new immigration.

This potential might well account for one fifth to one fourth of the general vote.

During Haider's campaign for his referendum, the parties in the government claimed that they had already adopted the right-wing policy of strong action against foreigners, and this was not only electoral rhetoric. A brochure published by the Interior Ministry in 1991 explains in detail that the 'anxieties' of the people were not considered by the authority as 'an expression of god-given xenophobia among Austrians'. Instead they are explained as 'real fears and apprehensions', so that a policy on foreigners has to defend the rights of the Austrian citizens in the labour and housing market against 'competition from immigrants'.[23] The 'real measures' against 'real anxieties' promised in this brochure became several pieces of legislation already by the following year, several months *before* the Liberal leader confronted the government with his ultimatum. By then, the law on asylum was amended, together with a new 'law on foreigners', both severely criticised by a large range of civil rights organisations and even some exponents of the Catholic Church as being too restrictive. The centrepiece of the new legislation was a law concerning 'the sojourn of foreigners in Austria',[24] which produced an outcry by its critics. Its ideological guideline, the critics said, was 'to provide that foreigners remain foreigners' and not be allowed to integrate.[25]

First drafts for this legislation still spoke of a law on 'immigration', then the title was changed to 'right of domicile' before becoming a law dealing with the 'sojourn of foreigners'. It provides that the government lay down yearly quotas for naturalisation, but that asylum figures have to be added to the number of those looking for naturalisation. In very detailed articles, it allows the possibility of temporary exceptions to provide cheap seasonal jobs for the tourist industry. The term 'immigration', however, is not mentioned at all in the new law.

The authorities deal with it exclusively and purely in terms of administration. There is no room left for explicit political or humanitarian considerations with the one exception of war refugees, who can be accepted for a clearly limited time of transition.

Yet especially in the Austrian and in the wider Central European context, this recalls the largely authoritarian and nationalistic traditions of *technical control* instead of a democratic policy enjoying broad visibility to the public. By the same token, most of Haider's 12 points in his referendum are calling for *administrative* action, and only the first point – 'Austria is not a country of immigration' – is *political*.

The parallel between Haider's suggestions and the response of the Interior Minister can even be more detailed. In his commentary, the exponents of the referendum mention that the regulations they suggest were even in the interest of illegal immigrants as 'many foreigners are forced to live in miserable quarters with unbearably expensive rents.'[26] In an address to the Budapest Conference on 'Uncontrollable Migration' in February 1993, the Austrian Interior Minister Franz Löschnak, who himself largely defines the governmental policy on this issue, said: 'The rapid and efficient deportation of illegal immigrants [. . .] is in the interest of the migrants', and he added that, the quicker the process, the easier would be their 'reintegration' back home.[27]

With this policy on immigration, the government is trying to uphold the ethnic homogeneity of the country without ever admitting the ambivalent history of both the national consensus and the national identity of (with the exception of tiny Slovene and Croatian minorities in border regions) an ethnically homogeneous, only German-speaking Austria. The measures to impose this stance – especially in this time of deep change and controvery – are again similar to those of the period of mass migration caused by political change and large-scale modernisation around the turn of the century; *administrative regulations* prevail instead of an *open policy* that accepts the challenge of the situation and deals with it with foresight. The *foreigner* – the immigrant – is not accepted and invited to integrate slowly into an open society. Instead, a strict distinction between the alien and the native is enforced. And the natives, whose ancestors might have been of quite different nationalities, are supposed to present themselves as *one* people, whatever the political cost.

The destruction of ethnic and cultural bridges between new residents and old ones through one-dimensional legislation and an ethnocentric policy lends high legitimacy to the public exponents of nationalist resentments. And, of course, to legitimate such a social construction, the authorities of the state and the representatives of its administration need to adopt much of the vocabulary of the populist argument. By the same token, the native population will hardly become prepared for societal changes the country is heading for anyway. Obviously, the fact is that immigration itself is not the agent of change, but the much larger and complex process of European political integration and therefore the new definition of borders towards those regions and countries of the continent that will supposedly lie *outside* even a much larger European Union of the future.

Thus the general pattern is 'typically Austrian' only in some of its secondary and more practical aspects. The policy on immigration follows the path of European integration as a whole. Purely technical and bureaucratic regulations are not tools within a political and intellectual framework of what 'Europe' might become some day. Instead, the political leaders dump the vital and difficult question of patterns of future European identities on the desks of technocratically orientated administrators who cannot do much besides define quotas and establish procedures of technical control. There is no working mediator between them and the many competing layers of a society in the middle of complex change and anxiety.

In the case of Austria, the same lesson is disregarded for the second time within one century. For the people directly involved, the emergence of a competitive multi-ethnic society through processes of peripheral modernisation and subsequent migration is certainly a difficult challenge, and not the appealing ideal of rising multicultural communities. The political response, however seems to be anything but convincing. Therefore the next confrontations with the nationalist and populist forces of Jörg Haider or – more probably – a successor, are already under way.

NOTES

1. *Kurier*, Wien, 12 Oct. 1989.
2. According to a study by the conservative 'Fessel & GFK Institute' from Feb. 1990 it is second in popular concern only to the preservation of the environment. The 'IMAS Inst., Linz, found that 45 per cent of all Austrians are thinking 'often' how one could preserve the country from 'alienation' by foreigners ('*Überfremdung des Landes*'). Andreas Weber, Christa Zöchling: Die geteilte Republik. *profil*. Wien, Nr.46, 11 Sept. 1992, p.15.
   'Fear of new wave of refugees' ('*Angst vor neuer Flüchtlingswelle*') was the headline of the daily newspaper '*Kurier*', quoting a poll by 'Market' Inst. which says that 54 per cent of the population fear refugees from the East and a rise of criminality, 49 per cent are scared of losing their jobs due to growing competition, 48 per cent fear growing environmental damage caused by transit traffic crossing through Austria. *Kurier*, Wien, Nr.4, 1 April 1992.
3. '*"Österreich zuerst" durch Schaffung gesetzlicher Maßnahmen, die das Recht auf Heimat für alle österreichischen Staatsbürger dauerhaft sichern und unter diesem Gesichtspunkt eine zurückhaltende Einwanderungspolitik nach Österreich gewährleisten.*' ["Austria first" by establishing legal measures that guarantee the native rights for all Austrian citizens in permanence and with special emphasis on a restrained policy on immigration to Austria.' – so the text in the official application to the Home Secretary]. Antrag auf Einleitung eines Volksbegehrens. Bundesministerium f. Inneres, Zl. 8.119/1. 23 Nov. 1992.
4. Heinz Fassmann, Rainer Münz: 'Aufnahmefähig, aber noch nicht aufnahmebereit. Österreich als Aus- und Einwanderungsland: Bestandsaufnahme, Aufgaben, Perspektiven.' *Die Presse*, Wien, 6–15/16–1991, [suppl.] p.III. Also, with more detailed data and tables: Fassmann, Münz: '*Einwanderungsland Österreich? Gastarbeiter – Flüchtlinge – Immigranten.*' Bundesministerium f. Unterricht und Kunst and Austrian Academy of Sciences, Inst. of Demography. 5th ed., Wien 1992.
5. The city of Vienna had planned to host a 'World exhibition' together with Budapest in 1995 with the general theme of 'Bridges to the Future'. But the plan had to be cancelled after a referendum in 1990. During the Cold War, Austria was a major place

for trade between the West and the socialist countries, but during the late 1980s the EC had started to establish more and more direct contacts with single countries of Eastern Europe so even at this level Austria's role as a mediator began to diminish in importance.

6. Leon Botstein showed for instance that 'with the exception of Schnitzler, Wittgenstein and Stefan Zweig most of the Jews who at the turn of the century played a major role in [Viennese] cultural life were persons whose families had come to Vienna only after 1860.' Botstein, *Judentum und Modernität* (Wien, Köln: Böhlau, 1991), p.42. See also the essay 'Moderne Migranten' in my book *Karpaten. Die dunkle Seite Europas* (Wien: Kremayr & Scheriau 1992), pp.161–81.
7. In 1910 only 18.2 per cent of the 'fathers' of Viennese Jewish families were born in the city, 34.7 per cent came from Galicia, 19.4 per cent from Hungary. Marsha L. Rozenblit, *Die Juden Wien 1867–1914. Assimilation und Identität* (Wien, Köln: Böhlau 1989), p.29.
8. All data following the official census figures. For their interpretation: Karl M. Brousek, *Wien und seine Tschechen* (München R. Oldenbourg 1980). Monika Glettler, *Die Wiener Tschechen um 1900* (München, Wien 1972). And Heiko Haumann, Gottfried Schramm (eds.), *Zentrale Städte und ihr Umland. Wechselwirkungen während der Industrialisierungsperiode in MittelEuropa* (St. Katharinen Scripta Mercaturae 1985).
9. Victor Adler: 'Die Lage der Ziegelarbeiter' in Friedrich G. Kürbisch (ed.), *Der Arbeitsmann, er stirbt, verdirbt, wann steht er auf? Sozialreportagen 1880 bis 1918.* (Berlin, Bonn: Dietz 1982), p.45–9 (orig. published in *Die Gleichheit*, Wien 12 Jan 1888).
10. Heinz Fassmann: 'Migration in Österreich: 1850–1900. Migrationsströme innerhalb der Monarchie und Struktur der Zuwanderung nach Wien' in Austrian Academy of Science, Inst. of Demography (ed.), *Demographische Informationen* (Wien 1986), p.34.
11. Glettler, *Die Wiener Tschechen um 1900* (note 8), p.310 passim.
12. *Wien im Zeitalter Kaiser Franz Josephs I* (Wien 1913). Quoted in Glettler *et. al.*, *Zentrale Städte und ihr Umland* (note 8), p148.
13. 'Peter Sipos', 'Die Rolle der Migration im Entwicklungsgang der Arbeiterklasse und in der Entfaltung der Arbeiterbewegung in einem von vielen Nationalitäten bewohnten Lande. Das Beispiel Ungarns; unpub. paper.
14. 'Ergebnisse der in den Ländern der ungarischen Krone am Anfang des Jahres 1891 durchgeführten Volkszählung I. heil. Allgemeine Demographie, *Ungarische Statistische Mitteilungn*, Neue Folge, Bd. I, Budapest 1893, 179*.' Quoted in Glettler *et al.* (note 8) p.149.
15. Elias Canetti, *Die Provinz des Menschen* (München: C. Hanser 1973), p.15. For more details see R. Wischenbart: *Karpaten*, p.171 *passim*.
16. 'Gesetz über die Staats- und Regierungsform von Deutschösterreich', 12 Nov. 1918. Reproduced in Norbert Schausberger, *Österreich. Der Weg der Republik 1918–1980.* (Graz, Wien: Leykam 1980), p.19.
17. Felix Kreissler, *La Prise de Conscience de la Nation Autrichienne 1938–1945–1978.* Vol.2 (Paris: PUF, 1980). p.648.
18. Fassmann, Münz, 'Einwanderungsland Österreich?' (note 4), p.11.
19. For a detailed account of the long list of scandals around Jörg Haider and his policy see Hans-Henning Scharsach, *Haider's Kampf* (Wien: Orac, 1992).
20. Austria Presse Agentur 191 5 II 0196, 28 Oct. 1992
21. Andreas Weber, Christa Zöchling, 'Díe geteilte Republik', *profil*, Wien, 9 Nov. 1992, pp.12–16.
22. Austria Presse Agentur, 'Volksbegehren – Regionale Streuung', 2 Feb. 1993.
23. Bundesministerium f. Inneres (ed.), *Keine Mauern gegen Flüchtlinge* (Wien 1991).
24. 'Erlassung des Fremdengesetzes und Änderung des Asylgesetzes 1991 sowie des Aufenthaltsgesetzes', Bundesgesetzblatt, 286. Stück, 29 Dec.1992. 'Regelung des Aufenthalts von Fremden in Österreich', Bundesgesetzblatt, 162. Stück, 31 July 1992.

25. Reinhold Gärtner, 'Neuordnung des Ausländerwesens' in *Informationen der Gesellschaft für Politische Aufklärung*, Vol.33, (June 1992), p.9.
26. 'Österreich zuerst'. Antrag auf Einleitung eines Volksbegehrens, p.7.
27. Franz Löschnak, 'Beitrag zur Budapester Konferenz zur Bewältigung unkontrollierter Wanderbewegungen', 15 and 16 Feb. 1993 [typed], p.4.

Immigrants as Political Actors in France

CATHERINE WIHTOL DE WENDEN

Immigrants have participated in politics in France in diverse ways, depending upon when they came to France, for what purpose, and where they were born. In addition, different roles have emerged in different periods, with some now fading and others reinforced by new generations of political actors. Different kinds of socio-political demands and policies are characteristic of different generations of immigrants. What is most striking since the mid-1980s is that terms of the political dialogue on immigration have changed, in part because of the initiatives of government and opposition, but also because of the initiatives of immigrants and immigrant associations themselves. Since 1985 the broad socio-political debate in France has focused on such questions as definitions of French identity and dual citizenship, as result of the political demands of the second generation of Franco-Maghrebians. However, after a brief 'passage au politique' at the national level, this generation has now focused its activity on local associations, with a stronger emphasis on civil rights.

As political actors, immigrants have participated in politics in diverse ways, depending upon when they came to France, for what purpose, and where they were born. Different roles have emerged in different periods; some roles are now fading, while others are being strengthened with the new generation. Any historical analysis must focus on these changing patterns of political participation. The types of political actors are both a result of the historical evolution of immigrant settlement as well as each particular stage of migration in its context.

Foreign immigration to France began in the middle of the nineteenth century, but really developed during and after World War I (1918–29) and after World War II (1945–74). It was first introduced to compensate for a decline in the birth rate which had begun in the eighteenth century, long before that of other European countries, and which led to labour shortages at a time of industrialisation and major public works from 1850 to 1900. Migrants came principally from the neighbouring countries of Italy, Germany and Belgium. During World War I the recruitment of colonial workers to replace mobilised French workers took place, and after the war, migrants, mainly from Italy and Poland, came in great numbers to participate in the reconstruction of France. By 1932 there were 3 million foreign residents.

After World War II, foreign workers served another purpose. Wages were kept low and social pressure in large firms was reduced by a labour force characterised by high turnover, sometimes recruited directly by employers in the villages of origin. This segmentation of the labour market artificially stimulated the gentrification of French workers.

Another important change in France was brought about by the development of family reunification, mainly after the official end of labour migration in 1974. The unexpected results of this were the settlement of formerly temporary or 'turnover' migrants and the massive arrival of families, which raised new issues of multiculturalism and 'the right to be different'. Along with this came a subsequent focus on issues such as integration, Islam, secularism, and problems of the suburbs, and a renewal of the debate on citizenship and universalism. [1]

During the 1990s the arrival of middle class and elite migrants from the South and from the East served to alleviate shortages in the labour market, as many migrants assumed jobs as teachers, qualified technicians, and the like. Their arrival brought social change in the form of ethnic entrepreneurship, 'beur' fiction, and mixed marriages.

Different types of political actors correspond to these different waves of migration and settlement. France was built on the myth of homogeneity and for a long time supported the principle of equality of rights within the founding social contract, without group-specific policies. Foreign workers have in fact gradually obtained equality of rights in the workplace, as a result of laws passed in 1972 and 1975 on voting rights for works committees (*comités d'entreprise*) and in trade union elections for the union representatives (*délégués syndicaux*).

However, the debate shifted in the 1980s, gradually focusing less on workers and more on families; that is, less on the workplace and more on social issues. Integration appeared as an essential aim of the '*Vivre ensemble avec nos différences mais aussi avec nos resemblances*' campaign, launched in 1983. Yet specific policies intended as tools to aid in the attainment of equal social rights were formulated in terms which addressed such collective problems as education for immigrants and obtaining social services, as well as specific urban policies entailing a coordination of various government departments in areas of extreme deprivation (70 pilot areas were so defined by Prime Minister Michel Rocard in 1989). If specificity is provisional rather than permanent, however, it creates the risk of trapping the people concerned in a culture of dependency, and of stigmatising 'differences', thus providing arguments to opponents of the presence of foreign communities.

On the basis of these different kinds of socio-political demands and policies, we can distinguish among several generations of immigrants (and children of immigrants) in their roles as political actors as follows:

1. *Immigrants as foreigners and workers:* Migrant workers were first organised according to their country of origin in the 1960s and 1970s, with a focus on home-country issues, sometimes with strong links to French or foreign unions.
2. *Immigrants as mediators of socio-political traditions:* For Turkish, Portuguese, black African and even Italian first-generation immigrants, the associative tendency has been to maintain the traditions of their village or region of origin (in the case of Italians and Portuguese), to engage in political and religious debates and struggles from abroad (for Turks) or to recreate family social life (for Africans). We should also note the existence of roughly 1,000 Islamic associations of various types. Most of these associations have contributed to the internal cohesion of foreign families but have not integrated them into French society. Some, particularly the more politicised and radical religious associations, have brought about local conflict with the French authorities.
3. *The children of immigrants as local political actors:* In the 1980s the associative movement of the second generation of Franco-Maghrebians, created after the freedom of association was given to foreigners in 1981, generated new forms of struggle and participation. The fight against racism, the struggle for civic rights and a new definition of citizenship, the promotion of socio-cultural integration in the suburbs, the call for the meeting of students' needs and assistance in the job market and with new business ventures, were all prominent demands, which were related directly to new policy initiatives.

Initially restricted to a narrow political space in France, and thus limited to being political actors in social conflicts, immigrants have gradually become actors in the realm of urban conflict through the politicisation of social demands, and now their children have entered into politics.

IMMIGRANT POLITICAL ACTORS AS FOREIGNERS AND WORKERS

From the beginning of the organised recruitment of foreigners after World War I to the end of the period of growth in 1973, immigrants

TABLE 1

IMMIGRANTS IN FRANCE, 1990

NATIONAL ORIGIN	FOREIGNERS BORN OUTSIDE OF FRANCE			NATURALISED FRENCHMEN BORN OUTSIDE FRANCE		
	NUMBER - IN 1990 (th)	VARIATION 1962-90 (%)	DIST. OF NATIONALITIES, 1990 (%)	NUMBER IN 1990 (th)	VARIATION 1990-92 (%)	DIST. OF NATIONALITIES, 1990 (%)
TOTAL	2650	-11	100	1308	141	100
EEC	1099	-184	36.4	740	9	56.6
Spanish	190	-77	6.7	223	4	17.0
Italian	223	-50	7.8	300	-25	22.9
Portuguese	505	-82	17.7	101	44	7.8
Other EEC	181	+34	6.3	116	-14	8.9
E.EUROPEAN*	104	-27	3.6	163	-12	12.5
OTHER EUROPEANS	33	+2	1.1	25	+4	1.9
N. AFRICANS	1004	+18	36.2	167	+34	12.7
Algerian	473	-51	16.6	69	+9	5.3
Moroccan	396	+68	13.9	51	+21	3.9
Tunisian	135	+1	4.7	47	+4	3.6
OTHER AFRICANS	204	+69	7.1	57	+32	4.4
INDO-CHINESE	92	-3	3.2	67	+37	5.1
Turks	147	+49	5.1	12	+1	0.9
OTHERS FROM ASIA	106	+46	3.7	53	+23	4.1
OTHERS	70	+19	2.4	25	+13	1.9

* Includes Bulgaria, Hungary, Poland, Romania, Czechoslovakia, Yugoslavia, and all countries of the former Soviet Union.

Source: INSEE, *Recensements de la Population*

were first regarded either as traitors to the working-class movement, that is, as scabs or '*jaunes*', which referred to the supposedly docile Chinese workers introduced during World War I; as politically alienated or 'lumpenproletariat', devoid of political consciousness and absorbed in accumulating savings to further some project in the home country; or as political actors in the form of agents of their country of origin. They were therefore viewed as a political threat rather than actors in social conflict.

The period from 1945 to 1968 was the peak of the development and turnover of immigration in France. In 1945 the ONI (*Office national d'Immigration*) was created, which had a monopoly on recruitment of foreign workers except in the case of Algerians, who were residents of French *départements*. At the same time, a new nationality code was promulgated, in the context of a deliberate pro-immigration policy, in order to determine which foreigners should eventually become French and which should remain mere migrant workers. The authorities tried to select 'good' immigrants for permanent family settlement and possible naturalisation on the one hand, and 'turnover' or temporary workers on the other. The Italians, who had been widely criticised between the wars, had become 'desirable' in terms of population policy but fewer came than was expected. So, a rapid succession of migratory waves occurred: Spaniards in the 1950s, Portuguese in the 1960s, especially between 1968 and 1974 (in order to escape military service in colonial wars); Yugoslavs in the 1960s and 1970s, and Tunisians and Moroccans, along with Turks and black Africans in the 1970s. At the same time, Algerians, some of whom had been permanently settled since World War I, initiated the rise of family immigration before the Franco-Algerian War and after its end, in 1962.

The dynamics of this migration were largely outside state control. Recruitment was managed by the firms themselves, which hired workers directly in rural areas abroad, instead of using the ONI. By 1968 the ONI controlled scarcely 18 per cent of entries, which meant that 82 per cent were entering illegally and being legalised in the following months or years. However, beginning in 1966 the French state tried to give an institutional framework to its immigration policy. A Directorate of Population and Migration was created in 1966 within the Ministry of Labour. Its mission was to coordinate policy within the government.

In 1972 illegal entry was effectively restricted for the first time by the Fontanet-Marcellin circular, which instructed the relevant authorities to refuse legalisation to people who had entered France illegally after 31 December 1971. This led to protest in many immigrant areas, since this was an effective change in a longstanding policy. In 1973, following racist riots in Marseilles, Algeria decided to halt emigrant workers, and in July 1974 the new Secretary of State for Immigration, appointed by President Valéry Giscard d'Estaing, decided to suspend immigration of foreign salaried workers.

Between 1960 and 1970 three main analyses of this generation of immigrant workers as political actors were put forward.[2] The first of these can be summed up as 'the past explains the present'. The focus in this analysis is on the immigrant's itinerary, from the place of departure (supposedly rural and traditional) to the place of arrival (necessarily viewed as urban and modern). The immigrant is explained in terms of his place of origin and his cultural traditions, in order to understand his political alienation and the process of his socialisation. In most cases, national or regional affiliations are viewed as determinants of political involvement.

The second view can be characterised as 'the present explains the present'; the immigrant is described as a 'foreigner,' as well as a 'worker', or as a generally excluded person. The foreigner is above all described as a non-national, a non-member of the nation-state. What is key is this negative definition of the non-citizen, reinforcing a precarious status that is aggravated by illegal administrative practices which enclose the immigrant in an situation of political dependency with regard to the host society. In their role as workers, this view portrays immigrants as mainly unskilled and the emphasis is put on their place in the labour market, their lack of qualifications, and their social oppression. The immigrant is thus viewed as belonging to the lower working-class along with the rural population, women and the young, and may therefore have specific concerns and demands in the workplace. In contrast to a French trade-unionism threatened by corporatism and *embourgeoisement*, immigrants are seen as an emerging political force, an *avant-garde du prolétariat révolutionnaire avancé*.[3] This social status and behavior depend on the marginal position of foreigners as unskilled workers suffering from cumulative inequality and discrimination, and this explains their involvement in wildcat strikes and unofficial demands.

The last view presumes that 'the future explains the present'. This analysis focuses on the role and itinerary of the immigrant before and after the migration process. Migration, in this view, might be a temporary transition between two situations. The immigrant might be seen as a peasant aiming at becoming a 'petit bourgeois' after training as a proletarian. Owing to the myth of return, immigrants could be expected to settle for transitional precariousness, leading to passivity in social conflicts.

During the period of economic growth, immigrants were mainly defined as social actors in work conflicts whose demands had impinged on politics. They were mainly Algerian, Italian, Polish and Spanish. The ideal-typical political actor was the old Algerian immigrant: an unskilled worker, a man without his family, strongly linked to French trade-unionism (CGT), a foreigner willing to return home. His political participation was orientated towards the struggles of his country of origin or towards social movements in France. Accordingly, neither his religious belief (relegated to a hidden private sphere) nor his family life were seen as significantly influencing his political involvement.

Most of these characteristics which defined immigrants in the years of growth have now disappeared or are disappearing. The connection to the country of origin has weakened among North Africans and black Africans, and unemployment and de-industrialisation have had a major impact on migrant workers. Such images of immigrants as needing to be defended (according to a third-worldist or working-class analysis) or as a problem to be tackled (from the point of view of policy-makers) no longer fit. Gentrification of some long-settled immigrants and growing marginalisation of others are taking place in France, while new criteria have defined immigrants as political actors.

FROM THE POLITICISATION OF SOCIAL DEMANDS TO THE SOCIAL EXPANSION OF POLITICS

The period 1974–81 was a decisive turning point for 'immigrants in France'. A population which was considered a labour force of isolated men, viewed essentially as workers at the periphery of the socio-political spheres, gradually became a part of French society; because new entries were turned away, the 'turnover' of workers was replaced by family reunification. New problems arose from this unexpected result. Conflicts linked problems of work and residence, the most famous being the SONACOTRA strike between 1976 and 1980, which concerned the largest hostel-management authority for foreign workers. The rise to social salience of the 'second generations' and illegal residents asking for their legalisation gradually replaced the old stereotype of the foreign worker. In spite of family settlement, two junior Ministers for Immigration, Paul Dijoud and Lionel Stoleru, were still thinking of repatriation and in 1977 repatriation policies inspired by the German model were implemented. They failed however since most of the few who returned to their home countries were Spanish or Portuguese, the people that the government wanted to settle in France, while Algerians, in their overwhelming majority, refused the repatriation offered to them.

During this period, the term 'insertion', supposedly more respectful of links with the country of origin, supplanted the traditional idea of assimilation. The economic and social costs and benefits of immigration were discussed at the highest level (LEPERS report, 1976) and home-country links were made official by the teaching of languages and description of cultures of 'origin' at school. The teachers were provided by the countries themselves, which raised many debates on the legitimacy of the languages and cultures taught. At the same time, the struggle for equal rights was still in progress. Equal social rights in the workplace were granted by the 1972 law on elections to workplace *comités d'entreprise*, and the 1975 law on trade-union representation. Another 1972 law made manifestations of racism in public life illegal.

In 1980 legislation was passed which sharply restricted foreigners' right of entry and residence. This law, called loi Bonnet after the Interior Minister responsible, signified the end of a long period from 1945 to 1980, in which immigration 'policy' had been defined and implemented by administrative discretion, through circulars and administrative notes rather than by statute.[4] This shows that the topic had begun to leave the periphery of the decision-making process and had become a legitimate object of political debate.

Two groups of immigrants emerged as political actors in this period: the Portuguese and the Maghrebians. The Portuguese had gradually settled in France during the 1960s, mainly as illegal immigrants who sought to escape from both poverty and military service. They took part in French industrial conflicts in the early 1970s, the most famous case being at Pennarroya in 1972, and made political claims, including calls for freedom of expression and social demands. Yet the originality of their political involvement lay mainly in their participation in housing-related urban conflict. Many Portuguese, especially in the suburbs of Paris, were housed in shanty towns ('bidonvilles') which the government of Prime Minister Chaban-Delmas was committed to clear under a programme begun in 1969. Major conflict ensued as a result of protests against the expulsion from housing in the cities, which became highly politicised and led to the emergence of Portuguese leaders, mainly within the FASTI (*Federation des associations de soutien aux travailleurs immigres*). The Portuguese went on to assume political leadership among immigrant groups in France until 1974, when the revolution of 25 April occurred in Portugal. Their subsequent gradual ascendence to the ranks of the lower middle class in the 1980s, the maintenance of their links with Portugal as shown by the number of returnees, and the vitality of their community organisations in France have caused the French to forget their high degree of politicisation. Since the end of the 1970s, the

Maghrebians have begun to replace them as political actors, creating the image of the rapid and successful integration of the Portuguese.

Immigration from the Maghreb to France is long-established, especially in the case of Algerian workers, who were first recruited during World War I. The diversification of the social, economic and political presence of North African immigrants is rather new, compared to other groups. In autumn 1973, following racist incidents in Marseilles, Algeria decided to halt the migration of Algerian workers to France, and in July 1974 France decided to block the migration of salaried workers. One of the unexpected effects of these two decisions was the acceleration of family reunification, which had begun for Algerians in the 1960s. Before 1974 Maghrebian workers had a high rate of turnover, sending remittances to their families. They had organised their life in France around the firm, the hostel housing (*foyers pour travailleurs étrangers*), the trade unions, home-country organisations, both official and dissident, and the coffee shop, postponing identity and family life.

Since 1974 the socio-political situation of Maghrebians has slowly changed. First, family reunification has tended to accelerate because the workers feared that they would not be re-admitted to France if they stay too long in their country of origin, which would lead to their unemployment and illegal status. Between the census of 1975 and that of 1982, the proportion of European and non-European foreigners shifted for the first time in favour of non-Europeans, the majority being overwhelmingly from the Maghreb. Second, migration from Tunisia and Morocco, often illegal, has developed due to the decrease of labour migration from southern Europe (principally Spain). Third, as a result of family reunification, a second generation is appearing. Some of this group arrived in France as children; others were born there, and a part of this population has neither migrated nor ever been legally foreign.

Families, traditionally settled in old urban centres or districts with a high concentration of Maghrebians, began to acquire modern social housing in the suburbs (in HLM: *habitations à loyers modérés*) of large towns (Paris, Lyons, Marseilles, Lille-Roubaix-Tourcoing). At the same time, black Africans progressively took the place of Maghrebians in the 'foyers' for foreign workers. Under the first junior Minister for Immigration, Paul Dijoud (1974–77), a larger significance was accorded to 'the right to be different' and, as we have already noted, to the safeguarding of links with immigrant cultures.

The issue of immigration, which had previously been marginal, acquired political visibility at the end of the 1970s. In 1980 a period of heated controversy over immigration began; the Bonnet law was passed in January 1980 after a year of parliamentary debate. Hunger strikes in the suburbs of Lyons underlined the problems of the so-called 'second generation', and illegal residents (among them Tunisians and Moroccans) demanded the legalisation of their status. The election, in May 1981, of François Mitterrand to the presidency of the Republic brought many hopes. Immigration as an issue and immigrants as actors emerged in the political arena.

FROM ACCESS TO POLITICS TO LOCALISM, PROFESSIONALISM AND THE DE-LEGITIMATION OF POLITICS

The front of the arena is occupied by children of North Africans, owing to the freedom of association that they acquired in 1981, in line with the standard French law of 1901. As political actors, they raised new questions: citizenship, localism, Islam, problems of the suburbs, anti-racism, integration, professionalism of political actors. This was followed by the de-legitimation of politics, along with exclusion of some and access to the middle class for others. Most members of this generation have never been immigrants and are French or will become so. We can distinguish several periods in the evolution of these issues.[5]

The years 1981–86 saw the immigration question take heightened importance in French politics. The increasing centrality of immigration as an issue in French political life led decision-makers to insist on the symbolic dimension of legislation and on the expressive aspect of the measures adopted. Until 1981, emphasis was put on laws dealing with labour, and later with legislation fostering the equal treatment of foreigner and national. In contrast, during the first years of the socialist period (1981–83), the emphasis shifted to human rights. This included the suspension of the expulsion of young immigrants, reaffirmation of the right to family reunification, and the confirmation of freedom of association for foreigners. The main measures took the form of laws, and attempts were made to encourage self-expression on the part of immigrants and the second generation.

This policy unfolded in two parts, the second of which was regarded as conditional upon the first. The two aspects were the struggle to suppress illegal immigration, and the improvement of the living conditions of those immigrants who had already settled in the country. Such aims were not without contradiction, and had unanticipated effects, mainly in terms of immigration control, which degenerated to the policing of frontiers with limited results, and to the regularisation of illegal immigrants in 1982–83, which attracted new migrants.

Although these matters are far from resolved, what did seem to change in terms of the political debate in France during the years 1981–83 was the significance of immigration in the social imagination and political mythology. The local elections of March 1983, marked by the electoral breakthrough of the National Front, revealed that the issue of immigration had become a central object of bargaining between political leaders. The summer of 1983 heralded a turning point in immigration policy: stricter border controls, as well as internal controls, were introduced in order to convince public opinion that the repression of illegal immigrants was effective. Other measures adopted in 1984 against illegals involved family reunification and asylum-seekers, and reinforced the contradictions of such a policy.

At the same time, the rise of social movements and the marches of 1983 and 1984, encouraged by the freedom of association granted in 1981, gave a great impetus to new forms of political participation and intervention in French society by the second generation. The ten-year residence permit, acquired by immigrants in 1983, was automatically renewable, and broke the link (which was to some extent an element of legitimacy) between employment and residence. As a result of their participation in local politics, some immigrant activists gained professional status and became part of the middle class. Some elites have emerged and become mediators between the working-class suburbs and elected politicians.

The structure of the Maghrebian immigrant population has also changed, and now tends to be divided into two general types. The first is older, and is increasingly threatened by unemployment in the car, steel and mining industries. The other segment is younger and, in spite of such difficulties as delinquency, unemployment, insufficient vocational training, failure at school and drug-use, is better disposed towards economic, social, cultural and even political self-organisation. The Maghrebian population in France is an increasingly heterogeneous group. Socially, economically, culturally and juridically it is becoming more diverse. Some Maghrebians still belong to the first generation, while others are French citizens well-integrated into their social groups.

The rise of the movement brought by the freedom of association granted in 1981, and the acceptance of the legitimacy of collective identity claims, including Islam, have provided the impulse behind new forms of participation by the second generation in French society. Many in this group, however, were hesitant to accept French nationality when the choice was possible, especially Algerians.[6] Most young people are of Algerian descent among the Maghrebians, because Moroccan and Tunisian immigration is more recent.

Some industrial conflicts in the 1980s, especially the strike at Citroen in 1983, demonstrated links between strike action and Islam. The increasing number of Islamic associations, with roughly 650 declared in the *Journal Officiel*, point to the fact that Islam has become the second largest religion in France, with three million believers. At a time when working-class mobilisation had lost some of its potency, the religious dimension has abruptly appeared as an aspect of the changes which have affected Maghrebians in France.[7] The struggles in the car industry were presented as being connected to the emergence of Islam at the work-place; a kind of 'social syncretism' distinguished by the appearance of a joint religious and trade-union leadership.

Islam had for the most part not been a theme in conflicts, although it had been present in the work-world for a long time. Prayer rooms were created inside factories, along with ones established in urban suburbs in the 1970s; the first factory mosque was opened at Renault-Billancourt in October 1976. It began to acquire visibility and legitimacy and its exponents moved from assimilationist tactics, aimed at gaining individual acceptance, to a game of tactics and identity used to negotiate as a collective entity. The main union, the CGT, decided to 'go along with' Muslim Renault workers, devising a unifying strategy in the name of culture and dignity.

What is most striking since the mid-1980s is that the terms of political dialogue on immigration have changed, in part because of initiatives by the government and opposition, in part because of initiatives from immigrants and immigrant associations themselves. Consider the focus put on citizenship and civil rights. Some forms and definitions of a new citizenship appeared in urban suburbs among Franco-Maghrebians who liked to say that some of them were citizens by participation without necessarily being nationals. From the municipal elections in 1983 until 1986, the rise of racism stimulated mobilisation around the theme of citizenship based on residence and participation in local affairs, with an increasingly central place in political debate devoted to immigrants both as actors and as objects of policy.

In 1986 the new conservative majority in the National Assembly introduced several important changes affecting the place of immigration in political debate. These included the Pasqua Law of September 1986, which limited foreigners' rights of entry and residence, the highly publicised expulsion of 101 workers from Mali, the emphasis placed on French identity, on security, and on the threat of Islam, followed by the reform of naturalisation proposed by the National Front. This all occurred against the backdrop of the latter's slogans.

The proposed reform principally concerned the acquisition of French nationality by the French-born children of foreigners residing in France.

According to Article 44 of the Nationality Code, such children acquire French nationality by right between the ages of 16 and 21, if they have lived in France for the previous five years. Both the Right and the Far Right wanted to withdraw this right, arguing that such people were '*Français de papier*' or even '*Français malgré eux*'. They also argued that Franco-Maghrebians did not deserve to become French because of their adherence to Islam, the memory of the Algerian war, and suspicions about their behaviour and their intentions with regard to the acquisition of French citizenship.

The proposal thus sought to suppress the principle of *jus soli*, long established in French law and an important tool of integration since the end of the nineteenth century. Consequently, the debate on immigration was transformed into a debate on nationality and came to focus on complex legal texts that were of little interest to the public, not least because they were difficult to understand. A Committee of Wise Men (*Commission Des Sages*) was appointed in June 1987, which finally recommended that the Nationality Code should not be significantly changed. At the end of 1987 the reform was postponed and the question of immigration was avoided during the presidential campaign of 1988, except when François Mitterrand stated that he was not hostile to giving voting rights to foreigner at the local level. Following his re-election, the Pasqua law was abrogated, and, after much equivocation, replaced by the milder Joxe law in 1989.

Still other challenges were brought by the protests of the second generation and by the 'Foulard affair' in October 1989, an event which was rapidly transformed into a national debate on secularism and multiculturalism, and which was solved by the Council of State, the Ministry of National Education and the King of Morocco, in a speech on French television.

In spring 1993 the coming to power of the Right was finally followed by a reform of the Nationality Code, which followed most of the guidelines originally proposed in 1986. It suppressed automatic access to French Nationality (Article 44) and limited access to French citizenship for some categories, such as spouses of French citizens, and Franco-Algerian youth offenders. At the same time, a new Pasqua law on residence and entry encouraged 'stop and frisk' actions by the police and placed greater emphasis on the tightening of border controls.

The complexity of government concerns with citizenship and identity can be seen by the evolution of integration policy after the elections of 1988. A new policy of integration was implemented with the appointment in December 1989 of Hubert Prévot as a '*M. Intégration*' to head a '*Haut Conseil à l'Intégration*', composed of nine 'sages' appointed in

1990, and with the creation of a representative structure for Islam in France (the CORIF). New measures were proposed in spring 1990 to combat illegal immigration and to promote local integration in the suburbs. At the end of 1990 and the beginning of 1991, the Gulf War raised anew the question of allegiance and legitimacy, illustrated by debates about military service for Franco-Algerians and Islamic solidarity as a threat to internal security. With the change of prime minister in 1991, integration policy tended to merge with urban policy and with general measures dealing with the marginalised and the young.

Within the associations run by young Franco-Maghrebians, the planned reform in 1986 contributed to their return to the mainstream of French politics. It put an end to the hesitation over the choice between French or Algerian nationality and over French allegiance. It also decisively moved their struggle from the cultural to political concerns. A collective movement of 110 associations in 1988 advocated the abrogation of the Pasqua law of 1986, and led to a new law regulating the entry and residence of foreigners, the Joxe law, which was passed in 1988. The definitive entrance of this new generation into French politics was also marked by this movement, which addressed such themes as new forms of citizenship, strongly promoted during the bicentennial of the French Revolution, and Islam as a collective identity to be expressed as a basis on which to negotiate in France.

The 1986 law also led Franco-Maghrebians to reaffirm their support for François Mitterrand in the presidential election of 1988; in the second round, he obtained the vote of more than 80 per cent of those Maghrebians who voted, according to some exit polls. This support was also extended to the Socialist Party, and its various factions, as it was viewed as a '*parti dominant*', able to give both grants and legitimacy.

Some 400 Franco-Maghrebians, children of immigrants or *harkis*, were candidates in the local elections of 1989 and some 200 were elected as municipal councillors, or '*élus beurs*'. The political parties thus cannot ignore them, a fact which was hotly debated during the 1991 Gulf War when they appeared to belong in part to another political sphere, in spite of their allegiance to the French position and their diversity of views. This was an argument analogous to the one made about communists during the Cold War. It was exacerbated by the fact that some, the most marginalised, wanted to provoke the French government with ostentatious pro-Saddam sentiments.[8]

This rethinking and co-ordination of their position is also noticeable in their position with regard to Europe: most of these groups' leaders have firmly established themselves in the broader European context, a position which can be used as a weapon against the nation-state, and they intend to gain from it.

Thus, since 1985–86 the broad socio-political debate in France has also focused on such questions as definitions of French identity and dual citizenship, and these have emerged as political demands of the second generation of Franco-Maghrebians. Yet, after a brief '*passage au politique*' at the national level, they have focused their activity on local associations, with themes such as civil rights for their parents and citizenship. (The *Etats généraux de l'immigration* in 1988 focused on such demands.)

The theme of citizenship emerged in 1986, centring on a new definition of the criteria for membership and participation, within the local associations of Franco-Maghrebians. It was viewed as an answer to a crisis in a democracy threatened by the rise of individualism and the intensification of collective identities The debate on the reform of the Nationality Code led primarily to the questioning of the association between nationality and citizenship, a central theme in the idea of 'new' citizenship.

The second generation demanded a notion of citizenship based more on participation and residence than on nationality and descent, in a multicultural society. The emergence of local associations (nearly 3,000) promoted the idea of citizenship 'for those who all have the same problems', referring to such things as the difficulties of life in working-class suburbs. It also fostered the notion that a grassroots process of politicisation might appear based on the concrete concerns of unemployment, local life, housing, education and the defence of rights.

The challenges posed to these local organisations by such issues as the 'Foulard affair', the Rushdie (*Satanic Verses*) Affair, the integration at the local level of associations fighting against exclusion and ghettos, and the progressive gaining of legitimacy by their leaders, have all served to integrate the Franco-Maghrebians, despite the fact that their individual social positions have not necessarily improved. Some of them have in fact entered the professional and middle classes, in tandem with the gentrification and entrepreneurship of the elites.

Yet the problem of Maghrebians and Franco-Maghrebians in France is that French public opinion does not tend to perceive this. Some members of the second or third generation call themselves, humorously, the 'beurgeoisie'. In reality however, this group is very heterogeneous; some are French, while others belong to one of the three nationalities of the Maghreb. Some define themselves as Muslims, other as secularised or simply belonging to an Islamic culture; some are *harkis* (Muslims who served in the French Army during the Algerian War) and define themselves as such, while others are Berbers and focus on this identity as distinct from the Arab world. Still others are of mixed descent.

Gender is an important category in this self-identification: among women, especially those who belong to associative movements, attitudes towards their country of origin and Islam are much more clear-cut. In public life, girls and women fight more for secularism, for integration into French society, for equality with men and the French, and for access to birth control. They tend to vote for the Socialist Party. Some want to reject their native culture and they are more likely to define themselves as European. However according to some surveys they have been less affected than their brothers, in their private lives, by the experience of migration. The practice of Islam is more respected by women than by men, although men define themselves more readily as Muslims, as women stay at home when they are young instead of being educated 'by the street'. We find among women many 'soft' feminists who expect rewards from work, school and secularism, while men and boys express issues more often related to ethnicity, Arab and Islamic 'belonging', and mixed identity.

Identity is in most cases reconstructed, or *bricolée* (do-it-yourself). Nationality is no longer the main divide; instead, the line between socio-economic exclusion and success is the more salient one. Maghrebians and Franco-Maghrebians are defined less and less as foreign workers, and increasingly as French nationals integrated into towns and suburbs, where unemployment has destroyed the traditional aims of social involvement and mobility, and for whom their 'native' countries have ceased to represent a possible future. Thus localism serves as a central part of identity for many Franco-Maghrebians, and is more than a mere focus for political activity.

Membership in local associations by Franco-Maghrebians is now facing a crisis due to lack of involvement from the younger generation, since leadership is in the hands of their older siblings. Another conflict has arisen between the leaders of local movements trying to promote grassroots participation and integration, and the national leaders of large associations such as France-Plus and SOS-Racisme. This has taken the form of competition for legitimacy and leadership between those who consider themselves the foundation, performing the unsung task of mobilisation at the local level, and those who act as mediators between the Franco-Maghrebians, government departments and the media. Another recent trend in Franco-Maghrebian political participation has been the use of activist experience acquired in organisations as a tool for social mobility. In contrast with the situation in 1981, politics has ceased to be seen as the most legitimate and autonomous struggle. It has become a tool in the service of other aims. Local interest groups have tended to manage the social economy and action in the suburbs, aided by para-institutional schemes financed by public funds that have been implemented to fight against marginalisation, exclusion and violence. In addition, forms of 'beur' media have been born in the press and local radio stations.

All of these institutionalised forms of collective action have fostered the rise of new leaders; the political, economic and cultural leaders are the most visible.[9] Willing to integrate, but without disappearing, and sometimes maintaining their positions on both sides of the Mediterranean, they have progressively acquired professional skills in mediation and publicity, which they use to negotiate between political actors and the grassroots, as well as between centre and periphery, in urban areas. Their context is often defined as Mediterranean, based on communities and traditional collective solidarities, but using modern communication tools.

Their aim is the convergence of cultures, collective integration, and the building of bridges between France and the Maghreb at a non-governmental level. The means of achieving this are the creation of social links, and the instructing of the population in the ways of 'soft subversive' activity. This strategy could offer them greater benefits than discrete assimilation and individual social mobility. While the leaders of the 1980s were absorbed in local associations as a substitute for political action or as a stepping-stone to politics, these associations serve now as a route to entrepreneurship and gentrification. Some penetrated the economy through associational links, mainly through forms of 'Islamic entrepreneurship'. These included the selling of halal meat, books, and Islamic clothes. Community radio stations have been started. Other new ethnic businesses have emerged, such as in communication and computers, as well as chic restaurants, and services such as vocational training and business advice, all of which used associations as a step to economic activity. The name *associations business* given to some of them reflects this shift.

Some initiatives have also been directly conceived as answers to institutional needs, in the form of 'multicultural' businesses aimed at exhibitions and publications, the provision of educational training, and sport and leisure for children. In some cases one can say that there has been an adaptation of the actions undertaken to the funding available, mainly from the Social Action Funds, or FAS. In order to profit from such funding, associations focus more on identity and on its creation than would have been the case without public funding. In other instances, the institutions have become federated and have channelled informal local initiatives. At the same time, new elites are coming directly from their native countries, as students or under bilateral employment agreements, mainly as teachers of mathematics, and they are trying to remain in France. They are part of a new brain-drain from the Maghreb countries and have a strong desire for integration and mobility.

CONCLUSION

In looking at these three generations of political actors which are linked to successive stages of development in the immigrant communities, we can focus on the role of politics as a decisive factor in integration, as well as the trend towards its instrumentalisation. From workers' conflicts to the urban conflicts of the Portuguese and Maghrebians, we move from social to political action. Now, however, political actors tend to use politics for social and cultural aims. The local nature of integration and the domination of immigration policy by political or electoral concerns have both served to de-legitimise political activity, except for the roughly 200 beurs elected to office in the municipal elections of 1989. Meanwhile, identity based on community and ethnicity is in fact a new frontier in the arena of French society and politics. With the emergence of new types of literature, music, and dance (the 'roman beur'[10] and 'beur' music groups are two examples), the memory of immigration is becoming a legitimate social fact, no longer perceived as a social rupture (revolutionary or 'miserabilist') as it was in the 1970s, but something more influenced by the supposed 'American' or 'British' model.

With the persistence of new immigration, coming mostly from black Africa, can we envisage new actors, after the Europeans and the Maghrebians? And in describing all these actors, whose politics often shift between cultural mediation and urban violence, will we be able to speak of a social movement, of ethnic lobbies, or merely of new citizens? One thing which can be asserted without hesitation is that in the end, most of them are merely asking for respect and dignity.

NOTES

1. For historical background see Catherine Wihtol de Wenden, *Les immigrés et la politique* (Paris: Presses de la FNSP, 1988) Part 1.
2. Catherine Wihtol de Wenden, *Citoyenneté, Nationalité et Immigration* (Paris: Arcantere, 1988), pp.146–58.
3. Mark Miller, *Foreign Workers in Western Europe* (NY: Praeger, 1981).
4. Danièle Lochak, *Etrangers, de quel droit?* (Paris; PUF, 1985), pp.205–32.
5. Catherine Wihtol de Wenden, 'Immigration Policy and the Issue of Nationality', *Ethnic and Racial Studies* 14/3(July 1991), pp.319–32.

6. Since the recent reform in June 1993 of the French nationality code, the access of Franco-Maghrebians to French nationality has been restricted to:
   - children born in France after 1 Jan. 1963 whose parents were born in Algeria before that date (i.e., when Algeria was composed of French *départements*), who benefit from the so-called double *jus soli*, if their parents have been living in France for five years before their birth
   - the children of *harkis* (forces of the French Army between 1954 and 1962) and of other Muslims repatriated to France since 1962 and whose parents were already French or could ask for French nationality until 1967,
   - the other foreigners (i.e., Tunisians and Moroccans) if they were born in France and have resided there without any interruption between the ages of 13 and 18. Since June 1993, they can become French if they willingly ask for French nationality between the ages of 16 and 21. The have no rights to French citizenship if they have been imprisoned for more than 6 months.

   We estimate the population of Maghrebian origin in France at:
   1.5 million Algerians, Moroccans and Tunisians, 500,000 *harkis* and their children, and a million French nationals of Maghrebian origin. (The census is barred from asking about religion, which makes estimates difficult.)
7. Catherine Wihtol de Wenden, 'Trade Unions, Islam and Immigration', *Economic and Industrial Democracy*, Vol.9, (1988), pp.65–82.
8. Catherine Wihtol de Wenden, 'Les beurs et la guerre', *Esprit/Les cahiers de l'Orient*, No.6 (May 1991), pp.102–7.
9. 'Immigration: a la recherche des intermédiaires culturels', *Migrations société* 4/22–23 (July–Oct.1992).
10. Alec Hargreaves, *Voices from the North African Immigrant Community in France: Immigration and Identity in Beur Fiction* (NY, Oxford: Berg, 1991).

Integration in Theory and Practice: A Comparison of France and Britain

PATRICK WEIL and JOHN CROWLEY

The authors compare the integration of immigrants in France and Britain in terms of the theoretical models, politics and practice in each country. In France, the tradition of republicanism is emphasised, and thus a legacy of integrating immigrants under this banner is proclaimed; in Britain there is no real analogue to this, and no common myth which is shared across the spectrum of political opinion, though historical conditions have also shaped policy. The political debate in France has centred around the concepts of insertion versus integration, while in Britain debate has revolved around the concept of 'race relations'. In both countries the practice of integration is threatened by economic dislocation, however, in Britain citizenship and political rights for immigrants have not been challenged and thus are not salient issues as they are in France.

An important strand of current European debate about the implications of mass migration is the perception that the process of 'integration' in the various countries has reached an impasse. Integration is a word derived from social and political theory which has been caught up in the very peculiar and contemporary political debate about the absorption of migrants.

The concept of integration comprises two distinct strands. On the one hand, integration is the opposite of disintegration. In this classic sociological Durkheimian sense, integration derives from shared beliefs and practices, social interaction, and shared goals;[1] some subsequent writers have suggested that, of these conditions, shared practices and social interaction are in fact largely sufficient.[2] In terms of political theory, integration may be seen as what makes standard majoritarian democracy possible. Conversely non-integration implies some other, non-majoritarian, political order such as communitarianism or consociationalism, and indeed may, at the limit, make democracy impossible. Integration may also be thought of as the opposite of segregation.[3] Finally the two meanings can be linked: not only is segregation unlikely to be conducive to integration (in the first sense) but, more generally, social inequality is destructive of integration.

These concepts form a common background (often implicit) to political and policy-orientated discussion in France and Britain about the absorption – to use a very general term – of immigrants. At the same time, however, major differences in historical tradition and in political context divide the two countries. The results are often seen as embodying two competing and incompatible 'models' of integration. Furthermore, each model is used polemically to denigrate the other. In the British literature, a description of the French model as 'ethnocentric', leading to the racist *front national* and relying on a coercive process of assimilation, is sometimes used to highlight the pluralist, liberal and anti-racist British model.[4] Conversely the same British model, redescribed as communitarian, multi-culturalist, mixophobic, and leading to religious fundamentalism, is frequently used in France to highlight the secular, egalitarian French model, with its respect for individual identity and social mobility. Yet, in many ways, the problems actually faced by France and the Britain, as well as the policy options available, are similar.

The purpose of this article is to clarify the nature of the models of integration in their theoretical background, to examine convergences in practices in the two countries and, by distinguishing common elements from genuine differences, to assess the reality of the crisis of integration in the Britain and in France.

THE THEORETICAL MODELS: THE NATIONAL ORIGINS OF PUBLIC POLICY

There are points of comparison between the British and French experiences of immigration. In both countries the migrants at the centre of current debates came originally from former colonies to meet the economic needs of the former imperial power, where they were entitled to settle and to acquire citizenship. Yet policy and politics on either side of the Channel have also been influenced by profoundly dissimilar, historically rooted, traditions.

France

France, with the longest history of immigration in Europe, is proud of its ability to assimilate immigrants into its 'republican' society. In the theoretical model, ethnic or national origins are erased by the second generation. The child of a Italian, Polish, Spanish, or British foreigner born in France cannot be distinguished from a child with French ancestors. There is therefore no social basis for stigmatisation: structural or institutional racism, in the British sense, is inconceivable.

This tradition of assimilation has its roots in the pre-Revolutionary *ancien régime*. The Kingdom of France was unified by the gradual consolidation of an ever larger territory as, over the centuries, the Crown integrated into the French state the inhabitants of the various counties, duchies and regions.[5] Pre-Revolutionary law gave easy acccess to nationality for children of foreign parents on condition that they were Catholic and born and resident within the realm (residence being viewed as a sign of allegiance). The Revolution removed the religious discrimination and replaced allegiance to the Sovereign by allegiance to the nation and to the ideals of the French Revolution. French policy towards the immigrants that France has welcomed on a large scale, for demographic or social reasons, since the middle of the nineteenth century[6] is, in this view, an attempt to integrate them into the nation by putting into practice the ideal of the French nation-state, as derived from the Enlightenment and the Revolution. The Third Republic implemented that particular tradition through strict separation between individual culture and religion (confined to the private sphere) and the secular state which inculcated in both French and foreign children, via the schools, a common civic culture.[7]

Britain

Historical tradition plays a less significant role in British debate, although such myths as the self-perception of Britain as a country of toleration and individual liberty[8] have fuelled liberal rejection of radical anti-racism, to the point of being occasionally promoted as a distinctive British 'model'.[9] There are however two important ways in which Britain differs from France. First, the French parallel between immigrant integration and nation-building (the former being seen in the republican myth as in some sense a special case of the latter) has no real analogue in Britain. In theoretical terms, this no doubt reflects the fact that the construction of the (English) nation as a geographic and cultural entity was historically almost completely unrelated to the construction of the (British) nation as a democratic political entity. This reinforces the view of immigration as a 'new' problem, to which no solution derived from past experience can be applied. Second, and perhaps more strikingly, there is no common British myth, widely shared across the spectrum of political opinion: conflict between competing conceptions of integration policy has been particularly sharp.

British policy did not, however, develop in a vacuum. For instance, the political compromises that put an end to 150 years of religious and constitutional strife at the beginning at the eighteenth century were predicated on accommodation, usually based on pluralism and group representation. Accommodation has also been at the centre of British involvement in a variety of overseas conflicts, particularly in India and in Ireland. Thus the willingness to envisage community-based solutions to minority issues (called 'indirect rule' by many of its critics[10]) is in no way specific to recent race-relations policy. Similarly, the preoccupation of early British policy with a 'liberal' agenda – that is, keeping both minority demands and xenophobia out of politics as far as possible – was partly related to the peculiarities of the issues, but may also be seen as a consequence of a general desire (equally visible in other areas) to preserve autonomy on the part of the state elite. One could also argue that short-term pragmatism as such is a British policy tradition, contrasting sharply with the often more ideological French approach.

THE POLITICS OF INTEGRATION

The politics of integration and the integration policies implemented on either side of the of the Channel have not primarily been determined by abstract models. Short-term problems, sometimes unrelated to immigration, have been solved in ways that have had a major unplanned impact. For instance, in both Britain and France, colonial and post-colonial policy has had major consequences for immigration. In general terms, politics must be analysed as the interplay between concepts and the requirements of action.

France

That a French 'melting pot' functioned effectively in the first half of the twentieth century to integrate large numbers of immigrants from a wide variety of origins is not really in question. At this time the legitimate name for the process in official discourse was *assimilation*, implying the idea of unilateral adaptation of the immigrant to the laws and the customs of France and of the French, the superiority of French culture and national identity, and the requirement that the immigrant renounce his or her identity and culture. When in 1974, after immigration of new workers was suspended, a political debate started on the status of immigrants and the future of legal non-European migrants, the concept of *assimilation* lost much of its legitimacy. A rival concept – *insertion* – was dominant from 1974 to 1985.

It was the product of two contradictory but converging processes. After World War II, for the first time in its history, French immigration and integration policy was endowed with a coherent, formally egalitarian and liberal, legal framework. The ordonnance of 2 November 1945 introduced a permit system that gradually guaranteed security of settlement for any new immigrant. In addition, the ordonnance of 18 October 1945 guaranteed liberal access to French nationality. From 1945 to 1968, during the postwar economic boom, immigration was not an issue. Yet, when the social condition of marginalised foreigners was taken up by the left-wing parties, there was no question of demanding assimilation, the connotations of ethnic superiority of which were frequently related to imperialism or fascism. The intellectual mainstream of the time was well represented by Lévi-Strauss's plea for recognition of the equality of different cultures.[11] *Insertion* was used in this context to designate the right to refuse assimilation, to defend and to preserve collective identity, and to refuse to adapt to dominant French culture.

At the opposite end of the political spectrum, *insertion* became legitimate for very different reasons. While, in reaction to Nazi ideology, the legal framework for immigration defined in 1945 made no mention of ethnic preference, it is important to recall that most immigration-policy specialists had defended ethnic quotas. As immigration to France was, for demographic reasons, already viewed as permanent, selected European workers were preferred to supposedly 'unassimilable' North Africans.[12] Nevertheless Algerian workers soon afterwards obtained freedom of movement, albeit for political rather than for economic reasons. French colonial policy led to French citizenship for Algerian Muslims and consequently, in 1947, to freedom of movement between Algeria and the metropolis. Again for political reasons, citizens of newly independent Algeria obtained the right by the treaty of Evian (1962) freely to travel to, and settle in, France. After the interruption of new immigration in 1974, along with unemployment and recession, would they be allowed to settle permanently in France? Many right-wing leaders were hostile to their assimilation, or simply considered it impossible.

Thus assimilation was rejected, and *insertion* supported, by both proponents and opponents of permanent settlement. The right for non-European immigrants to retain their own culture (an aim of anti-racist organizations) could be seen as preparing them to leave France (desired by some right-wing leaders) and to make their deportation easier than if they were already mixed in French society. Thus, paradoxically, the deliberate protection of minority culture was a policy shared by pro- and anti-immigrant groups. The concept of *insertion* preserved an ambivalence on the future of the migrants which prevailed until 1984. At that point the failure of forced repatriation of non-European immigrants – and the unforeseen and perverse effects of the left-wing concept of insertion – led to a loss of interest in the concept and its replacement in political debate by *intégration*.

In 1979 President Giscard d'Estaing failed in his attempt to repatriate by force 500,000 Algerians, opposed by the left-wing parties, the labour unions and the churches, as well as by the Gaullist and Christian-Democrat right-wing parties and the *Conseil d'Etat*.[13] In July 1984 a new law, passed unanimously by Parliament, reasserted the primacy of the legal principles of the 1945 ordonnance, and granted most foreign residents, whatever their origins, a renewable ten-year residence permit which guaranteed to them and to their families the right to settle in France.

Communitarian insertion had now become in the mind of the xenophobic right a threat to French national unity rather than a mechanism for eventual repatriation. For the left the threat was somewhat different. After 1983 Jean-Marie Le Pen, leader of the *front national*. astutely converted the claim to the right to the maintenance of cultural collective difference (*droit à la différence*) for non-European immigrants, promoted by the left, into a right for the French to be different from the non-European immigrants (i.e., ultimately the right to deport them).[14] Faced with this threat, anti-racist organisations and political leaders redirected their efforts from 1986 towards the fight for foreign residents' right to equality – that is, to stay in France and to become French.

This shift in political debate was embodied in a change of vocabulary: *intégration* became – and is still – the legitimate, albeit in many ways ambivalent, political concept. For a part of the right it is undoubtedly a mere euphemism for the virtually taboo assimilation, and the concept itself is sometimes dismissed on these grounds. In fact, this charge ignores the distinctive content of integration. The reinforcement of the secular and assimilationist tradition implemented by state action – which is, as Dominique Schnapper stresses,[15] an end-state principle, not a description of society – goes hand in hand with the abandonment of the traditional assumption of France's superiority compared to other nations or cultures. Integration as defended by present-day republicans is an interactive, rather than self-evidently one-way, process. The rejection of cultural coercion means that immigrants and their descendants will transform French society and culture – as a consequence, to take just one example, of the religious freedom enjoyed by millions of Muslims – and the legitimacy of this transformation is now increasingly accepted. The pronouncements of bodies such as the *Commission de la Nationalité* and the *Haut Conseil à l'intégration* reflect an elite consensus on such an interpretation of integration, in which the debate about settlement is over, and in which equal and straightforward access to French nationality is seen as a key element of the French liberal tradition.

Despite its ambiguity, *intégration* in this sense is a bulwark against the xenophobia of the National Front. While the far right was happy with the *droit à la différence*, it can find no place for integration in racist discourse. On the contrary, it is deeply worried that integration may be taking place and destroying the identity of France and its ideal objective is still the departure of non-European immigrants and their children. It is thus understandable that integration should have become a core slogan of the anti-racist movement. It is an effective weapon in the hottest current battle – about the right to be French. Far from being an expression of French racism or xenophobia (of which there is unquestionably an ample supply, as there always has been), it is perceived (and was constructed) as the political negation of it.

Britain

Like France, and for very similar reasons, Britain had a major debate on immigration in the immediate postwar period. As in France, the consequent decisions were taken within the state elite, with little public discussion. British debate, however, produced no clear, coherent policy framework.

That immigration was an appropriate response both to short-term labour shortages and to long-term demographic requirements was widely accepted in principle, as shown by the settlement schemes directed in the 1940s at refugees and prisoners of war from Eastern Europe. The underlying ideology was explicitly assimilationist, the criterion of long-term success being defined as inter-marriage. Assimilation was however generally understood in strongly racialised terms. The same prejudices that had led to the tacit collusion of the British authorities in the maintenance of segregated civilian facilities for the US Army on British soil during the war now led to the view that some migrants were, because of their 'race', unassimilable and therefore undesirable.

Such concerns, expressed in much the same way in France, could have been met either by embodying racialisation in immigration policy, or by defining policy so as to reject it unequivocally. In fact Britain did neither. The prewar legal framework – in which colonial and Commonwealth migration was *de facto* treated as internal on the basis of common nationality – was left virtually unchanged, with the result that no discriminatory policy could be applied. Yet, beyond lip-service to the imperial ideal of the 'mother country', no serious attempt was made to challenge the preoccupation with 'race', constantly, albeit often secretly, expressed in government circles throughout the 1940s and 1950s.[16]

This fundamental contradiction structured early public debate on immigrant absorption. As hostility to 'coloured' Commonwealth immigration became a significant political issue in the late 1950s, an elite consensus gradually emerged that without immigration control (on conventional nation-state, rather than imperial, lines), integration, absorption or assimilation – the terms were used more or less interchangeably – would be impossible. The Labour Party lagged behind the Conservative Party in this respect and opposed the first piece of restrictive legislation – the Commonwealth Immigrants Act of 1962 – , but by 1965 a significant degree of bipartisanship on immigration policy had been achieved, surviving intact, broadly speaking, to this day. Bipartisanship, however, was a response as much to party-political pressures as to concern for integration,[17] and its ultimate foundations were deeply ambivalent.

While the word 'integration', along with its quasi-synonyms, was quite common in early debate, and is still occasionally used, British political vocabulary has been dominated by the very different phrase 'race relations'. While its meaning in racist discourse is clear enough – relations between 'races', which are assumed to exist as well defined biological and social entities – its general usage is puzzling, indeed meaningless if the concept of race is dismissed as invalid: nevertheless even its critics end up in practice using it.[18]

In the 1960s and early 1970s the concept of 'race relations' served as a battleground for the liberal and xenophobic fractions of the elite, who still had a virtual monopoly on political debate. The 'respectable' xenophobic position, most articulately and influentially represented within the Conservative Party by Enoch Powell, was that race relations are necessarily a bad thing because they lead (as supposedly in the US) to violence and ultimately to civil war. The only solution is cultural assimilation. Assimilation, however, is impossible when the concentration of people to be assimilated is too great. Therefore solving the race relations problem requires halting immigration, encouraging repatriation and vigorously promoting mainstream culture. Although Powell himself was sacked from the Shadow Cabinet in 1968 because of his anti-immigration speeches, and subsequently left the Conservative Party, these views have for the past 25 years been widely shared on the right, despite the virtual disappearance of the word assimilation, although they have not usually been in the policy mainstream. They are in many ways similar to the views of the xenophobic right in France (see previous section), as shown anecdotally by the links between such right-wing Conservative groups as the Monday Club and the *front national*.

Many features of this analysis had, by the mid-1960s, been accepted by mainstream liberal opinion. Certainly the view of immigration as a problem and a threat to the social order was the impetus behind the further restrictions introduced by the Commonwealth Immigrants Act of 1968 (under a Labour governement) and the Immigration Act of 1971 (under a Conservative government), and is still the basis of a discreet bipartisan consensus. The emphasis on assimilation was however rapidly abandoned in favour of 'good race relations', namely, peaceful coexistence through tolerance, diversity and pluralism. There is an obvious contradiction between the belief in stringent immigration control and in diversity as contributing ipso facto to social order,[19] but the compromise was driven by party-political necessity as much as by intellectual consistency. The content of this ideological position is similar in many ways to that of *insertion*, particularly in its suspicions about the neo-imperialism of assimilation (see above), with the major differences that it is the British mainstream position (whereas it was confined in France to the extremes of the political spectrum) and that it is seen as a dimension of citizenship and of full participation in British society rather than, as in France, as a substitute for them. It is very much the second plank of the bipartisan consensus and is embodied in anti-discrimination and equal-opportunities legislation (the oddly, but significantly, named Race Relations Acts of 1965, 1968 and 1976) and in quasi-governmental bodies such as the Commission for Racial Equality.

In its own terms, 'race relations' policy has been largely successful. In particular, the political neutralization of the far right – whether within the Conservative Party or in such organisations as the National Front – has been more effective than in mainland Europe, although it can be argued that the price has been a general racialisation of politics that is strongly detrimental to British black people.[20] The terms set by the elite were however very restrictive, since they tended naturally to marginalise minority demands. In a context of acknowledged citizenship, this was unsustainable, and the most striking development since the mid-1970s has been the gradual minority appropriation of the minority agenda.

Academic analysis, which has developed distinctively compared to France, has played a major role in this respect. There is no hegemonic British race-relations paradigm: on the contrary, many key issues remain matters of fierce debate. Yet, it is at least possible to sketch out a dominant analytical framework, influenced to varying degrees by black nationalism and Marxism, that still commands wide acceptance. The briefest summary that is not a gross caricature would be describe it as a class-centred paradigm, sensitive to status differentiation in a complex industrial society and to the central importance of colour-based racism in the social definition of status.[21]

This framework has been of great political significance because of two key implications. The first is that ethnic minorities (a phrase that has steadily supplanted 'immigrants' as the British-born population of immigrant descent has grown) are affected more by the (shared) consequences of immigration and racism than by cultural particularities. The second is that the natural core of black politics is relations with the white working class, that is, in practice, with the trades unions and the Labour Party. These principles had by the early 1980s become the basis of a distinctive radical political agenda, strongly opposed to mainstream 'race relations' policy, before themselves being challenged in recent years.

The single most characteristic word of this radical agenda is *black*, conceived as a political rather than an anthropological category, that is, defined by reference to oppression. It is also the best illustration of the ambivalence of the whole paradigm. If the oppression of black people is simply a special case of generic capitalist oppression, the radical agenda promotes a fairly straightforward form of integration on the basis of a common class position. If, on the other hand, black oppression is qualitatively distinctive, so must black liberation be, in which case the radical agenda takes on a strong tinge of separatism.[22]

The anti-racist movement that flourished in the 1980s encapsulates this ambivalence. Its contention that British society as a whole is structurally racist, rather than simply affected by some people's individual racism, could in theory have been framed in terms of integration (the aim being to build a new, egalitarian, genuinely non-racist culture). In practice, however, the heightened colour-sensitivity supposedly necessary for the eradication of racism has tended to be seen as desirable *per se*, with separatist implications. This has led to, in addition to predictable attacks by right-wing Conservatives on its excesses,[23] damaging criticism from black radicals concerned about its preoccupation with culture, which they see as dangerously similar to that of the racist right.[24] Confirming their fears, the revival of cultural politics has produced in recent years a growing tendency to reject the central tenet of radicalism: the political conception of 'blackness'. The single most important reason is the new insistence of many British Muslims on being designated by reference to religion and/or national origin (cf. the Rushdie affair). This is both a political and a theoretical challenge to the radical paradigm,[25] which appears to have been disproved in its analysis of common economic positions as the major determinant of identity or, more accurately, to have failed to provide, on the basis of this analysis, an effective framework for political mobilization.

INTEGRATION IN PRACTICE

It is arguable how much impact abstract models and political debates have on practical policy and social reality. The greater part of the process of integration takes place beyond the reach of state policy, at the levels of social and economic structure and of individual action. Significantly, the situations in the Briitain and in France are far closer in this respect than might be inferred from political debates.

France

Many of the factors that contributed to the success of integration in France in the very specific historical circumstances of the two postwar periods are no longer operative. While in terms of legal status the current situation is actually an improvement,[26] social integration is in decline. In both postwar periods immigrants could easily find employment in an expanding labour force. In the last 20 years, on the contrary, immigrants and their children are faced with an unprecedented, and apparently irreversible, rise in unemployment. Housing shortages have increased as the building of low-income housing has decreased in the last decade. In this context it is impossible to meet the needs of the adult second generation and of new legal migrants, including the beneficiaries of family reunion, political refugees and selected skilled workers.

The school system is facing a general crisis that affects the children of immigrants disproportionately but certainly not exclusively. François Dubet has shown the perverse effects of successive reforms of secondary education.[27] In the 1960s only 6 per cent of working-class children were able to go to the university while 10 per cent were admitted to the *collège* (the first four years of secondary education). The system was, *de facto*, sharply segregated for the benefit of the children of the bourgeoisie. However, while the social system that excluded working-class children was perceived to be unfair, the school system itself preserved its legitimacy. Since the 1975 education reform, essentially all children enter the *collège* while a virtually unchanged 6 per cent of working-class children go to university. This leads to destructive competition between 'winners' and 'losers', based on the feeling that school has become a machine designed to exclude those who have not been educated to use it. The capacity of the school system to contribute to social mobility has been delegitimised, a perception obviously enhanced by chronic unemployment. Failure at school thus leads to individual loss of self-esteem, marginalisation and, in the slang term used by Dubet to summarise his research, *la galère*.[28] (The 'galley' in the sense of servitude). There is little ground for thinking that the breakdown of integration provides the basis for an innovative form of multiculturalism. *La galère*, as described by Dubet, is not a new form of culture but rather an absence of culture.

Thus, the actual social context is far more complex than any of the abstract models would suggest. Depending on differences in both structural constraints and personal strategies, a wide variety of configurations can be observed. Some French-born children of immigrant parents have followed the traditional republican path of social mobility through school success and exogamy, while others have cultivated their ethnicity and still others have turned to individual delinquency. While these tendencies may be apparent, the future cannot be predicted.

Social factors are fully operative as a basis for integration only when combined with a specific historical setting. On the eve of World War II, Polish, Spanish and Italian immigrants suffered in the face of intense xenophobia. It was the war that enabled their political integration because the political cleavages within French society were modified. The legitimate conflict, defined before the war as that between Frenchman and foreigner, was replaced in 1945 by the opposition between *collaborateurs* and *résistants* (with reference to Nazi occupation). Thus the real or fictitious commitment of many immigrants to the Resistance reinforced the liberal immigration strategy chosen by the authorities. The united front of French people and foreigners facing the occupying Germans was officially presented as a sign of assimilation that justified the explicitly egalitarian legal status implemented at the time. Economic growth did the rest.

The past 20 years offer a very different picture. In addition to economic crisis, the French national future is seen to be threatened by European integration. The common historical identity (real or mythical) that is the implicit basis of integration[29] is obscured by divisive memories of the Algerian War of Independence. The xenophobic battle against integration has been astutely conducted by Jean-Marie Le Pen, and his *front national* remains a significant political force ten years on, while the anti-racist organisations formed to oppose it are reduced to struggling against their own decline. Xenophobia has already borne fruit in the field of nationality law. French nationality for 'undesirable' or 'unassimilable' foreigners is sometimes judged to be illegitimate,[30] both by politicians such as former President Giscard d'Estaing (who argues for France to endorse the German tradition of citizenship exclusively by descent) and by experts, who have focused their attacks on dual nationality and on the 'instrumental' use of French nationality by some applicants.[31] In this context, access to French nationality at the age of 18 for all French-born foreign residents, regardless of national origin, which has traditionally been automatic, has now been restricted.

Yet to categorise 'France' as racist because of the political importance of Jean-Marie Le Pen is a travesty. The French have always been deeply divided on this very subject, and the fact that the ideological battle took place is not in itself a bad thing: debate opposing French citizens of divergent political views (irrespective of national origins) was unquestionably a contribution to the process of integration.

Britain

As in France, the descendants of Commonwealth immigrants in Britain have been disproportionately affected – partly because of discrimination, partly because of the long-term consequences of migration – by general social problems, aggravated by the fiscal crisis caused in the industrialised countries by the economic changes of the 1970s and 1980s, and related in various ways to inadequate public investment. Britain, however, was hit earlier than most European countries by this crisis and its effects have been visible for longer. Among the most important are chronic unemployment, especially in the unskilled segment of the labour market; housing decay; and the crisis of the state education system. All these tend to the disintegration of society generally, and can hardly promote integration in the special sense it has acquired with reference to immigration. The key issue from this point of view is marginalisation, that is the confinement of those affected by disadvantage to an increasingly separate 'sub-society'.[32] Not only does this promote, as has been extensively documented, a subjective feeling of 'unbelonging', of *anomie* in the Durkheimian sense; it also, more subtly but ultimately more damagingly, erodes the common (material and symbolic) interests that are the objective basis of belonging. The *reductio ad absurdum* of this erosion is reached when relations between the 'underclass' and mainstream society are seen as collapsed onto the interface between the victims and perpetrators of crime.[33]

Other factors, on the other hand, point to a context for integration that is distinctively favourable. For instance, citizenship is largely off the political agenda. No serious attempts have been made to prevent the children of migrants born in Britain from becoming British citizens (the supposedly radical British Nationality Act of 1981 made only – from a French perspective – minor changes). Furthermore political rights are not related to citizenship in the legal sense, so that even first-generation (Commonwealth) migrants are effective political participants. This has had a major impact on the social process of integration. Over the past 15 years, black[34] politicians, activists, academics and intellectuals have acquired a range of political resources; black MPs and local councillors have been elected; and black activists have come to exert considerable influence in the Labour Party. Similarly, the black presence in the media, the professions (notably law) and business is significantly greater in the Britain than that of the French population of recent immigrant origin. Not only does this guarantee the British black population a voice, it also contributes directly, by promoting social interaction and shared practices – including, crucially, shared debates and constructive political conflict[35] – to integration in the Durkheimian sense.

While the French situation can be summarised without caricature by the tension between effective citizenship and social exclusion, a description of the Britain in these terms is incomplete. In the 1980s the separatist interpretation of the radical agenda achieved considerable influence, not only through the initial emphasis on the specificity of black experience but also through the main challenge to it in the name of cultural (religious, linguistic, etc.) specificity. Minority demands that could not have been expressed a decade earlier took a prominent place on the agenda, including such controversial issues as same-race adoption, separate schooling, specific family law, black sections in the Labour Party, etc. Despite considerable debate, mainstream opinion acquired, by French standards, a remarkable tolerance for such demands: official multiculturalism moved from the denial that diversity is a threat to the quite different claim that diversity is in itself a value that must be promoted. And, while the participants in public debate may not be representative, there is considerable evidence of support for some aspects of separatism among the minority population generally. What is striking from a comparative perspective (recall that in France insertion derived from the negation of citizenship) is that this shift in debate is a direct consequence of citizenship (which is not to say that it is unrelated to social exclusion), which by its very nature legitimates minority demands. Ideally, multiculturalists might claim that Britain thus provides a model for a successful, democratic, culturally non-integrated society, and therefore that the whole debate on integration is somehow passé. It remains to be seen how plausible this 'model' is.

CONCLUSIONS: PROSPECTS FOR INTEGRATION IN BRITAIN AND FRANCE

The most obvious common experience of France and of Britain is that systematic social exclusion is an insuperable obstacle to integration in any sense. That society is minimally successful in providing for all its members is not a trivial assumption, but general social disintegration would make specific discussion of immigrant/minority integration entirely academic.

If France and Britain remain broadly integrated societies, the key question is whether either is likely to be more successful in the integration of its minorities of immigrant origin. If factors common to the two countries, and independent of ideological discourse, are dominant, one might expect the future to show convergence. Some common features between France today and Britain a decade or two ago (preoccupation with immigration control, the 'youth' issue, Le Pen/Powell, *hijab*/turban, etc.) suggest that France might move towards a British situation. On the contrary, one could argue that France's adoption (in the 1970s) and subsequent abandonment of multiculturalism shows that community-based integration does not work and points to an inevitable evolution in British thinking. If, on the other hand, the two countries genuinely have distinctive models of integration, rooted in their histories (as ideological discourse claims), there is no reason for convergence. France and Britain would preserve their respective anti-communitarian and communitarian biases and the future would show which, on balance, is more successful.

While it is likely that profound theoretical differences will restrict future convergence, the gap in practice should not be exaggerated. The key problem of integration is common to Britain and France: taking equality seriously, and being perceived as taking it seriously by those most likely to suffer from inequality. Equality – as distinct from purely formal non-discrimination – cannot be created by decree, but must have a credible social basis, which implies active and successful social policy. Here more than anywhere, there is abundant Franco-British common ground behind the smoke of ideological battle.

NOTES

1. John Crowley, 'Ethnicité, nation et contrat social', in Gil Delannoi and Pierre-André Taguieff (eds.), *Théories du nationalisme* (Paris: Kimé, 1991), esp. pp.189–94.
2. An influential discussion on these lines is T.H. Marshall, 'Citizenship and Social Class' in *Citizenship and Social Class and other Essays* (Cambridge: Cambridge UP, 1950).
3. Cf. US legal terminology. For a theoretical interpretation, see Brian Barry, *Political Argument* (London: RKP, 1965), pp.119–35.

4. A good recent example of this criticism is Maxim Silverman, *Deconstructing the Nation: Immigration, Nation and Citizenship in Modern France* (London: Routledge, 1992).
5. Peter Sahlins, *Boundaries: the Making of France and Spain in the Pyrenees* (Los Angeles: Univ. of California Press, 1989).
6. Gérard Noiriel, *Le Creuset français* (Paris: Le Seuil, 1988).
7. Examples of the quasi-official formulation of these ideas may be found in the reports to the Prime Minister of the Commission de la nationalité (*Étre français aujourd'hui et demain*, 2 vols (Paris: La Documentation française, 1988) and of the Haut Conseil à l'intégration, *Pour un modèle français d'intégration* (Paris: La Documentation française, 1991).
8. Cf. Colin Holmes, *A Tolerant Country? Immigrants, Refugees and Minorities in Britain* (London: Faber, 1991).
9. For a typical example, see Russell Lewis, *Anti-racism: A Mania Exposed* (London: Quartet, 1988).
10. See, e.g., Ira Katznelson, *Black Men, White Cities* (London: OUP, 1973); Anthony Messina, *Race and Party Competition* (Oxford: Clarendon Press, 1989).
11. Claude Lévi-Strauss, *Race et histoire* (Paris: UNESCO, 1952).
12. Patrick Weil, *La France et ses étrangers:(L'aventure d'une politique de l'immigration. 1938–1991* (Paris: Calmann-Lévy, 1991), Ch.1.
13. Ibid., Ch.20.
14. See, e.g., Pierre-André Taguieff, *La force du préjugé – Essai sur le racisme et ses doubles* (Paris: La Découverte, 1987); and Silverman, *Deconstructing the Nation*, (note 4).
15. Dominique Schnapper, *La France de l'intégration* (Paris: Gallimard, 1991).
16. For this period, see among others Zig Layton-Henry, *The Politics of Immigration* (Oxford: Blackwell, 1992); Robert Miles and Annie Phizaclea, *White Man's Country – Racism in British Politics* (London: Pluto Press, 1984); Paul Rich, *Race and Empire in British Politics* (Cambridge: CUP, 1986); Shamit Saggar, *Race and Politics in Britain* (Hemel Hempstead: Harvester Wheatsheaf, 1992).
17. Cf. John Crowley, 'Paradoxes in the Politicisation of Race: A Comparison of the UK and France', *New Community* 19/4 (July 1993), pp.627–43.
18. Cf. the usage of 'race' (always in quotation marks) in the work of Robert Miles, Annie Phizaclea, John Solomos, Paul Gilroy and others.
19. Barrie Axford, 'United Kingdom', in Jay A. Sigler (ed.), *International Handbook on Race and Race Relations* (NY: Greenwood, 1987); Clifford Hill, *Immigration and Integration*, (Oxford: Pergamon Press, 1970); Miles and Phizaclea, *White Man's Country* (note 16).
20. Miles and Phizaclea, (note 16).
21. The single most influential writer on this subject has been John Rex. Of particular importance in terms of influence are his early works: John Rex and Robert Moore, *Race, Community and Conflict: a Study of Sparkbrook* (London: OUP, 1967). John Rex, *Race Relations and Sociological Theory* (London: Weidenfeld, 1970); *Race, Colonialism and the City* (London: RKP, 1973).
22. For the orthodox class-based analysis, see in particular Miles and Phizaclea, *White Man's Country* (note 16); Robert Miles, *Racism* (London: Routledge, 1988); John Solomos, *Race and Racism in Contemporary Britain* (Basingstóke: Macmillan, 1989). For more ambiguous perspectives on black specificity, see Paul Gilroy, 'Steppin' out of Babylon – Race, Class and Autonomy' in Centre for Contemporary Cultural Studies, T*he Empire Strikes Back – Race and Racism in 70s Britain* (London: Hutchinson, 1982); and *There Ain't no Black in the Union Jack* (London: Hutchinson, 1987); A. Sivanandan, *A Different Hunger – Writings on Black Resistance* (London: Pluto, 1982).
23. Paul Gordon, 'A Dirty War: The New Right and Local Authority Anti-racism', in Wendy Ball and John Solomos (eds.), *Race and Local Politics* (Basingstoke: Macmillan, 1990).

24. Paul Gilroy, 'The End of Anti-racism', in Ball, Solomos, *Race and Local Politics*. As discussed in the previous section, the same criticism has been made in France of the double-edged *droit à la différence*. Cf. Taguieff, *La force du préjugé* (note 14).
25. Roger Ballard, 'New Clothes for the Emperor?: The Conceptual Nakedness of the Race Relations Industry in Britain', *New Community* 18/3 (1992), pp.481–92; Malcolm Cross, 'Editorial', *New Community* 17/3 (1991), pp.307–11; Tariq Modood, *Not Easy Being British – Colour, Culture and Citizenship* (Stoke-on-Trent: Trentham Books, 1992).
26. For the historical detail see Patrick Weil, *La France et ses étrangers*; and, in English, 'Immigration and the rise of racism in France: the contradictions of Mitterrand's policies', *French Politics and Society* 9/3–4 (1991).
27. François Dubet, *Les lycéens* (Paris: Seuil, 1991).
28. François Dubet, *La galère, jeunes en survie* (Paris: Fayard, 1987).
29. Ernest Renan, 'Qu'est-ce qu'une Nation?', lecture given at the Sorbonne on 11 March 1882, in *Oeuvres Complètes* (Paris, Calmann-Lévy, 1946).
30. Abdelmalek Sayad, *L'immigration et les paradoxes de l'altérité* (Bruxelles: De Boeck, 1991).
31. Jacqueline Costa-Lascoux, 'L'acquisition de la nationalité française, une condition d'installation', in S. Laacher (ed.), *Questions de nationalité. Histoire et enjeux d'un code* (Paris: CIEMI, L'Harmattan, 1987); and 'Appartenance d'origine et choix de nationalité', in Dro*it et politique de la nationalité en France depuis les années 60*, Actes du colloque organisé à Nantes par le Ministère des Affaires sociales et de l'intégration, direction de la population et des migrations (Aix-en-Provence: Edisud, 1993), pp.107–8. In fact, instrumental attitudes to nationality are neither new nor necessarily a good indication of allegiance. See Sahlins, *Boundaries* (note 5).
32. Cf. the Anglo-American debate on the so-called 'underclass' (for a convenient summary, see Malcolm Cross, 'The Ghetto and the Underclass', *New Community* 17/1 (Oct. 1990), pp.141–9).
33. John Solomos, *Racism, Black Youth and the State – The Politics of Ideology and Policy* (Cambridge: CUP, 1988).
34. It is important to note that this standard use of the word 'black' presupposes the British radical agenda, and is open to serious criticism in this regard.
35. Crowley, 'Paradoxes in the Politicisation of Race', (note 17).

The Debate on Immigration and the Crisis of National Identity

DOMINIQUE SCHNAPPER

The legacy of mass labour migration to Europe in the 1960s is a considerable permanent 'foreign' population. Now recession and industrial restructuring have cast doubt on that population's economic, social and political legitimacy; simultaneously, the nation state is under pressure from both above and below. Despite historically very different approaches to the role of immigration in Britain, France and Germany, there has emerged a common problem of national identity. Across Europe there remains strong popular attachment to the national cultural identities, and it is this inertia which denies the logic of adaptation and change.

Since the end of World War II, different peoples have migrated to the democracies of Western Europe: refugees and people displaced after the war, such as the Poles in Great Britain, or the tens of millions of Germans who fled from the eastern provinces to the West; nationals and 'indigenous' people linked to colonial government returning to the mother country following the dissolution of the French, Dutch and British colonial empires; immigrant workers from southern Europe and the Third World who came to find work during the 'thirty glorious years' of economic growth (1945–1975). This movement of population was unprecedented in every respect – its scale and national diversity as well as the minimal restrictions placed upon it by most European countries during the 1960s. It is estimated that between 20 and 30 million foreigners – around eight per cent of the total population – took up permanent residence in Western Europe, compared with the six per cent of the population of the United States which was born abroad. Yet even these figures fail to convey accurately the real situation. Apart from naturalisations – which have been numerous in countries like France and Sweden, and have become increasingly common in countries which have modified their rights to nationality (the Netherlands and Belgium, for example), there is the complication of migration from former colonies. Certain immigrants into Britain, France and the Netherlands either have enjoyed an automatic right to nationality, or were already nationals and not therefore considered as 'migrants'. Such a massive and – outside France – new phenomenon has been at the centre of debate since the 1970s.

In all European countries, and for both economic and political reasons, the debate has centred on the former 'indigenous' peoples and on workers from southern European countries and the Third World. Confirmation of this can be found in the fact that they alone are referred to as 'immigrants'. The white-collar employees of multinational companies have never been branded with this term, which is restricted almost entirely to poor migrants. During the 1950s and 1960s, when the importation of foreign labour was organised bureaucratically, and when in almost all cases immigrants immediately found a low-skilled job that nationals did not want, their presence was not a political issue. Both useful and marginalised, and seen purely in terms of their economic role (whose utility was never disputed), immigrants were neither the objects nor the participants of democratic debate. Besides, everyone – including themselves – considered their presence as only temporary.

Political reactions to these massive population movements have been determined less by their numerical scale than by the capacity of societies to absorb them into their economies, and by the actual political and historical forms of migration. The absorption of tens of millions of refugees from eastern Germany at a time of economic reconstruction did not trigger debates in Germany or anywhere else: the refugees found jobs. Furthermore, just after the end of World War II, Germans did not have the political legitimacy to debate the eventual problems that could be created by the acceptance of their eastern compatriots expelled by the victory of the Red Army.

It was only in the 1960s in Britain, and a decade later in France and Germany, that the issue of the 'immigrant presence' came to the centre of political debate. Economic recession and industrial restructuring meant that there were fewer jobs for low-skilled migrants: their presence, which, until then, had been legitimised by their economic contribution, was perceived henceforth in new political, economic and cultural terms. In all European countries, taxes and social charges doubled as a proportion of GDP between 1960 and 1975, and it was argued that immigrants now cost more than they contributed to national economies and that their employment had retarded the modernisation of numerous industrial sectors. However, the cost-benefit analysis of immigration was quickly sidelined: most people who adhered to democratic values were not attracted to an argument which characterised the role of man too crudely in terms of his contribution to production. Instead, the political debate developed, focusing on the possibility of 'assimilating' or, even better, of 'integrating' immigrants, and on the danger that their presence might pose for the functioning of democracy.

During the 1980s it became clear that the repatriation policies implemented in Germany and France after the Oil Crisis were failing. It was now accepted that immigrants had ceased to be temporary workers and that they would stay in Europe. Part of public opinion felt that once permanently in place, the presence of these foreigners and colonial nationals would undermine cultural uniformity – the condition for national unity – and pose a direct threat to democracy. It was thought that Muslims in particular, who were often perceived as foreign to and even hostile to the Christian foundations of modern Europe, could never be assimilated. It was considered in certain quarters that new immigrants had neither the desire nor the capacity to conform with accepted patterns of life, as their claims for the recognition of cultural diversity seemed to confirm. In Germany and above all in France, the 1980s saw part of the extreme right directly accuse immigrants of undermining national identity and begin to use this issue as a means of nourishing its ideology.

This article does not attempt to assess the degree of truth or fantasy in these allegations. I have tried to do this elsewhere in the case of France.[1] My aim here is to show that whatever the objective problems (whose existence I do not wish to deny) the debate on immigration reveals another, perhaps more fundamental problem – the question of national identity. In different ways, all European nations are experiencing a crisis created by the impact of modernisation on national integration and by the need to rethink the relationship between the market, society and the State.

In Great Britain, in contrast to Germany and France, a single ballot, first-past-the-post electoral system has excluded from political representation an extreme right openly hostile to immigrants, of the type that Enoch Powell created inside the Conservative Party at the end of the 1960s. But this exclusion has not removed the problem of 'immigrants' from the political agenda. Access to the United Kingdom – which had been ensured for all Commonwealth citizens until the beginning of the 1960s – was restricted by a series of immigration and nationality laws between 1962 and 1981. The practical effect of these regulations was to prevent the Citizens of British Dependent Territories and British Overseas Citizens – members of the non-white Commonwealth, that is – from entering the country. Only British Citizens were free from immigration control and enjoyed the right of access and residence.[2] Successive reforms of nationality laws have therefore led the United Kingdom to redefine herself as a nation state and to develop, for the first time in her history, a notion of national citizenship. It goes without saying that the redefinition of nationality and citizenship has not been sufficient to resolve the social problems experienced by non-white immigrants; nor has it provided any answers to the issue of their position and role in society or the means of combating 'racism'.[3]

In effect, British policy has defined itself in terms of 'ethnic minorities' and their rights, 'race relations' and 'racism'. Relations between the British population and those referred to (significantly) as blacks are based on the traditions of colonial politics which, by and large, observed the principle of Home Rule. In other words, it respected the structure of local society and limited itself to consolidating and controlling the power of traditional leaders. These relations are also based on the tradition of a democracy which has always been shaped by the collective expression of local and social entities, classes and interest groups. Furthermore, policy and practice in the United States – where the 'black problem' is a major political issue – has had a direct influence on the British situation. The British have concentrated on controlling migratory movements from the coloured Commonwealth and on struggling against discrimination and racism.

A series of Race Relations Acts (1965, 1968, 1976) has ensured that the immigrant population enjoys equality of opportunity in British society. The institutions and legislation used to fight discrimination – in response to demands from a well-developed network of associations which is regularly consulted by the authorities – have made the struggle against racism one of the most important mobilising themes of the political system. They have also had the perverse effect of creating an obsession with the subject. A campaign by the Greater London Council in 1984 had a slogan posted on the walls of the capital which stated: 'Racism affects all of us. We are either the victims or the perpetrators'. This active anti-discrimination policy has had the effect of interpreting a range of problems in terms of race – the failures of the education system, the financial difficulties of the health system and all social conflicts. However, even if inter-ethnic riots and criminal attacks have periodically ravaged the centres of the old industrial cities, clearly not all social problems have been generated by the 'ethnicisation' of British life.

The former 'nations' or 'kingdoms' brought together within the United Kingdom by the Crown have always kept their collective identity, based on cultural and legal entitlements. They have their own regiments in the British Army and their own sports teams.The survival of Irish, Scots and Welsh identities within British society may well have helped the assertion, in turn, of Muslim and Pakistani identities. In the

British tradition the logic of citizenship combines with that of minorities: one can be both a British citizen and a member of a minority, or even a citizen *by virtue* of belonging to a community. This helps us to understand the part played by 'minority' or 'community' politics.

Those referred to as Asians in British society – those, that is, with origins in the Indian subcontinent – have a strong collective identity. They have created genuine communities – in the sociological sense of the term – organised, for example, around the mosque which serves simultaneously as a religious, social, cultural and political centre. Their leaders intervene in local and even national politics in the name of the 'community' and call for and obtain policies to ensure the preservation of its collective identity. This includes, for example, special measures for schools, allowing the imam to enter, allowing girls to conform with the rules of Islamic modesty, and the recognition of Islamic holidays. After the Rushdie Affair began in 1989 there was a demand for an 'Islamic parliament'.

Beyond the basic issues, the intensity of debates, the proliferation of institutions and legislation and the obsession with racism in society can all be seen as the symptoms of a crisis of national identity. This crisis seems especially acute to the British themselves.[4] A country which was once nationalistic and imperialist, Great Britain's role in the world has been substantially diminished. Her participation in the 1991 Gulf War was probably one of the last attempts to play a role on the world stage. For over a year now, the UK has even been modifying her special relationship with the United States – through which she had attempted to keep alive the memory of a now-defunct empire. She has simply become one more member of the European Union – one that is neither the most powerful, nor the most prosperous. She has experienced significant economic decline. The crisis of the welfare state common to all European countries has been especially acute on her self image, given that after World War II Britain had been the pioneer of a model of social organisation which subsequently was imitated throughout Europe. Divisions of class, gender, region and 'race' – which are no longer transcended by a grand imperialist project, or by confidence and pride in a political system which was for a long time the model *par excellence* of parliamentary democracy – seem to threaten the unity of the country.

In the future, could the Muslim population, whose presence is linked to the colonial past, constitute a special entity in the political system as do the Irish and the Welsh, given that the latter are also demanding a greater recognition of their distinct identities? The historical identity defended so ardently by the Scots or Irish is closer to that of the English than is the identity of British Pakistanis. The latter are a people formerly colonised by British imperial power, but remain faithful to an Islamic culture and religion: they retain both real and symbolic links with their country of origin. The obsession with problems of racism has produced a plethora of anti-racist legislation – although it is difficult to prove its efficacy.[5]

Books dedicated by social scientists to the theme of 'the division of the country' are numerous[6] and echo the phrase coined by Prince Charles in 1985 when he declared that Great Britain was a 'divided realm'.[7] The economic crisis is compounding the transformations and fragmentation wrought by the modernisation of society: in creating conflict, for example, between the regions of the South East which have benefited from the policies of the Thatcher governments and the old, threatened industrial regions of the North West; between the middle classes and the unemployed; and between blacks and others. The thread of national unity is unravelling.

The situation in France is comparable in many respects. Belonging to a nation which has long thought of itself as invested with a universal mission, the French recognised that their country had become a secondary power only at the end of the Gaullist period and after the events of May 1968. Even if her leaders still aspire to an independent foreign policy, as shown by France's symbolic participation in the 1991 Gulf War or by the pretence of having invented humanitarian policies, the French no longer believe in the exceptional character of their nation – a notion propagated by all nineteenth century historians, from de Tocqueville to Michelet.

The weakening of the nation state, although not specific to France, does present a special challenge: France has been the most state centred of all European nations. Although Eugen Weber[8] has shown that the population was 'nationalised' just before World War I, her 'statocracy' has been the most developed and the construction of the nation has been a state project for centuries.[9] The state built the nation. Society has been infused with the ethos of national identity. Collective national pride is based in large part on the idea that France invented the very concept of 'nation'. The objective situation is no different from that of other European countries, but the end of the grand ideological debate between Left and Right, and the questioning of the legitimacy of the regime and the nature of collective identity has also thrown into question the integration of French society which, since the Revolution, has been based on participation and sometimes violent political opposition.

The fact that, alone in Europe, an openly xenophobic, extreme right party – the *front national* (FN) – has managed to attract as much as

16 per cent of the vote would seem to indicate that the 'immigrant problem' is particularly acute. However, the reverse is actually true. The emergence of the FN must be explained first of all in purely political terms: by the transfer to the FN of a part of the protest vote which has supported the French Communist Party for decades; by the 'social democratisation' of the conventional Right; by disappointment with the Socialist government after initial excessive expectations . . . and, in the background of course, by the economic crisis and high unemployment.[10] It is often noted that xenophobia is at its greatest when the integration of immigrant children brings them up against, and puts them into direct competition with, the poorer parts of the population. The impoverished lives of poorly integrated people in the suburbs of the large cities is expressed in an xenophobia which the leaders of the FN seek to exploit and reinforce.

Because France was a country of immigration one hundred years before the other European nations, since World War II she has continued with her traditional immigrant policy: to transform immigrants, or at least their children, into French citizens.[11] French policy towards immigrants has a long historical tradition. Since the French Revolution, the logic of individual citizenship has been imposed on, and opposed to, the political recognition of minorities, whoever they may be. Since the nineteenth century, France has 'assimilated' – to use a term from that era – successive waves of immigrants of all origins into a common political project. Originally formulated by the Revolution, this is based on the idea of individual citizenship, and uses powerful national institutions (schools, the Army, the Church, political parties and trade unions). Politically, it is referred to as the 'Republican' model.[12] In reality, this model has never had the success which is often attributed to it – if only in order to condemn it: the actions of the state are, by definition, limited in a democracy. The policy of 'assimilation' was an idea, an ideal, a programme of action, a desired objective, but it was never a concrete, historical reality either in France or in the colonies. It was never completely enacted, never completely successful; it failed to eliminate xenophobic passions. However, in France at least, it did transform foreigners into French men and women over two generations: today, 18 million French citizens have at least one foreign grandparent. The 'Republican model' retains its political importance. Its principles continue to inspire government policy towards immigrants. Moreover, by and large, these principles are still being implemented to good effect. Sociological studies have shown that, overall, the children of the last large wave of immigrants (1960–75), like those of previous waves, have been integrated at their respective social levels into French society.[13]

The principles of 'French integration' continue to be applied: the tradition of individual integration is so strongly entrenched that those measures which have sought to recognise particular ethnicities have always failed.[14] Those concerned – the immigrants and their children – have never called for the recognition of their ethnic rights in schools or public life. After a short period at the beginning of the 1980s when the 'right to difference' was demanded by certain young immigrant associations, the 'right to indifference' – in other words, the 'Republican model' – has been reaffirmed.

This policy of individual integration is strongly criticised in other European countries for denying the specific needs and aspirations of immigrants and their children. According to this argument, formal integration through citizenship denies social reality. The dialogue between European nations is not simply an intellectual one: it is shaping the construction of the European Union. The model of 'French integration', through an individual citizenship which is universal and 'colour-blind' and which is linked to the tradition of the Revolution and the long French experience of immigration, is unique in Europe. Within EU institutions, where the northern European democracies are dominant and where national representatives speak the language of 'communities' and 'minorities', and demand the recognition of the 'rights of minorities', the French representatives could be forced to revise this traditional policy and to replace it, for example, with multicultural education, cultural rights for minorities and respect for the customs of such and such a group in the public realm. The meaning of policies must therefore be related to national tradition. Policy measures which are the product of a specific national history would undermine, in another country, the notion of social cohesion. The politics of 'minorities' – which is normal and even desirable in countries like Great Britain and the Netherlands – would break with a long tradition of national integration in France and weaken (and perhaps even dissolve) the social fabric.

Even in France the validity of the 'Republican model' – and the national project which it underpins – have been questioned. Prioritising individual citizenship can only be efficacious if the political project remains clearly and resolutely defined. Nowadays, in France as in any other modern democratic society, the political will must bend to aspirations for equality in education, housing and unemployment and for social protection. In these circumstances, is the traditional 'Republican model' still capable of integrating the different groups in the national population, including those of foreign origin? If the very idea of 'citizen' has lost its real, political meaning, is it not useless and even dangerous to employ it as a privileged means of national integration, especially in so far as foreigners are concerned? Perhaps it would be more realistic and effective to recognise the reality of ethnic differences. To borrow a Marxist distinction, in attempting to respect the universal values of a citizenship which no longer has any clear meaning, this policy can really only create a 'formal' rather than a 'real' level of integration. Sociologists like Alain Touraine who consider that the 'Republican' response is outdated, and also the leaders of self-proclaimed 'communities' who wish to become publicly-recognised group representatives, consider that new forms of integration should be substituted for the obsolete 'Republican model'. This collective reflection on the crisis of the 'Republican model' – which has been triggered by the issue of immigration – is in reality a debate on national integration as such.

The case of Germany is no less symptomatic of the national crisis of European countries. Although the problem of immigrant workers has been on the political agenda for more than a decade, the upheavals created by the decline and fall of the Soviet empire have revealed the extent to which that specific debate has obfuscated other critical issues. Until reunification, German policy towards immigrants consisted of maintaining a legal and political distinction between nationals and foreigners. The *Gastarbeiter* policy was adopted during the 1960s when the number of immigrants from the East ceased to provide sufficient additional manpower for the economy of the Federal Republic. Foreign workers were recruited subsequently through recruitment agreements with Italy, Spain, Greece, Turkey, Tunisia, Morocco and Yugoslavia. Measures were adopted to ensure that they remained temporary guests who, in line with the formula of Simmel, 'arrive today and leave again tomorrow'. Yet this policy, which was based on the idea of a rotation of manpower, proved impossible to implement. It was economically impracticable. It was contrary to human rights provisions which were consecrated in German law and European conventions and it clashed with common values. It ignored the essential fact that the immigrants, who were transformed by their participation in German society, also became at least partially assimilated into it. The policy adopted after the mid-1970s oil crisis of returning immigrants to their countries of origin proved to be a failure. As in the rest of Europe, it had the perverse effect of accelerating the reunification of families and settling the immigrants.[15] Even if the great majority of immigrants today are permanently established in Germany, and even if an increasingly large number of them have been assimilated into German society and culture, German policy remains essentially that of the original *Gastarbeiter* project, based on an ethno-cultural conception of the

German nation.[16] Significantly, in Germany one does not speak of immigrants but of foreigners, of *Ausländer*, *Ausländische Arbeitskräfte*, of *Fremdarbeiter*, or simply of *Fremde*. The German Federal Republic has never officially recognised itself as a country of immigration. Inevitably, the authorities have had to carry out a policy of integration, if by that one means a policy which aims to encourage the participation of migrants and their children in public life. Yet the right to nationality, based on the law of 1913, is strictly linked to the principle of blood rights – *ius sanguinis* – and gives practically no possibility for the acquisition of German nationality to foreigners or their children, however long their settlement in the country. In Germany, neither immigrants nor their children are transformed into citizens.[17]

This policy of integrating immigrants through their participation in economic and social life alone, without giving them citizenship, is in a sense the logical outcome of the German national project. At the end of the 1940s, the memory of the crimes committed in the name of the unitary Nazi state and the separation of Germany into two sovereign states effectively compromised the very notion of 'the nation'. Even the objective of reuniting the two Germanies, as inscribed in the Basic Law of the German Federal Republic, was criticised by many. For 40 years, the Federal Republic was a social and economic democracy but not a real nation.[18] It was a perfect example of what Max Weber, referring to Switzerland, called an 'incomplete nation': notable features included federalism, respect for the law of the state, a priority given to economic activity, a cautious foreign policy until the *Ostpolitik* of the 1970s, and even, for a long time, a hesitation to create an army. In 1983, 20 per cent of the age group required for military service were conscientious objectors. The abstention of the most prosperous European nation from any active role in the 1991 Gulf War – in the name of a legality inherited from the defeat of Germany in 1945 – clearly illustrates the nature of the West German political project. By contrast, alongside France, Germany has been one of the main instigators of the construction of the European Union – a political project beyond the confines of the national framework.

Reunification – imposed by the collapse of the communist system and the dissolution of the Soviet empire in 1989 – profoundly challenged the Federal Republic's conception of itself. The government rapidly made a political choice which committed it to a new project – that of including the states of the former East Germany as new *Länder* of the Federal Republic, and recreating a national, economic and cultural unity by imposing material sacrifices on the population of west Germany in the name of the union of the German peoples. The national identity which

Germany is experiencing today derives not just from the evident collapse of the political project of the former East Germany – to build a communist society – but also, and much less obviously, that of the prosperous, egalitarian and decentralised Federal Republic which had no ambition to intervene in international affairs.

The effective integration of immigrants and their children into German society has also been undermined by the political consequences of the Berlin Wall's collapse. West Germans have suddenly become aware that foreign workers – the great number of which have been settled in Germany for more than 15 years – had become more integrated into their society than their 'compatriots' from the east. Contrary to what many imagined before reunification, Turks have created fewer political and identity problems for West Germans than have the East Germans. For the citizens of the Federal Republic, the latter are the heirs to the Prussian tradition which, under Bismarck, created the military and bureaucratic Wilhelmine *Reich* during 1860–80 after the failure of the liberal and bourgeois project which emerged from the Rhineland regions. The West Germans think that the East Germans have had no experience of democracy since 1933 and that they have no conception of the rules of the modern economy or of the spirit of enterprise which, together, are the basic conditions for prosperity. For their part, the East Germans – humiliated by their political and economic backwardness compared with the West Germans (and even with the Turks and other immigrants settled in the West) are undergoing a profound economic crisis (unemployment has massively increased with the closure of unprofitable firms) and also a crisis of morale and identity.

If one adds to this the world economic crisis and the massive influx of asylum-seekers – who profit from the exceptionally liberal legislation adopted by the Federal Republic after World War II until July 1993 – then one might begin to understand the explosions of xenophobic violence over the last two years which seem to have spread from east to west. The democratic Germans of the west are worried about forging links with a past which the political tradition of West Germany after World War II had apparently broken with. Racist outbreaks are not caused by the presence of foreigners. The latter provide the occasions, 'arguments' and even 'justifications' for explosions of violence which reflect the more general crisis of national identity in all its dimensions: the crisis of the Federal Republic, the crisis of the German Democratic Republic, and the economic, social and identity crisis created by making a new political union from two national identities whose historical paths have been diverging for two generations.

It is less the objective difficulties of integrating migrants – even if they do exist – which explain the passion of the European debates on 'immigrants' than the crisis of the nation state itself. Its values and institutions are being challenged by both subnational pressures and by European construction and integration in the world economy. Subnational groups – the Scots, Welsh, Basques, Flemish and Corsicans – are making cultural and even political demands. The explosion of nationalism which followed the collapse of the Soviet empire has even provided some models. The 'velvet divorce' by which Czechoslovakia was divided into two independent nations has been invoked by those Belgians who wish to denounce the 'federalism' which, since 1970, has united the communities of Wallonia, Flanders and Brussels. The construction of Europe, on the other hand – which is limiting the legal and economic sovereignty of the member states – has undermined the independence of the nation-state even if political sovereignty as such has yet to be challenged. Objectively at least, Europeans are increasingly being integrated into a European union and a global economy.

Yet at the same time, the sentimental tie which binds the people to the nation as the locus of historical continuity and democratic expression, had been under-estimated under the influence of Marxism, as revealed by the campaigns on the ratification of the Maastricht Treaty in France, Great Britain and Denmark. To use the words of Norbert Elias, there is a lag between the objective integration of people and their social habitus: 'This evolutionary force . . . has clashed with the contrary force of national identity, and until now the latter has proven the most powerful.'[19] Regardless of their objective integration into larger units, national peoples remain attached to the historical community – the nation – forged by centuries of common history. It is this, rather than the immediate issue of the participation of non-citizens in West European societies, which lies at the heart of the debate on 'immigrants'.

NOTES

1. Dominique Schnapper, *La France de l'intégration: sociologie de la nation en 1990* (Paris: Gallimard, 1991).
2. Ann Dummett and Anthony Nicol, *Subjects, Citizens, Aliens and Others: Nationality and Immigration* (London: Weidenfeld, 1990).
3. Charles Husband, 'Les communautés musulmanes et la société britannique', in Bernard Lewis and Dominique Schnapper (eds.), *Musulmans en Europe* (Poitiers: Actes Sud, 1992).
4. Vincent Wright, 'Immuable Angleterre?' in Dominique Schnapper and Henri Mendras (eds.), *Six manières d'être européen* (Paris: Gallimard, 1990).
5. Richard Jenkins and John Solomos (eds.), *Racism and Equal Opportunity in the 1980s* (Cambridge: CUP, 1987).

6. See, e.g, Ray Hudson and Allan M. Williams, *Divided Britain* (London: Pinter, 1989); Linda McDowell, Philip Sarre and Chris Hamnett (eds.), *Divided Nation: Social and Cultural Change in Britain* (London: Hodder, 1989).
7. Hudson and Williams, *Divided Britain*, p.vii.
8. Eugen Weber, *La fin des terroirs: la modernisation de la France rurale 1870–1914* (Paris: Fayard, 1983).
9. This is a well-known theme in the literature since de Tocqueville. Principal references are: Charles Tilly (ed.), *The formation of National States in Western Europe* (Princeton: PUP, 1975); Bernard Guenée, *L'Occident aux XIV et XVe siècles: les Etats* (Paris: PUF, 1971); Colette Beaune, *Naissance de la nation France* (Paris: Gallimard, 1985); Pierre Rosanvallon, *L'Etat en France de 1789 à nos jours* (Paris: Le Seuil, 1990).
10. Monna Mayer and Pascal Perrineau, *Le Front national à découvert* (Paris: Presses de la Fondation nationale des Sciences Politiques, 1989).
11. Jacqueline Costa-Lascoux, *De l'immigré au citoyen* (Paris: La Documentation française, 1990).
12. An analysis of this model can be found in Schnapper (note 1) Part 2.
13. See, e.g., Rémy Leveau et Gilles Kepel (eds.), *Les musulmans dans la société française* (Paris: Presses de la Fondation nationale des Sciences politiques, 1988); Didier Lapeyronnie, 'Assimilation, mobilisation et action chez les jeunes de la seconde génération de l'immigration maghrébine', *Revue française de sociologie* 28/2 (1987), pp.87–318; François Dubet, *La galère, jeunes en sursis* (Paris: Le Seuil, 1987).
14. E.g., in the case of the introduction of indigenous languages and cultures in schools.
15. Dominiquc Schnapper, *L'Europe des immigrés: essai sur les politiques d'immigration* (Paris: François Bourin, 1992), pp.15 and 74ff.
16. See the literature on the difference between the ethnic conception of the German nation and the civic and political conception of the French nation. For recent discussions, see Schnapper, *La France de l'intégration*, p.33ff and W. Rogers Brubaker, *Citizenship and Nationhood in France and Germany* (Harvard, MA: Harvard UP, 1992).
17. L. Hoffman, *Die unvollende Republik: zwischen Einwanderungsland und Deutsche Nationalstaat* (Cologne: Papyrossa, 1990).
18. See the special ed. of the *Revue française de Science Politique*, June 1987.
19. Norbert Elias, *La société des individus* (Paris: Fayard, 1991), p.288.

Towards Understanding State Capacity to Prevent Unwanted Migration: Employer Sanctions Enforcement in France, 1975–1990

MARK J. MILLER

The implementation of employer sanctions in France along with problems and issues related to their enforcement are chronicled in this article. Bureaucratic structures and legal aspects of the issue are analysed, as is overall effectiveness of the sanctions, in order to assess whether state capacity did in fact increase over the period 1975–90. It is found to have increased incrementally, but obstacles to the measure's effectiveness remain. These include the reluctance on the part of the courts and labour inspectors to impose fines in some cases, the lack of sufficient resources devoted to enforcement, and the difficulty of monitoring employers in general. In addition, the issue of discrimination and employer sanctions is not found to have been a salient issue in France.

All Western democratic, industrial states confront challenges in regulating late twentieth century international migration. Globalisation of economies, demographic disequilibria, enormous disparities in wages, socio-economic opportunities and life chances, growing ethnic conflict and political disorder in the post-Cold War era and advances in communication and transportation all combine to render industrial democracies susceptible to unauthorised entry. Powerful forces within advanced capitalist societies compound and complicate regulation of international migration. A growing number of studies are serving to advance our understanding of unauthorised migration and its effects upon states and societies.[1]

One of the key policy-related research questions pertaining to Western democratic efforts to prevent unauthorised migration involves analysis of the effects of laws prohibiting and punishing unauthorised employment of aliens. Curiously, given the acrimony of debate in the United States over the wisdom of imposing employer sanctions, which at long last were provided for under the controversial Immigration Reform and Control Act (IRCA) adopted in 1986, only scant research has been conducted on enforcement of employer sanctions in Western Europe. Several North American attempts to assess the effects of employer sanctions in Western Europe as part of the debate over IRCA reached mixed, contradictory conclusions.[2] Western European scholars have accorded little attention to analysis of the effects of employer sanctions. This may in fact be due to a laudable prudence, as interpretation of the effects of such laws is no easy task. Does the upsurge, for instance, in citations for illegal employment of aliens in France after 1987 signify growing illegal migration or better application of the law and thereby more effective deterrence? This disinterest, however, may also arise from the paucity of debate about enforcement of employer sanctions. There appears to be a striking transatlantic contrast in this issue area, as employer sanctions enjoy broad political support in Western Europe. The chief criticism one hears is that they are insufficiently enforced. Most Americans also support employer sanctions, including about half of the Hispanic population, but there has been bitter resistance to them by some Hispanic organisations, employers, civil liberties advocates, supporters of migrants and other groups.

In recent years, some American and European students of migration have expressed viewpoints on employer sanctions enforcement, but largely in passing. James F. Hollifield is sceptical of the capacity of Western governments to regulate internation migration in general, principally due to the extension of rights to migrants and to the complexity and extensiveness of economic interdependence.[3] He is dismissive of employer sanctions. In an important chapter on illegal migration in Western Europe, Catherine Wihtol de Wenden found them to be weakly enforced.[4] Georges Tapinos, Yann Moulier-Boutang and Jean-Pierre Garson have similarly scoffed at the seriousness of employer sanctions enforcement in France.

One of the most detailed and widely available examinations of French efforts to curb illegal alien employment and residency is made by Patrick Weil. He holds that ' . . . the application of repressive laws has revealed itself to be particularly difficult.'[5] He regards enforcement of the panoply of French laws designed to curb illegal migration as a 'failure'.[6] At one point, echoing a charge made by the French specialist on foreign seasonal agricultural workers Jean-Pierre Berlan, Weil suggests that there is an understanding between enforcement agents, various ministries and employers not to apply employer sanctions.[7] Such charges have also been levelled, off the record, by some generally highly knowledgable officials of international organisations, and even by some

French government officials. However the charge is also heatedly denied by many others.

Other experts on immigration to France have been more upbeat in their assessments. Jacqueline Costa-Lascoux has taken exception to the viewpoint that such laws are merely symbolic by pointing out that laws are supposed to have an educational, symbolic function and that it is a rare law that eradicates the ill that motivated its promulgation overnight. Claude-Valentin Marie, who has been following enforcement of laws against illegal employment, including illegal alien employment, for the French government, also has been more positive in his assessment. In conversations with the author in early 1993, he pointed to significant progress in enforcement since 1987 and especially since 1990. In this respect, he echoed earlier optimistic assessments made by experts at the inter-ministerial mission charged with monitoring and facilitating the application of laws against illegal employment.

The following analysis is based on field research and interviews conducted intermittently between 1980 and 1993. France, Switzerland and Germany were the principal foci of inquiry, although, due to space limitations, the emphasis here is on France. Can Western democracies prevent unwanted migration? The answer to this critical question is unclear, but examination of employer sanctions enforcement is one way to begin to shed empirical light on it.

THE HISTORICAL AND EUROPEAN CONTEXT

Illegal migration in Europe is not uniquely a phenomenon of the period after immigration was curbed. Some analysts appear to establish an unwarranted cause and effect relationship between the recruitment curbs from 1972 to 1975, which were never complete, and subsequent illegal migration. This is then used to support the assertion that states cannot control immigration, or to suggest that those putatively ill-considered curbs had perverse effects.

Illegal migration, however, has a long history in Europe. It was a problem for Imperial Germany's foreign seasonal labour policy. It was commonplace in interwar France. Between 1946 and 1981, technically-illegal entry followed by legalisation was the rule, rather than the exception, for immigrants to France. Across the Rhine, illegal migration also was fairly widespread, although Germany did not develop an explicit legalisation policy. Generally speaking, though, illegal migration did not become a salient public policy concern until the period of the recruitment curbs. The laws enacted during the mid-1970s have since typically been revised and enforcement strategies have also evolved. European modifications of employer sanctions invariably involve either the strengthening of penalties or the rewriting of laws to facilitate punishment of illegal employment of aliens. They also encompass administrative steps including enhanced inter-agency coordination and the commitment of increased budgetary and/or personnel resources to enforcement.

As indicated in Table 1, most Western European states had adopted employer sanctions by 1980. Ireland and the United Kingdom were important exceptions. However, in the United Kingdom, employers of aliens not entitled to work could be punished for non-payment of employment-related insurance premiums and taxes, as well as for illicit harbouring of illegal aliens. It should be noted that several regional and international organisations adopted instruments including employer sanctions during the 1970s, which probably influenced decisions taken by European member states to enact employer sanctions. The International Labour Organisation's convention 143 of 1975 includes a provision for employer sanctions. A draft directive of the European Community issued in 1976 similarly encouraged adoption of employer sanctions. British resistance to this draft directive effectively killed it.

The British objected to the draft directive on the principle that the criminal sanctions envisaged by the draft directive would infringe on the United Kingdom's sovereign prerogatives. The United Kingdom also objected to the draft directive on the grounds that it did not need employer sanctions, as illegal immigration was not a significant problem, and on the grounds that employer sanctions might exacerbate employment discrimination against minorities. A high-ranking British official of the EC with responsibilities in the employment and manpower area, interviewed in 1987, did report that he did not think that the draft directive would ever be resurrected.

Employer sanctions did not become a significant policy issue in Switzerland until the early 1980s. Swiss employers long were subject to minor fines for illegal employment of aliens but these penalties were little known and seldom invoked. Illegal alien employment was long not viewed as a serious problem, although this was contested by those familiar with the problem of false seasonal workers and the plight of illegal alien children back in the 1960s and 1970s. As in France and Germany, employer sanctions were embraced as a significant component of immigration-related policy only when illegal migration and illegal alien employment were perceived as a serious problem.

TABLE 1
EMPLOYER SANCTIONS IN WESTERN EUROPE

Country	Local Basis	Fine	Imprisonment	Cancellation of Recruitment	Payment of Deporation Transportation Costs	Closure of Business	Penalties for Violation of Social Laws (Health Accident Pension Ins.)	Penalties for Illegal Alien Employment in Leasing and Temporary Work	Other
AUSTRIA	Aliens Police Law Social Insurance Act	Yes		Possible			Yes		
BELGIUM	Law of 22 July 1976	1,000 to 2,000 B.Fr per worker Max of 150,000 B.Fr	Possible	Possible	Yes (including family of worker)	Yes	Yes		
DENMARK					Yes				Provision of false information to authorities punishable by fine and imprisonment up to 6 months
FRANCE	Labour Code Law of 17 Oct. 1981	2,000–20,000/ worker court fine, 40,000 Fr. for repeat. 30,200 Fr. admin fine per worker	2 months– 1 year 3 years for repeat	Possible		Materials and goods may be seized	Yes	Fines of 4,000 to 20,000 Fr. 8,000 to 40,000 for repeat offenders and/or 2–6 months imprisonment for hiting illegal alien temp. worker or for leasing	2 months to 1 year imprisonment and 2,000 to 20,000 Fr. fine for violation of OMI recruitment monopoly, up to 3 years in prison and 40,000 for repeat offense. 4,000 to 20,000 Fr fine for reimbursement of recruitment costs, 8,000 to 40,000 Fr. and up to 6 months for repeat
GERMANY	Employment Promotion Act Temporary Employment Act Act to Combat Illegal Employment of 1981	100,000 Marks/worker Fine may be increased to deter employers	For employment in conditions worse than German, 3 to 5 years (+fine)		Yes		Yes	Up to 3 years and 100,000 fine, up to 5 years in serious cases for leasing illegal aliens, max. fine may be increased	

TABLE 1
CONTINUED

Country	Local Basis	Fine	Imprisonment	Cancellation of Recruitment	Payment of Deporation Transportation Costs	Closure of Business	Penalties for Violation of Social Laws (Health Accident Pension Ins.)	Penalties for Illegal Alien Employment in Leasing and Temporary Work	Other
GREECE	Basic Law 1346183	Min 30,000 drachmas per worker	Minimum 3 months		Yes				
ITALY		2,000 to 10,000 Lira						Use of intermediary other than Employment Office subject to 2,000 L fine per worker per day of employment	Violation of Employment Office monopoly fine 100,000 to 1,000,000 L and imprisonment for 15 days to 1 year
LICHTENSTEIN		Up to 10,000 Sw.Fr.	Up to 6 months	Yes	Yes				
LUXEMBOURG	Regulation of 12 May 1972	2,501 to 50,000 Fl.	8 days to 1 month						
NETHERLANDS	Foreign Workers Employment Act of 1984 and the Economic Offenses Act	Up to 10,000 Fl.	Up to 6 months						
NORWAY	Working Environment Law	Yes	Up to 2 years						
SPAIN									
SWEDEN	Aliens Act	Up to 20,000 SEK	Yes			Damages may be paid to Unions for violation of collective agreements			
SWITZERLAND	Law on the Sojourn & Establishment of Aliens of 1988	Up to 5,000 Sw.Fr. for intentional violation, up to 3,000 Sw.Fr. for negligent hiring, up to 10,000 Sw.Fr. for housing illegal employee.	Up to 6 months for housing illegal employee or for recividism within 5 years	Possible			Yes		
UNITED KINGDOM		No	No			Yes		Employer might be prosecuted for harbouring aliens	

Source: Council of Europe, OECD.

Implementation and Major Revisions in France

In France, a judicial mission aimed at suppressing illegal immigration and employment was established in 1975. By 1976 the Interministry Liaison Mission to Combat Manpower Trafficking was formally created and a law passed in July of that year reinforced penalties against individuals who aided illegal migration and created an administrative penalty for employers of aliens not entitled to work. Employers who hired aliens illegally were required to pay a sum equivalent to 500 times the minimum hourly wage to the National Immigration Office for each worker illegally employed. In 1980 the fine was approximately $1,000 per worker. In principle, imposition of the fine was automatic and offending employers also could be imprisoned for one to two months or longer, in the case of recurrent offenders.

A major difference between French and German administration with regard to enforcement of employer sanctions was the inclusion of enforcement of employer sanctions against illegal employment of aliens within the broad mandate of the German Ministry for Labour and Social Affairs, to combat the underground economy in general. The mandate of the French Interministry Liaison Committee to Combat Manpower Trafficking was far narrower and limited to suppression of illegal alien entry, residency and employment. This administrative contrast came to an end in 1989, when the French Interministry Liaison Committee to Combat Manpower Trafficking was renamed the Interministry Liaison Ministry to Combat Illegal Work, Undeclared Employment and Manpower Trafficking.[8] It thereby had its responsibilities extended to the entire underground economy, as in the German case. The expanded mandate had long been advocated by officials of the former Interministry Liaison Mission to Combat Manpower Trafficking.

A major function of the Interministry Liaison Mission was to keep track of enforcement of the panoply of laws aimed against illegal immigration and employment. Employer sanctions are only part of an impressive legal arsenal that has been built up. In Figure 1, an overview of overall legal enforcement between 1976 and 1984, as measured by communicated legal complaints (*proces-verbaux*) made by various enforcement agencies, (the top line representing the combined total) is presented. The graph reveals a 1976 upsurge in enforcement followed by a decline, precipitous in 1977, 1978, and 1981, followed again by a resurgence in 1982 and 1983. The number of legal complaints (*proces-verbaux*) communicated by each of the four agencies involved in the enforcement of French laws against illegal immigration and employment shows a correlation between the increased levels of enforcement by police and labour inspectors and the overall number of complaints.

Figure 2 shows the number of infractions by employers of section L 341–6 of the Labour Code, which specifically penalises employers for hiring irregular-status aliens. The level of enforcement of employer sanctions, strictly speaking, corresponded to the up and downs in overall enforcement of laws aimed against illegal immigration and employment, and centrally affects those variations.

The Interministry Liaison Mission summarised the first four years of enforcement of the 1976 law reinforcing employer sanctions as follows in its 1979 annual report:

> After four years of functioning, it is necessary to recognise that the objective was not totally attained and that irregular-status alien employment remains an important problem both with regard to the employment situation and on the social conditions for those workers themselves. On the other hand, it is difficult to evaluate the number of clandestine foreign workers, and thus to know whether it is more important in 1980 than it was in 1976.[9]

Implementation of employer sanctions over the period was complicated by various factors. The first of these was the continuation of legalisation despite the intent announced during the period of the Fontanet-Marcellin-Gorse decrees in the early 1970s to terminate the practice. Some 'exceptional' collective legalisations occurred during this period, particularly in spring 1980 when some 4,000 Parisian garment industry workers, primarily Turks, were granted legal status. The legalisations diverted manpower resources, since a good number of labour inspectors, who are always in short supply, were involved with the legalisation efforts.

There was also a notable surge in deportations over this period. A 1975 law made working illegally punishable by deportation, and a 1980 law appreciably increased the government's deportation powers. Deportation seems to have become a major means of penalising illegal employment by 1980. According to Garson and Moulier-Boutang, 'With the law of January 10 1980, deportation had become simultaneously a priority means of combating clandestine immigration, and a means of rendering precarious (the legality) of alien sojourns in France.'[10]

The French law of 17 October 1981 made employment of irregular-status aliens a criminal offence subject to fines of 2,000 to 20,000 francs and imprisonment from two months to a year. For repeat offenders, the prison term could reach two years and the fine 40,000 francs.

FIGURE 1

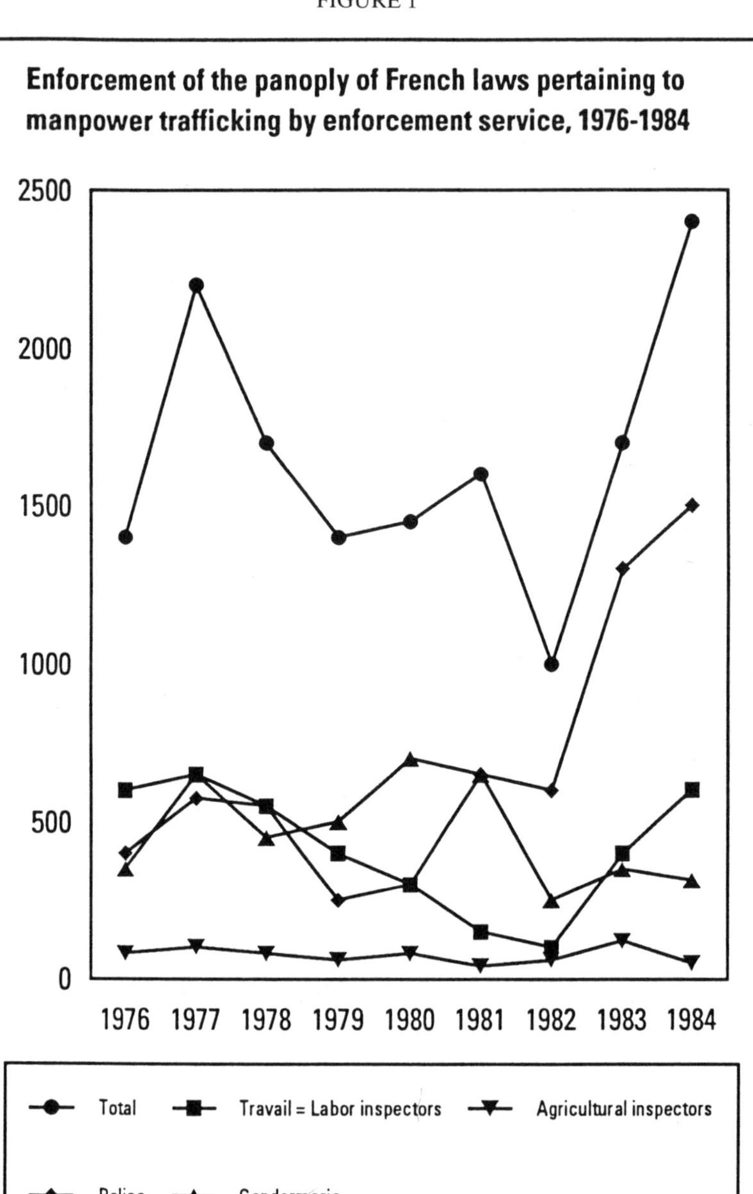

Source: Adapted from Mission de liason interministérielle pour la lutte contre trafics de main-d'oeuvre

FIGURE 2

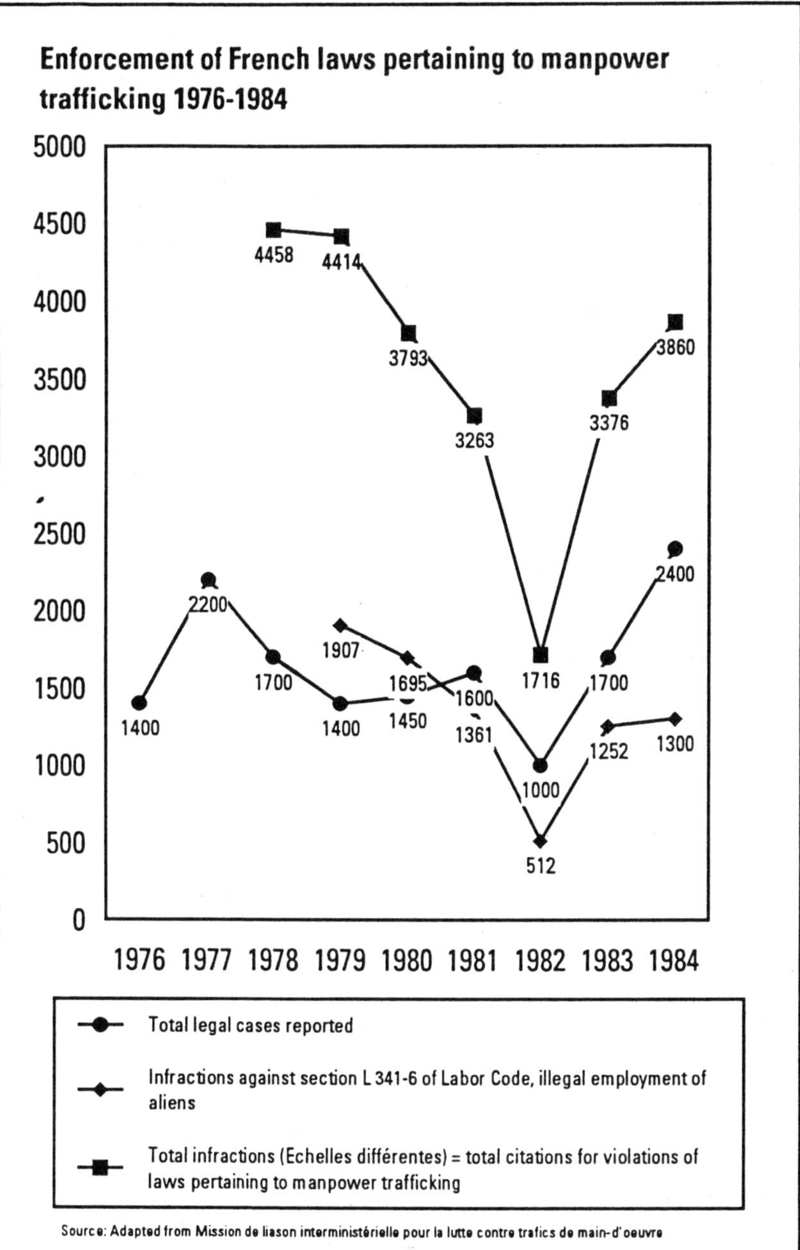
Enforcement of French laws pertaining to manpower trafficking 1976-1984
5000
4500
4000
3500
3000
2500
2000
1500
1000
500
0
4458
4414
3793
3263
1716
3376
3860
2200
1400
1700
1400
1450
1600
1000
1700
2400
1907
1695
1361
512
1252
1300
1976 1977 1978 1979 1980 1981 1982 1983 1984
Total legal cases reported
Infractions against section L 341-6 of Labor Code, illegal employment of aliens
Total infractions (Echelles différentes) = total citations for violations of laws pertaining to manpower trafficking
Source: Adapted from Mission de liason interministérielle pour la lutte contre trafics de main-d'oeuvre

The fine could be imposed as many times as there were individual aliens involved. However, a legalisation programme was simultaneously announced, and employer sanctions were not to be enforced until after the termination of the legalisation period. Contrary to expectations, the legalisation period was prolonged as additional categories of aliens, such as seasonal workers, were permitted to apply for legalisation. The marked drop in enforcement of employer sanctions in 1981 as indicated in Figure 2 was thus directly linked to French legalisation policy.

Enforcement of employer sanctions did not begin again until well into 1982. On 31 August 1983 the French government adopted a series of measures proposed by the Interministry Liaison Mission which were aimed at both reinforcing the effort to curb illegal alien residency and employment and promoting the 'insertion' of legally-resident alien communities in France. This linkage was made explicit in the 1983 annual report of the Interministry Liaison Mission.

> Stopping clandestine immigration, combating employers of irregular-status aliens and controlling migratory fluxes effectively constitute a priority objective (for the French government). Failure in this case would put in doubt the insertion of legally resident alien communities in France.[11]

The 31 August 1983 measures increased the administrative fine for employers of irregular-status aliens from 500 to 2,000 times the minimum hourly wage for each alien illegally employed. Beginning on 1 January 1985, the administrative fine was 26,340 francs, roughly $3,000. The Interministry Liaison Mission staff was increased, allowing the Mission to open up a regional office in Marseilles. The number of specialised labour inspectors was authorised to increase to 55. In September the Minister of Justice addressed a memorandum to all public prosecutors which reiterated the government's viewpoint regarding the grave consequences of illegal alien employment, and called upon prosecutors to step up enforcement of laws prohibiting it. Prosecutors were also asked to 'rigorously apply' the text of the laws concerning penalties.

In June 1984 the first of 23 priority departmental coordinating committees came into being. These co-ordinating committees were authorised by a governmental memorandum (*circulaire*) of 21 November 1983, and were designed to facilitate the exchange of information so as to more effectively detect and punish violations stemming from illegal alien employment. The Parisian area co-ordination committee included representatives from the police, fiscal authorities, the Department of Labour and Employment, the Department of Sanitary and Social

Affairs, the National Employment Agency, the National Immigration Office, the enforcement arm for social security and family allowance taxes (URSSAF) and the departmental authority for state finances and economic affairs. Representatives from other public organisations and the prosecutor's office were also invited. The Paris-area co-ordinating committee has since served as the model for the coordinating committees established in other priority areas.

The termination of legalisation combined with the measures taken in 1983 and 1984 resulted in an increase in enforcement of laws against illegal immigration and employment as measured by legal complaints communicated to the Interministry Liaison Committee. The 2,245 *proces-verbaux* communicated to the Mission in 1983 was the highest number ever. The number of *proces-verbaux* for infraction of article L 341–6, which prohibits employment of irregular-status aliens, rose from 549 in 1982 to 947 in 1983. The increase in legal complaints was matched by increased court action, enforcement of the administrative fine, and penalties against employers of irregular-status aliens. About 1,300 court decisions ordering employers to pay fines of at least 2,000 francs were made during 1983. In Paris, the first six months of 1984 witnessed a 50 per cent increase in the number of persons found guilty of employing illegal aliens relative to the 1983 period. The Director of the Interministry Liaison Mission summed up the judiciary's handling of employer sanctions over the first six months of 1984 as follows:

> The sampling of judgements rendered during the first half of 1984 by various courts appears to us as very indicative of the current trend toward the hardening of legal counteraction *vis-à-vis* employers of irregular-status aliens. The great majority of fines are to be found from now on above the minimum provided by the law, which denotes a clearcut understanding by the courts of matters connected to manpower trafficking.[12]

There clearly was an official perception that enforcement of employer sanctions was beginning to bear fruit by 1985. The 1981–83 period was seen as a stage where the policy instruments decided upon in 1981 were 'broken in' and when the policy outlined in 1981 on paper had taken concrete form. In March 1985 Madame Georgina Dufoix, the Minister of Social Affairs and National Solidarity and the spokesperson for the French government, declared that the results of enforcement of laws against illegal immigration and employment had a '. . . very encouraging balance sheet'.[13]

The Interministry Liaison Mission report on the 1986–87 enforcement period included a revised summary of enforcement as measured by legal

TABLE 2

Infractions Communicated to Interministry Liaison Mission to Combat Manpower Trafficking

	1981	82	83	84	85	86	87**
Employment of Aliens Without Permits	1366	513	1255	1538	963	1397	1716
Violation of ONI* Recruitment Monoply	25	NA	9	94	36	67	103
Violation of ban against employee reimbursement of recruitment expenses	20	NA	4	24	4	1	5
Underground Labor	NA	NA	135	214	533	141	328

*National Immigration Office
** Incomplete
Source: Interministry Liason Mission to Combat Manpower Trafficking 1986-87 Report, p. 21

complaints. This statistical series, presented in Table 2, excludes citations for illegal housing of aliens. Table 2 reveals a dip in infractions communicated, particularly for employment of aliens without permits and illegal (underground) labour in 1985 and 1986. French officials and labour inspectors interviewed in 1987 and 1988 spoke of a 'demobilisation' over this period, linked to the changes in the French government and to the uncertainty created by a decision not to prosecute a large case because of the ambiguity of the law under which the citations had been made (the provision of the Labour Code prohibiting illegal or underground labour, *travail clandestin*).

In an October 1987 address of unusual candour, the new director of the Interministry Liaison Mission maintained that the level of legal complaints '. . . is of little impact and unrevealing of a mass of legal contentions which is *a priori* surprising since illegal employment is a widespread phenomenon.'[14] She singled out for criticism the disjuncture between statistics on condemnations of aliens for illegal entry and/or residency and the number of infractions for manpower trafficking.

	Condemnations for Illegal Entry & Residency	Infractions
1984	15,120	4,131
1985	10,404	3,608
1986	16,506	3,655

She was also critical of the regional imbalance in enforcement, noting that more than 84 per cent of the legal complaints originated in three regions. Moreover, two thirds of the legal complaints for illegal alien employment were dismissed by provincial courts, as opposed to less than 10 per cent in the Paris region. Parisian area courts assessed fines of over 10,000 francs on 53 per cent of the individuals punished and condemned 56 per cent of them to a prison term, as opposed to only two out of every seven such individuals in the provinces.[15]

The speech concluded with questioning of the efficacy of the effort being made to curb illegal employment, of which illegal alien employment is a significant component. Were the means utilised appropriate and sufficient? Was an essentially social and repressive approach to the problem a wise choice? Was the oft-affirmed political will to curb illegal employment truly there? Did enforcement services possess sufficient understanding and know how to implement policy? Overall, her assessment was that the action undertaken to date was unsatisfactory since legal complaints were insufficient and negatively perceived by enforcement services themselves. The results were not proportional to the effort being made.[16]

The demobilisation of the 1986 to 1987 period seems to have marked a nadir. In 1987 a revised legal text was adopted redefining illegal employment and the period of cohabitation in French government ended. This led to a 'remobilisation' reflected in an upsurge in citations communicated in 1987, particularly for employment of aliens without permits. A dramatic increase in enforcement as measured by legal complaints for illegal employment of aliens continued in 1988 and 1989.[17]

Employers convicted under the panoply of laws aimed at curbing illegal alien employment and residency in France were expressly excluded from the pardons traditionally extended at the onset of a new presidential term. This exclusion was intended by the government to underscore the gravity of the social harm caused by illegal employment of aliens and the seriousness of the intent to combat illegal alien employment and residency. The following summarises the principal steps in the development of French policy against illegal alien employment and the underground economy between 1972 and 1990.

Principal Steps in the Evolution of French Policy to Curb Illegal Alien Employment and the Underground Economy

Date	*Measure*
11 July 1972	Illegal employment made an indictable offence
1972	Initial *ordonnances* promulgated concerning temporary work, trafficking of labour and manpower leasing.
July 1974	Non-seasonal alien worker recruitment suspended
31 Dec. 1975	Civil law regulating subcontracting in public and private markets adopted.
1974–1976	Laws which provide for the hiring of labour inspectors specialising in control of foreign labour in 23 'priority' departments adopted.
10 July 1976	A 'special contribution' civil fine payable to the National Immigration Office for illegal employment of alien workers instituted.
10 Aug. 1976	Interministry Mission to Combat Manpower Trafficking created.
1980–1983	Four governmental studies of illegal work and the underground economy completed
17 Oct. 1981	New law makes illegal employment of aliens a more serious offence (misdemeanour subject to police courts).

2 Feb. 1982	New *ordonnances* reinforce regulation of manpower leasing
31 Aug. 1983	Cabinet reinforces policy against illegal alien migration and employment by – the creation of 55 new positions for labour inspectors specialising in control of foreign labour – the creation of department-level interagency committees to combat illegal alien migration and employment in 23 'priority' departments – creation of a branch office of the Interministry Liaison Mission to Combat Manpower Trafficking in Marseilles – Augmentation of the 'special contribution' civil fine from 500 to 2,000 times the minimum hourly wage (30,200 francs as of 1 Jan. 1990).
25 July 1985	Illegal work made a misdemeanour.
16 Jan. 1986	Laws pertaining to illegal alien migration and employment extended to overseas departments.
14 March 1986	Decree replaces department-level interagency committees created 31 Aug. 1983, with similar committees with a broader mandate to combat illegal work (the underground economy) in addition to illegal alien migration and employment.
27 Jan. 1987	Law redefines illegal employment infraction
21 July 1988	Amnesty law expressly excludes those punished for illegal work, illegal alien employment and manpower trafficking and leasing.
13 Jan. 1989	Law again redefines the definition of an illegal employment infraction
16 Jan. 1989	Interministerial decree extends the competency of the Interministry Liaison Mission to the underground economy
10 July 1989	New labour law measures adopted which – newly incriminate illegal alien employment through intermediaries – redefine and more severely punish violation of the prohibition against reimbursement of fees paid to the International Migrations Office for foreign worker recruitment

2 Jan. 1990	Labour law amendment enables officers of the Judiciary police, after court authorisation, to enter workplaces on the presumption of illegal employment or illegal alien employment

Source: Gervaise Hue, 'Legalité, Efficacité et Travail Clandestin', unpublished paper, March 1990, pp.4–7.

Madame Gervaise Hue, who succeeded Denis Moreau as the head of the Interministry Liaison Mission in 1986, observed that it took the French government over 30 years to develop laws and enforcement capacities fully adapted to combating the illegal alien employment phenomenon.[18] The capacity emerged incrementally as it took time to draft and pass laws, reorientate and train enforcement personnel and develop interagency co-operation. Requests for more budgetary and personnel resources for enforcement had to be balanced against other governmental priorities and budgetary constraints. Despite setbacks, particularly in the domain of the writing of laws which would enable successful prosecution of offending employers in the court system, a plausible state capacity to punish illegal employment of aliens did develop, whereas it had been tolerated some 15–20 years earlier. This incrementally enhanced governmental capacity to punish illegal employment of aliens was reflected in the enforcement statistics compiled by the Interministry Liaison Mission in the late 1980s which confirmed the remobilisation apparent in the statistics for 1987.

However, despite extensive 'fine-tuning' of employer sanctions in France since the 1970s, the effort to curb illegal alien employment still appeared to be an uphill struggle by 1990. The balance was tilting more and more against effective enforcement of employer sanctions for various reasons.

PROBLEMS AND ISSUES IN ENFORCEMENT OF EMPLOYER SANCTIONS: THE COURTS

Authorities charged with enforcement of employer sanctions complain that the response of legal systems to the social harm done by illegal alien employment has been inadequate. In France, an extensive effort has been made to inform judges about the problem of illegal alien employment with a view to getting stiffer sentences against employers. This educational effort can claim some success, particularly in Paris-area courts. In the mid-1980s court sentences were viewed as growing stiffer by the director of the Interministry Liaison Mission. However, it is clear that provincial courts are far less likely to prosecute and punish employers who illegally hire aliens.

Another problem adversely affecting court action against employers was the severity of the administrative fine assessed them. By 1990, the fine stood at 32,000 French francs per illegal alien employee. The complaint written by a labour inspector against an employer for illegal employment of aliens has the force of law until proven otherwise. Employers can appeal against the fine, but, unless the appeal succeeds, an employer must pay the full sum to the Office of International Migrations (OMI). Recovery of the administrative fine or special contribution by the predecessor of the OMI, the National Immigration Office, was haphazard but has improved significantly in the 1980s. Many courts regard the administrative fine as punishment enough for employers and therefore do not prosecute, even though administrative sanctions are in principle independent of penal sanctions. The steady augmentation of the administrative fine since 1976 was seen by some French observers of employer sanctions as a barrier to effective court action and overall enforcement. They therefore advocated reducing the mandatory administrative fine or giving department-level administrations the discretion to set fines at levels commensurate with the offence. In fact, regulations to this effect had been prepared by 1990. Yet the political climate was such that any measure that could be construed as evidence of governmental laxity towards illegal immigration could not be pursued.

Some opponents of the proposed plan to 'modulate' administrative fines by granting greater discretion to departmental authorities feared that modulation would result in a downward spiral of reduced fines and enforcement. Proponents argued the contrary, maintaining that labour inspectors were reluctant to write up complaints because of the severity of the administrative fine and courts were reluctant to prosecute for the same reason. As the fixed fine does not take into account the size of a firm, a 32,000-franc fine usually had a far greater effect on a small firm than a large one. They argued that administrative and penal punishment had to be proportionate to the harm caused society in order for employer sanctions to be enforced more effectively. Courts were slow to respond to the new laws punishing illegal employment of aliens. Such a lag probably was to be expected and, in the French case in particular, suggests an unexpectedly healthy separation of the legislative, executive and judicial branches of government.

The French government responded incrementally, and ultimately constructively, to the reluctance of public prosecutors to pursue charges against employers by revising legal texts. In one noteworthy case that adversely affected overall enforcement of sanctions in France in 1986, a public prosecutor found the provisions in the Labour Code prohibiting illegal employment, under which charges had been brought against an employer employing some 350 aliens, ambiguous.[19] Therefore, all 350 charges were dropped with a resultant demoralising effect upon those charged with enforcement. The dismissal led to redrafting of the legal provision in question and its subsequent adoption as law, and the subsequent remobilisation suggested by the upsurge in citations made by labour inspectors beginning in 1987.

Whatever the shortcomings in the responsiveness of French courts to employer sanctions, it must be recalled that a great deal of enforcement is not recorded in statistics kept on court cases. Administrative and other sanctions, such as fines collected for nonpayment of mandatory health insurance premiums, are not recorded. And many enforcement activities have a deterrent effect even if they do not result in the writing up of complaints and successful prosecution of employers in the courts.[20]

Laws which prohibit illegal employment of aliens seem to be adhered to by many, if not most, employers, and thus are not a negligible deterrent to greater illegal migration. A minority of employers either ignore or consciously violate the prohibition. And there is reason to believe that this minority is growing despite enforcement efforts.

Prosecution of violations of social legislation is always difficult. Agricultural law inspectors in particular tell of workers, presumably illegally employed, running into the fields as they approach.[21] Labour and agricultural inspectors need the co-operation of the police to apprehend the employees in situations of this nature. Prosecution of employers under criminal law must of course comply with standard rules of evidence and procedure. Complaints generally are not written up unless all the elements of a successful case, in the opinion of an inspector or other enforcement agent, are there. Several enforcement agents pointed out that investigations and visits that did not result in the writing up of complaints and prosecution undoubtedly had a deterrent effect upon employers, nevertheless.

INSUFFICIENT ENFORCEMENT PERSONNEL AND RESOURCES

An upsurge in criminality over the last several decades has fed anti-immigrant sentiment and profoundly affected politics in most Western European states. Court systems and law enforcement agents have been sorely tried by the resultant mass of litigation. In contrast to the corps of specialised labour inspectors in France, which is under strength, and whose principal responsibility is the inspection of alien labour, enforcement agents generally have far broader responsibilities, above and beyond enforcement of laws prohibiting illegal employment of aliens. For many labour inspectors and police officers, enforcement of employer sanctions is a low priority. Labour inspectors in particular often do not write up complaints for infractions that they detect because there are other enforcement priorities in their eyes. It is for this reason that the Interministry Liaison Mission in France devotes most of its effort, in addition to studying illegal migration and illegal alien employment, to informing enforcement agents about the various laws penalising illegal alien employment and the priority attached to their enforcement by the government. Members of the Marseilles branch office of the Interministry Liaison Mission have noted an increase in the number of citations, particularly enforcement by the Gendarmerie or national rural police, in the wake of their visits.[22]

Labour inspection has historically been based on inspections of factories. As most illegal alien employment is not to be found in large factories, which often have a substantial union presence, and is instead concentrated in in small businesses, this discrepancy affects enforcement of laws prohibiting illegal alien employment. By training, labour inspectors look for unsafe working conditions more than illegal alien employment; enforcement of laws prohibiting illegal alien employment is largely incidental to routine enforcement of social legislation. Enforcement agents must have a reason to suspect illegal alien employment, say a letter of denunciation or a telephone tip, before launching a nonroutine investigation.

Inadequacy of enforcement personnel and resources is the problem most cited by authorities in charge of enforcement of employer sanctions in Western Europe. In the key agricultural department of the Vaucluse in France, for example, there were five enforcement personnel with a budget of some 38,000 French francs. The agricultural inspector explained that budgetary constraints greatly limited the number of inspections that could be made. While enforcement of employer sanctions was thought to have a deterrent effect, it was clear that budgetary and personnel limitations have limited their impact. The Vaucluse example illustrates this.

Is there a gap between laws and governmental policies which call for steadily harsher punishment of illegal alien employment and the reality of limited personnel and other resources allocated to employer sanctions enforcement? To Western European critics of the level of employer sanctions enforcement, the answer is clearly yes. Yet this viewpoint tends to ignore a perceptible, if incremental, increase in personnel and other enforcement resources allocated to enforcement of employer sanctions over the past 15 years. Madame Hue of the Interministry Liaison Mission explained that the mission regularly requested greater resources. Usually most of their requests were denied, as the government had other priorities, but there was always an incremental increase in the capacity of the French government to punish illegal employment of aliens. However, it was difficult for the Mission to obtain additional labour inspectors specialised in enforcement of laws pertaining to aliens in a political atmosphere dominated by calls to reduce the presence of state regulation in French business activity. Enforcement of laws prohibiting illegal alien employment clearly is a function of the personnel and other resources allocated to it, and it seems clear that the level of enforcement could be increased if there were the political will to expand the commitment of enforcement personnel and other resources.

PROBLEMS OF PROPORTIONALITY, EMPLOYER ADAPTATION AND COORDINATION

Some enforcement agents are reluctant to write up complaints against employers because they feel that the illegal workers are more severely punished than their employers, and object to this disproportionality. Historically, employer sanctions were advocated by trade unions and progressive political parties because they made employers responsible for illegal employment that previously was punished by deportation and other penalties levied solely against the illegally employed alien.

The severity of the administrative sanctions in France, it has been seen, is another aspect objected to by those in favour of modulation. Labour inspectors interviewed from 1985 to 1987, particularly those in Paris and its environs, indicated that they often did not write up complaints or reduced the number of people that the employer was charged with hiring illegally for fear of putting marginal firms out of business. French labour inspectors enjoy a great deal of discretion, and they need not write up citations if it is not in the public interest, which they are free to interpret.

In the South, particularly in the department of the Var, a movement developed in the ranks of labour inspectors against enforcement of employer sanctions. A group calling itself the anti-racist collective distributed tracts and argued essentially that enforcement punished alien workers with deportation while their employers escaped punishment. This movement appeared to be specific to that region.[23] In the Midi, one of the complaints frequently heard is that deportation of the illegal alien worker prevents them from collecting the pay and employment-related benefits they are entitled to under French law. This, coupled with the perception that employers will not be punished, appeared to prompt the protest. The concern over the distribution of punishment, therefore, paradoxically appeared to affect enforcement in two ways, the fine against employers was seen by some French labour inspectors as a reason not to write up complaints while other inspectors felt that employers were not punished enough, and thus also did not write up complaints.

A further problem affecting punishment of offending employers arises from their ability to adapt to enforcement strategies. Some employers have thwarted enforcement by going, as it were, deeper underground. This has been the case, for example, in the Paris area garment industry where some employers of aliens ineligible to work have relocated out of the garment industry centre to the suburbs where underground factories are more difficult to detect. Another employer strategy has been to utilise subcontractors who hire illegal aliens. French authorities have revised their laws punishing illegal employment of aliens to facilitate punishment of the subcontractors and firms which knowingly dissimilate illegal alien employment through subcontracting.

This latter problem is particularly significant in the construction industry. Recent studies of the construction industry in France have pointed to widespread employment of illegal aliens through the subcontracting mechanism. The phenomenal growth of subcontracting in construction and service industries like cleaning and maintenance mitigates against successful enforcement of laws prohibiting illegal employment of aliens. As underscored in the 1986–87 report of the Interministry Liaison Mission to Combat Manpower Trafficking, the trend towards deregulation and greater flexibility in labour markets, as exemplified by the growth of temporary worker agencies and eased regulations concerning employment of non-permanent workers, tends to undercut governmental policies aimed at curbing illegal alien entry and employment.[24] Employer sanctions are therefore only one component of broader public policies affecting illegal migration; labour market trends and developments in the 1980s generally militated against successful enforcement of laws prohibiting illegal alien employment.

In the late 1970s a lack of co-ordination among various agencies charged with enforcement responsibilities against illegal alien employment constituted an important barrier. Information gathered by one service would not or could not be shared with another concerned service, and the limited personnel and other resources committed to enforcement of laws prohibiting illegal employment of aliens were thus ineffectively utilised. The response of French authorities was to establish interagency coordination mechanisms in targeted areas; a 1986 decree promulgated the creation of interagency committees to facilitate enforcement of laws against illegal alien employment and related offences in each department. By 1987 some 68 of France's 96 mainland departments had formally created departmental interagency committees, while another 18 had instituted informal ones.[25]

Interagency co-operation in enforcement of laws prohibiting illegal alien employment had improved in France over the period 1975 to 1990, although significant problems remained. In the Vaucluse, enforcement officials found the informal co-operation that ensued from department-level interagency meetings to be helpful.

A NON-ISSUE IN WESTERN EUROPE: EMPLOYER SANCTIONS-LINKED EMPLOYMENT DISCRIMINATION AGAINST MINORITIES

Several Western European states possess substantial foreign-born or immigrant-stock citizen populations. The relative ease of naturalisation in France and the legacy of French colonialism have combined to give France a substantial minority population of citizens and legally resident aliens of North African Muslim background. This population, which ranges between three and four million persons, over five per cent of the total population of France, is the target of widespread discrimination and racism despite longstanding French governmental policy to combat all forms of racism.[26] North African Muslims comprise a substantial share of illegal immigrants whose status was legalised in the early 1980s.

Under a 1972 French law banning all forms of discrimination, which is complemented by France's signature of various international treaties against racism and discrimination, minorities such as French citizens whose background is North African Arab, as well as legally established foreign residents, cannot be discriminated against in employment.[27] The 1972 law arose in response to anti-Semitism and it is most often invoked in response to racism in newspapers and books. In the aftermath of the desecration of graves at the Jewish cemetery in Carpentras in 1990, a movement to reinforce France's anti-racism law gathered strength and a measure proposed by the French Communist Party passed the Chamber of Deputies. Provisions of the 1972 law, in fact, are seldom invoked, a fact which defenders of the legal status quo maintain suggests the sufficiency, not the insufficiency, of the 1972 law.[28]

Under a relatively obscure 1932 law granting priority to the national or indigenous work force which was finally scrapped by the Socialist reform of immigration laws in 1981–82, an employer was supposed to prefer indigenous labour to immigrant labour. This law had little or no effect during the post-World War II period as the limitations it placed on alien employment in industries were obviously ignored. As late as 1975 to 1981, the government of Valéry Giscard d'Estaing pursued a policy aimed at attracting French workers to manual labour, or *revalorisation du travail manuel*. French employers were to give priority to indigenous job applicants over applicants who were not citizens or permanent resident aliens. This policy, which never had much effect, was dropped after the 1981 Socialist Party victories.

It is permissible for employers to prefer to hire an indigenous worker, a legal concept which includes longer-term aliens, over nonresident aliens. Indeed, this may be required of employers in periods of high unemployment although it rarely seemed to be during the long employment crisis of the 1970s and early 1980s. In France, it is clearly illegal for an employer to decline to hire or to fire a French citizen or legal resident alien of North African background solely because of the individual's ethnic or religious background.[29] However, French employers enjoy a great deal of legal discretion in personnel decisions and there is not a tradition of governmental regulation or monitoring of hiring decisions. Termination of employment, on the other hand, is subject to extensive regulation designed mainly to protect employees.

Under the 1972 anti-racism law, refusals to hire or decisions to fire motivated by racism or discrimination are subject to prison terms of two months to one year and fines of 2,000 to 20,000 French francs.[30] Very few complaints of employment discrimination have been made. According to Costa-Lascoux, a witness is required to prove discrimination, a requirement that is difficult to fulfill. Individuals, in addition, often find it difficult to register legal complaints due to the cost of doing so, although the 1972 law does enable recognised public interest associations, such as the Movement Against Anti-Semitism and Racism and for Peace (MRAP), to bring charges on behalf of an offended individual. The 1972 law provides various remedies for offended individuals. Depending on the gravity of the offence, justice can be sought through three alternative procedures.

Organisations like MRAP have not perceived a need to contest laws prohibiting illegal employment of aliens on the grounds that they give rise to additional discrimination against minorities. There is wide agreement that communities such as the North Africans encounter widespread discrimination, but laws prohibiting illegal employment of aliens are not perceived to be a problem. Virtually all observers concur that the problems of discrimination encountered by immigrants and citizens of immigrant background are to be found elsewhere. Many are quick to add that the status of illegally employed aliens is inherently discriminatory and that steps taken to curb it help guarantee equality of rights for citizens and legally resident aliens.

Document Fraud

A final issue that has affected enforcement is document fraud. In France, citizens are not required to possess a national identity card, although the vast majority of French citizens have one as they are widely used for identification purposes. All aliens who stay beyond a three-month tourism period are required to obtain residency permits and aliens must possess employment permits or their equivalent to work in France. Employers must keep a special registry of alien employees and make it available to inspectors on demand.

Alien residency and employment document fraud is a problem which has adversely affected enforcement of laws prohibiting illegal employment of aliens. There is a long history of politically-motivated counterfeiting of documents, stretching back to World War II and the Algerian conflict. Laws prohibiting illegal alien employment are premised on administrative ability to discern legal from fraudulent documents. While document fraud is a problem in France, it is not viewed as a significant obstacle to enforcement of laws prohibiting illegal employment of aliens.

SUMMARY AND COMPARATIVE OBSERVATIONS

Most Western European countries adopted or reinforced employer sanctions in the mid-1970s as concern over illegal alien migration and employment grew. Such policies were politically uncontroversial and reflected a broad political consensus that steps should be taken to deter illegal migration and employment. Laws sanctioning illegal employment of aliens were seen as an important component of a broader strategy to control illegal migration. As in the United States, European officials view the frontiers of their open societies as permeable and they regard employment as a key determinant of illegal migration.

Over the past 15 years, enforcement of employer sanctions has remained largely politically uncontroversial despite the marked trend towards politicisation of immigration issues in Western Europe. For example, immigration policy is arguably the most salient issue in French politics today. Yet enforcement of employer sanctions does not represent a significant issue. In France, Germany, and Switzerland, there remains a broad consensus that laws punishing illegal employment of aliens make sense. Indeed, they continue to be seen as an indispensable component of any coherent strategy to control illegal migration.

Criticism that is expressed generally holds that laws prohibiting illegal employment of aliens are inadequately enforced. There is less optimism today than there was five or ten years ago that employer sanctions can significantly curtail illegal migration, although they do have a limited deterrent effect. It is thought that illegal alien migration and employment in Western Europe would be significantly more extensive without employer sanctions. Consequently, there is virtually no discussion of eliminating employer sanctions in Western Europe. To the contrary, public discussion of employer sanctions invariably ends with calls for reinforcement of policies aimed at curbing illegal migration.

A gap between declared policies and the means to implement them has become more evident over the past decade. This is not to contend that enforcement of laws prohibiting illegal employment of aliens has not been refined and reinforced. Considerable progress has been made. Yet illegal migration and employment continues and it may be more extensive today than in the past. The pessimism expressed by some informants stemmed from their perception that the means allocated to enforce employer sanctions were insufficient in light of what is generally viewed, over the long run, as a growing problem of illegal alien migration and employment. Enforcement agents in Germany, Switzerland and France complain of inadequate manpower and insufficient budgets. They think employer sanctions could be a more effective means of controlling illegal migration if there were greater political support for expanded enforcement. One of the paradoxes of contemporary European politics is that broad public consensus on the need to curb illegal migration and employment has only been partially translated into policy. There are a variety of reasons for this.

Western Europeans adopted employer sanctions to (1) curb illegal migration, (2) protect jobs (less of a concern in Switzerland) (3) promote the integration of the legally-admitted alien population, (4) curb the abuse of disadvantaged illegal aliens by employers, and (5) to forestall the development of political extremism. These factors continue to be powerful arguments in favour of laws prohibiting illegal alien employment.

Most laws do not eradicate the phenomenon they are intended to counter overnight. The implementation of employer sanctions in Western Europe has proceeded incrementally and, in general, with limited efficacy. However, there is no reason to think that laws prohibiting illegal alien employment are draconian or incompatible with democratic ideals based on the European experience with them. Employer sanctions are seen as a necessary instrument within a broader strategy to control illegal migration, a phenomenon which is complex and perhaps intractable. All indications are that a more concerted effort to control illegal migration will be made in the future in that the creation of a single European market hinges on an acceptable level of control over illegal migration.

The development of a limited state capacity to prevent unwanted migration in Western European countries like France, Germany and Switzerland through employer sanctions and related deterrence measures seems to indicate that Western Europe will not be overrun by uncontrollable hordes of migrants as assumed in the most dire post-1989 scenarios. There are other reasons not to expect the worst to happen as well. On the other hand, this analysis also suggests that the much touted Fortress Europa of draconian immigration laws and hermetically sealed borders also should be regarded with a large measure of scepticism. Illegal and other forms of migration will continue into the foreseeable future. Yet only a small fraction of the millions of would-be migrants to Western Europe will succeed in their efforts; a selection process or sifting and winnowing occurs, as is evident by the fact that Europe in 1993 has not already been overrun by immigrants.

NOTES

The author wishes to thank the German Marshall fund of the United States and the European Community for supporting this research. He also wishes to thank two anonymous referees for their constructive criticisms of an earlier version of this manuscript.

1. See, for instance, Stephen Castles and Mark J. Miller, *The Age of Migration* (London: Macmillan and NY: Guilford Publications, 1993).
2. The General Accounting Office in Washington, DC published two reports on enforcement of laws seeking to curb illegal migration worldwide. The first one cast doubt on the efficacy of employer sanctions. The second found them to be effective in Europe. My testimony on employer sanctions in Western Europe is recorded in US. Committee of the Judiciary, *Knowing employment of illegal immigrants,* Hearings, 30 Sep. 1981 (Serial No J-97–61) (Washington DC: GPO, 1982), pp.199–217. I subsequently formally testified to the US Senate Subcommittee on Immigation and Refugee Policy on 10 April 1992 and to the House Subcommittee on International Law, Immigration and Refugees on 16 June 1993 in addition to several informal consultations.
3. James F. Hollifield, *Immigrants, Markets and States* (Cambridge,MA and London: HUP, 1992).
4. Catherine Wihtol de Wenden in Zig Layton-Henry (eds.), *The Political Rights of Migrant Workers in Western Europe* (London, Newbury Park and New Delhi: Sage Publications, 1990).
5. Patrick Weil, *La France et ses etrangers,* (Paris: Calmann-Levy, 1991), p.225.
6. Ibid., pp.223–7, esp. p.226.
7. Ibid., p.225.
8. Arrête interministeriel du 16 janvier 1989.

9. Mission de liaison interministerielle pour la lutte contre les trafics de main d'oeuvre, *Bilan. .pour l'annee 1979*, p.2.
10. J.P. Garson and Yann Moulier-Boutang, *Les Clandestins et la regularisation de 1981–1982 en France*, pp.21–22.
11. Mission de liaison . . . , *Bilan . . . pour l'annee 1983*, p.21.
12. *Le Quotidien de Paris*, 26 March 1985.
13. Agence France Presse dispatch, 25 March 1985.
14. Gervaise Hue, 'Travail illegal, emploi atypique', talk given at the Journees INRWFP-ENM, 13–15 Oct. 1987, p.4.
15. Ibid., p.4.
16. Interview with G. Hue, June 1990.
17. Ibid.
18. G. Hue, 'Legalité, éfficacité et Travail Clandestin,' paper written in March 1990, p.8.
19. Mission de liaison interministerielle . . . , *La Lutte contre les trafics de main-d'oeuvre en 1986–1987* . . . pp.18–19.
20. Interview with Alain Deille, Directeur Adjoin du Travail Avignon, 23 May 1990.
21. Interview with M. Lambert, Controleur divisionnaire des lois sociales en agriculture, 22 May 1990.
22. Interview with Gerard Demorg and Marc Lambert, 21 May 1990.
23. Interview with G. Hue, 6 June 1990.
24. Mission de liaison . . . ,*La lutte contre les trafics de main d'oeuvre en 1986–1987* . . . , pp.36–38. Also, interview with Claude Valentin Marie, 6 June, 1990.
25. Ibid., p.41.
26. See, generally, F.N. Bernardi, *et al.*, *Les Dossiers Noirs du Racisme*, Mouvement contre le racisme et pour l'amitie entre les peuples, *Chronique du flagrant racisme* and Michel Hannoun, *L'homme est l'esperance de l'homme.*
27. J. Costa-Lascoux, *De l'immigre au citoyen*, pp.98–107.
28. François Terre, 'Une proposition totalitaire, ' *Le Figaro*, 11 June 1990, p.2.
29. J. Costa-Lascoux, (note 27), pp.105–6.
30. Ibid., p.105.

European Union Immigration Policy: Phantom, Fantasy or Fact?

ALAN BUTT PHILIP

Moves to complete the single European market by 1993 together with worldwide migratory pressures have forced immigration onto the European Union's political agenda. Intergovernmental co-operation has been the preferred, but disputed method by which member states are developing a more co-ordinated immigration and border control policy. The EC institutions have become involved despite attempts by national governments to protect sovereignty and to promote subsidiarity. The Maastricht Treaty negotiations highlighted divisions between member states and policy development has been slow. Despite introducing more restrictive immigration controls, EU states have already become countries of immigration but have yet to acknowledge this.

There has always been a social dimension in the developing process of European integration and specific recognition of social policy concerns is to be found in the founding treaties of the European Community starting with the European Coal and Steel Community Treaty of 1951. The main obstacles preventing development of the EC's social policy have historically been the lack of support among member states for a strong Community profile in this policy area and a weakness of the phrasing of those parts of the European Economic Community treaty upon which the Commission might consider justifying any EC initiatives.[1] Nevertheless the founding treaties confer upon EC nationals certain economic and social rights – non-discrimination as between citizens of the EC states in economic and employment matters and free movement of workers within the Community, now Union, which are central to the concept of the modern EC, and yet which cannot easily be separated from immigration policy.

Immigration policy concerns at EC level thus fall to be dealt with under two distinct categories – the guarantee of the free movement of persons and social policy. While social policy issues have moved to the forefront of the EC's agenda only since the adoption of the 1985 White Paper on Completion of the EC's Internal Market,[2] the application of the principle of free movement of persons has been a constant subject for litigation before the European Court of Justice (ECJ).[3] The rights of EC nationals to free movement within the Community also proved to be one of the most contentious items in the enlargement negotiations leading to the accession of Greece, and of Spain and Portugal to the European Community treaties. Full free movement rights were not conferred upon Greek citizens until 1988, nor to Spanish and Portuguese citizens until 1992.

Three conditions have however reduced the potentially radical impact of the promise of free movement of persons within the EC. First, the EC in its early years was essentially the preserve of similarly developed high income and high welfare-providing states (with the exception of Italy) in which there seemed little to attract cross border movement of EC nationals except as a result of employment. Part of the original purpose of the European Social Fund was indeed to facilitate the integration of migrant workers into the host country through training programmes. In the mid-1970s, such movements of people, and even internal migration within EC states, declined sharply as the growth of employment in the industrialised core of the EC stalled.[4] Second, there has been surprisingly little mobility of persons within the EC states, the latest figures issued by the Commission showing that no more than 15 million out of the 344 million EC population are working in a state which is not the state of which they are citizens, and a large majority of these individuals are non-EC nationals (who may have lived nowhere else but in their current country of residence) and some 5 million EC nationals working in an EC member state other than that whose nationality they hold.[5] Only one EC member state has more than 10 per cent of its resident population who are not nationals of that state; a quarter of the population of Luxembourg are not citizens of the grand duchy, most of these being EC nationals employed in EC institutions and in the Luxembourg financial services industry (see Table 1). Third, control over the granting of nationality and citizenship of a member state remains exclusively in the hands of member states even though citizenship of a member state confers economic and social rights exercisable in all EC member states.

THE LOGIC OF THE SINGLE MARKET

The Commission's 1985 White Paper in effect relaunched the original plans for a European Common Market in which the free circulation of goods, services, capital and persons could be realised. The free movement of persons cannot readily be separated from the free movement of

TABLE 1

POPULATION BY CITIZENSHIP OF EC MEMBER STATES ON 1 JANUARY 1991

	Home State EC Nationals(%)	Other EC Nationals(%)	EEA Nationals (96)	Other Europeans(1) (96)	Others(2) %	Total Population (000s)
Belgium	91	5½	*	1	2½	9,987
Denmark	97	½	½	1	1	5,147
France	93	2	*	½	4	56,652
Germany	93	2	*	3½	1¼	79,753
Greece	99	*	*	*	1	10,120
Ireland	97½	2	*	*	½	3,524
Italy	98½	*	*	*	1	57,746
Luxembourg	70	27	*	1	2	384
Netherlands	95	1	*	1½	2	15,010
Portugal	99	*	*	*	1	9,859
Spain	99	1	*	*	½	38,994
UK	95½	1½	*	*	3	56,705
EC-12 Total(3)						
Number(millions)	328.8	5.0	0.34	3.8	6.0	343,881
%	(95.6)	(1.5)	(0.1)	(1.1)	(1.7)	(100)

Source: Table derived from data published in Eurostat, *Rapid Reports (Population and Social Conditions)*, 1993, No. 6.

Notes: (1) Includes Turkey and Switzerland. (2) Includes stateless and unknown nationals. (3) Some totals may not be reconciled exactly owing to rounding up. * = less than 0.45%.

goods, given that freight moving across borders is bound to be accompanied by people, and that people moving across borders inevitably take some possessions with them.[6] Even though the main thrust of the single market programme was to remove barriers to trade, there were elements in it designed to stimulate more cross-border movements of people, notably through the mutual recognition of professional and vocational qualifications and higher education degrees and diplomas.[7] The European Commission has also initiated programmes to encourage student mobility, foreign language learning, and young worker exchanges to facilitate free movement at several levels of industry, commerce and the education world. It may therefore come as a surprise to learn that the incidence of cross-border residence by nationals of one of the EC-12 states in another state has tended to decline since the 1960s. Nationals from poorer EC regions such as Southern Italy, Spain and Portugal have been returning to their countries of origin which have become relatively more prosperous and are offering better job opportunities than in the past.

In the early 1980s the population of Community residents who were not EC nationals also seemed to have stabilised, but it is this category which has begun to rise rapidly since 1988. Such residents are also not automatically entitled to legal and social rights conferred upon EC nationals, and risk becoming an underclass in their host countries. In the context of greater free movement of people within the EC, the non-EC nationals legitimately resident in one EC state have not had the automatic right to move to another EC state whether as a visitor or with the intention of taking up permanent residence. Strictly speaking these non-EC nationals have needed to obtain visas to travel to other EC states and these visas would be checked at or within national frontiers. Hence the drive to dismantle internal frontiers within the EC implies a harmonisation of visa policy or a reinforcement of internal checks in order to ensure that movements of non-EC nationals within the Community are regularised.

The Community's approach to the creation of a single market stipulated that there should be an 'area without frontiers' within the EC.[8] The removal of internal frontiers implied in the Single European Act of 1986 was predicated upon the strengthening of the external frontiers of the various EC states. Checks on goods and people as they crossed the borders of one EC state into another were to be abandoned, thereby speeding up the flow of goods across the Community, reducing industrial and commercial costs, and providing a powerful symbol to the individual EC citizens about the high degree of stability, security and European integration now achieved.[9] The single market in goods and services, given the standing down of EC border controls, would inevitably open up new opportunities for organised crime, terrorists, drug-traffickers and other undesirables – an aspect which Mrs Thatcher raised so strongly in her famous speech in 1988 to the College of Europe in Bruges.[10] Compensatory measures based upon EC-wide co-operation between the main law enforcement agencies (the police, customs and immigration services) have thus been considered to be an indispensable part of the realisation of the 1992 programme. The different EC national customs authorities have had a long history of cross-national co-operation, sometimes bilateral, sometimes in groups of neighbouring countries, or through the international Customs Co-operation Council. The police have been much slower to build up working relations with neighbouring forces despite the long-standing existence of Interpol, with its own European secretariat. No established cooperative network for immigration matters serving the EC members states existed before the single market programme was agreed. Accompanying such trans-national and EC-wide co-operation, checks previously carried out at the internal frontiers would have to some extent to be replaced by internal checks away from frontiers, including checks on individuals such as non-EC nationals, with or without rights of residence.

COMMUNITY COMPETENCE

Despite the confidence of EC leaders and the European Commission accompanying the launch of the 1992 programme and the signature of the Single European Act, it soon became clear that the EC institutions were legally in a very weak position to implement the ambitions for a single market, at least in those matters concerning the movement of people across the internal frontiers of the member states within the Community.

The EEC Treaty does set as one of the objectives of the Community the provision of free movement of persons within it, Article 3(c), but the treaty as a whole has almost nothing else to say on this matter; the treaty title dealing with free movement of persons in fact refers only to free movement of workers. Some members of the European Parliament have argued that Article 3(c) taken in conjunction with Article 235 of the EEC Treaty, which gives the EC institutions general powers to secure the realisation of a common market is sufficient for the EC to legislate for the dismantling of internal border controls. This view has yet to be fully tested in the European Court of Justice, but it is strongly resisted by several EC member states, notably the United Kingdom and Denmark.[11] Some independent legal authorities maintain that the

Community already has the legal competence to decide immigration policy issues.[12]

The EEC Treaty's social policy provisions, especially Articles 117 and 118 which set out the scope of the Community's social concerns, also offer an indirect route for the EC to develop aspects of an immigration policy, by virtue of the EC deciding collectively upon the needs and rights of migrant workers, many of whom are not EC nationals. When five EC member states challenged the legality of a Commission Decision of 1985 to set up a prior communication procedure on migration policies in relation to non-member states, the ECJ decided that migration policy could legally fall within the scope of the EC's social policy, but only to the extent that it concerned the situation of workers from non-member states in the Community and their impact upon working conditions or upon the employment market. Cultural integration issues were deemed to be beyond the scope of Article 118.[13] Nevertheless many EC co-operation or association agreements with third countries extend EC social rights to non-EC nationals.[14]

The view of the Commission on this legal issue is not far removed from the line taken by the European Parliament.[15] However, in the mid-1980s the Commission was thrown onto the defensive by an adverse ECJ ruling in regard to the conduct of administrative checks at internal frontiers.[16] After many months of inaction the Commission decided that rather than resolve this issue first through the ECJ, the best prospect for making progress on free movement of persons issues, so as to meet the deadline of 31 December 1992 set up for the single market, was to proceed by means of intergovernmental co-operation. At the end of 1988 a Commission communication to the Council of Ministers formalised this approach.[17] At the Rhodes summit in December 1988 the Council decided that a group of national co-ordinators, one from each member state, should be set up to guide the EC on the various free movement issues and to try to make progress where possible. The Commission was subsequently allowed to be represented on this group but without the right of initiative. By June 1989 the coordinators' group reported in the so-called Palma document to the EC heads of state and government that over 80 initiatives or pieces of legislation were needed to achieve free movement of people within the EC, and suggested that the EC institutions had competence to act in no more than one-fifth of these points.[18] Member states had already begun to dispute among themselves just how far the amendment to the EEC Treaty through the Single European Act (SEA) had moved the goal-posts on free movement of persons. The United Kingdom has argued that the general declarations attached to the SEA underline the individual member states' unrestricted competence to deal with terrorism, immigration and nationality matters.[19]

Although the jurisprudence of the ECJ has made clear that EC law applies in principle to EC nationals and not to non-EC nationals other than family members, a series of cases has led the Court to modify this stance in order not to jeopardise the rights of EC nationals under EC law. In the process the ECJ has on occasion felt impelled to overturn features of nationality and immigration law in individual member states, for instance, the 'primary purpose rule' introduced into UK immigration law in 1982 governing the acceptability of marriages between British nationals and non-EC nationals for the purpose of immigration into the United Kingdom.[20] The Court has repeatedly insisted that the right to free movement of EC nationals should not be impeded by national rules in regard to non-EC nationals, such as spouses or dependants of EC nationals.

Clearly immigration and nationality laws are considered in most EC member states to lie at the core of the exercise of national sovereignty. Yet individual features in such national legislation may obstruct the exercise of legal rights conferred upon EC nationals by EC law. The removal of EC internal frontiers, and the renewed drive to encourage free movement of persons within the EC (including the extension of rights of residence throughout the Community of students, retired persons and the unemployed), has highlighted the sometimes difficult overlap between the national and the EC jurisdictions. In cases where EC law and national law conflict, it is now well established that EC law prevails.

Member states have been unwilling to consider the long-term implications of European integration for immigration or nationality policy at national government level. Yet the single market programme, in addition to ECJ decisions on individual cases, has forced governments to rethink their position. While outwardly denying in the 1980s that there was any need for an EC-wide immigration policy, governments such as the French and the British were laying the foundations for just such a policy, as evidenced in the creation of the *ad hoc* intergovernmental Working Group on Immigration in 1986 and the terms of the Maastricht Treaty of 1992. Events following the collapse of Communism in central and eastern Europe together with increased asylum-seeker, refugee and migratory pressures from other parts of the world have forced the pace. Nevertheless, despite the reluctance to fan the suspicions of those who oppose a deepening of the process of European integration, the governments of the member states have continued to inch their way towards an ever closer union of their immigration policies.

Indeed the effects of economic and monetary union, as envisaged by the Maastricht Treaty, would be such as to demand much greater movement of the labour force across all EC internal frontiers, and in so doing to present ever more problems for national immigration law in regard to third country nationals.

THE GROWTH OF INTERGOVERNMENTALISM

The reluctance of EC member states to accept the jurisdiction of the Community in matters which are close to the core of national sovereignty has led to the growth of intergovernmental policy-making by the 12 EC states, avoiding the EC institutions and their legislative procedures. The development of intergovernmentalism can be traced back to the early days of European Political Co-operation, dealing mainly with foreign policy, instituted in 1970. The formation of the Trevi Group in 1975–76 enabled officials and ministers from the interior and justice ministries of the EC members states to concentrate upon issues demanding co-operation between governments and enforcement agencies dealing with internal security and criminal activities. Such processes have been developed under the umbrella of the European Council whose powers and functions are also not defined by the EC treaties. The first, albeit brief, mention of the European Council in the treaty base occurs in the Single European Act: the Maastricht Treaty develops this much further.[21]

Intergovernmental agreements between all the member states of the Community are thus governed by international law and do not use EC institutions for their interpretation or enforcement. Such agreements may however cover subjects that are within the legal competence of the Community but which member states prefer to deal with outside the EC institutional framework. Intergovernmental resolutions, such as the 1993 resolution on family reunification, have no standing under international or EC law.

The decision of the Council to set up an ad hoc Working Group on Immigration (WGI) in 1986 grew out of the European Political Co-operation, the work of the Trevi Group, and an increasing appreciation that the creation of the Single European Market would throw up immigration issues which ministers and their officials could resolve intergovernmentally.[22] In practice, several member states had already decided as a result of the Saarbrücken Agreement of 1984 (between France and Germany) and the Schengen Agreement of 1985 (whose original signatories were France, Germany and the three Benelux countries) to try to make faster progress in the dismantling of internal border controls, with all the resulting implications for visa and immigration policy, than the Community as a whole.[23] The negotiations in the intergovernmental conference of 1985 which led to the signature of the SEA were to demonstrate just how thorny and sensitive these issues were likely to be for EC member states to resolve jointly. These fast-track member states judged rightly that it would probably take the EC as a whole well beyond 1992 to resolve their differences. What they did not foresee was how difficult it was going to be even for those fully committed to removing internal border controls quickly to agree on all the various issues necessary before such controls could be safely removed.

The principal achievements of the intergovernmental machinery handling free movement of people issues since the ratification of the SEA have been the agreement of the Dublin Convention on Asylum in 1990 and the External Frontiers Convention initialled in 1991, both of which have implications for migration and immigration. The Dublin Convention is designed essentially to prevent multiple or successive applications for asylum in the EC states, laying down as a first principle that the decision on asylum should be made by the first country of application and that other signatories to the convention need not be obliged to reassess identical applications once assessment procedures had been mutually recognised. This approach did however present problems for Denmark, which required to be satisfied that member states' obligations to human rights under various international conventions were being maintained, and for Germany whose Basic Law appeared to demand that each application for asylum in Germany needed to be assessed in Germany.[24]

The External Frontiers Convention provides for the mutual recognition of national visas for non-Community nationals. It also abolishes the need for non-Community nationals legally resident in one EC member state to secure a visa to enter another EC member state for a period of less than three months, provided the purpose of such a visit is not to seek employment.[25] This Convention had not been formally signed by the EC member states at the time of going to press because the governments of Spain and the United Kingdom have reached an impasse in trying to reconcile for the purposes of the convention their conflicting claims of sovereignty over the international airport at Gibraltar.[26] The result has been to delay significantly the 'strengthening' of the EC's external frontier and so to provide grounds *inter alia* for national governments postponing the dismantling of EC internal border checks. There are increasing doubts whether the draft External Frontiers Convention will ever be signed and implemented.

RESISTANCE TO EC-WIDE INITIATIVES

Despite the initial euphoria and optimism occasioned by the 1992 programme and the application of the SEA, there have been sceptics in several countries from an early stage about the removal of border controls and the impact this would have on the free circulation of people both within the EC, and between the EC and elsewhere.

It is difficult to disentangle many of the strands of resistance, since some of the most important criticisms have been raised by groups and institutions which have challenged the process by which intergovernmental decisions in this general area (not exclusively in regard to immigration) have been arrived at. Some issues, such as the handling of asylum-seekers and refugees, are closely linked in practice to immigration policy and must be considered alongside the latter. It is also the case that concerns raised in the context of policy initiatives arising either from the Schengen Agreement of 1985 or from the EC directly have focused critical scrutiny on the course of discussions in *both* sets of forum. A powerful head of steam in opposition to many linked aspects of the implementation of the free movement of people within an EC without internal border controls has been built up and played a considerable role during the referendum campaigns in Denmark and France in 1992 and 1993.

General civil liberties concerns raised included the impact of the exchange of data across frontiers between enforcement agencies about individuals, especially so-called 'undesirables', and the means of securing access to and the accuracy of such information.

Much anxiety has been expressed about the impact of any reinforcement of the administration of identity checks upon immigrants and ethnic minorities, once internal EC border controls are dismantled. Organisations representing the interests of asylum-seekers and refugees believe that the harmonisation of procedures for dealing with applicants at EC level will only make it more difficult for those applying to find asylum or refuge. Representatives of ethnic minorities already resident within the EC are equally concerned about the impact upon their communities of more identity checks and greater difficulties in achieving family unification as EC co-ordination of policies on asylum and immigration takes effect. At a more practical level the passenger carriers in the airline industry are incensed by the growing demands of national governments in the EC that airlines be fined large sums of money for carrying passengers to EC destinations from outside the EC who do not have appropriate entry documents – according to the newly conceived doctrine of 'carrier liability'. This is forcing airline staff to act as immigration officers by proxy in order to minimise the financial liability.[27]

Parliamentarians meanwhile have begun to get increasingly anxious about the opaque and uncontrolled decision-making processes by which many of the new decisions at EC level on citizens' rights, asylum and refugee policy, and immigration matters are being made. The French Senate has complained bitterly about this problem in 1986 and 1993 in relation both to the Schengen Agreement and EC-wide developments. The Bundestag in the Federal Republic of Germany and the Dutch Parliament, as well as the European Parliament, have raised similar complaints since 1989. The problem of lack of democratic control over the decision-making processes arises from the sensitivity of many of the issues (inviting secrecy of discussion) and the conduct of negotiations on an intergovernmental basis, where the negotiators are not accountable to EC institutions, nor frequently to national parliaments, in practice. National parliaments have thus been presented with deals done by government ministers and officials behind closed doors and have been required to approve such deals without amendment because each is a delicate intergovernmental compromise. Both the Schengen Agreement (particularly the second agreement of 1990) and the Dublin Convention have run into difficulties in national parliaments as a result, and national parliamentarians have been alerted to what may be further down the EC pipeline on free movement of persons and immigration policy issues. The increased migration into Western Europe since the late 1980s and the rising incidence of racism and xenophobia in most EC member states have added to the anxieties of parliamentarians who had already begun to question the legitimacy of EC-wide decision-making in this policy field and its confinement to a small, largely unaccountable Community-wide policy-making elite of ministers and officials.[28]

POLICY DEVELOPMENTS SINCE 1988

The context in which the discussion of EC immigration policy issues has taken place has changed rapidly since the Hanover European Council of June 1988 addressed immigration issues; indeed, almost every EC summit meeting since has had to give consideration to such questions.[29] There has been an intensification of the migratory pressures from outside into Western European states.

Such events have been thrown into even sharper focus by discussions and forecasts at international level on migration, refugee and demographic trends. It has been estimated that some 30 official bodies and groups are discussing aspects of these issues in Europe alone.[30] The

Organization for European Economic Co-operation and Development has for some years highlighted the prospect of labour shortages and difficulties in funding social welfare systems emerging in states such as Belgium, France, Germany and Italy because the indigenous population is not replacing itself.[31] A few journalists as well as population experts have called for active encouragement to immigration in order to avert a substantial shrinkage in the labour force.[32] United Nations sources have claimed that in 1992 alone some 100 million people world-wide migrated from one country to another, most of them 'economic' refugees; in the four years from 1989 to 1992 the numbers of 'economic' refugees doubled, although only a small proportion of these reached Western Europe. 'The mass migrations of our times threaten to overrun our capacity to cope with them.'[33]

It took some time before the impact of this changing environment was felt by the core of EC states seeking a rapid dismantling of internal frontier controls through the Schengen Agreement. The five Schengen states were, however, unable to sign a second agreement in November 1989 as planned in order to deliver a frontier-free Schengen area by 1 January 1990. The ostensible reason for this was given as the need for more time to consider the impact on the external frontiers of the Schengen area of the fall of the Berlin Wall in November 1989. In fact there were several other unresolved points of difficulty such as the reconciliation of different national policies on the possession of soft drugs and in regard to data protection and bank secrecy.[34] Although the second Schengen agreement was signed in June 1990, many essential points were still undecided. The Schengen states revised their timetable for final implementation again and decided to set 1 January 1992 as the date. Again this target was not met, and the position at the time of going to press is that the implementation date will be 1 February 1994, delayed two months from the previously agreed 1 December 1993.[35] Earlier in 1993 one of the first acts of the newly-elected centre-right French government under Edouard Balladur had been to suggest that the implementation of Schengen should be indefinitely postponed until the Dutch abandoned their liberal approach to the possession of soft drugs in small quantities. More substantial reasons for delay could be deduced from the continuing failure to reach agreement on the External Frontiers Convention, the incomplete process of creating a computerised system of information exchange between the enforcement agencies (known as the Schengen Information System – SIS), and the highly-charged political climate in France which had led to much anti-immigrant sentiment among voters.

Nevertheless the Schengen system was gaining credibility, despite delays in its implementation, by the expansion of its membership to include Italy, Spain and Portugal, with Greece becoming a full member in November 1992.[36] The consequence for national immigration policies of these new members joining the Schengen group proved to be quite dramatic. Thus in 1991 the Spanish government imposed a requirement on visitors from the Maghreb states to obtain a visa before entry into Spain: this affects over one million travellers each year, many of whom are seasonal workers from Morocco. In the same year the Italian government sought to reduce greatly the number of illegal immigrants in the country by declaring an amnesty with full exoneration for employers from paying unpaid social security contributions for undeclared workers. Simultaneously a fourfold increase in personnel to police the Italian maritime frontier was announced. The Portuguese government meanwhile withdrew the previously automatic right of Brazilians to opt for Portuguese nationality, with attendant national and EC residence rights. As a consequence of EC and Schengen commitments to strengthen their external frontiers, all the southern European member states have increased coastguard patrols, police checks on third country nationals and deportations as part of the construction of similar Europe-wide immigration policies.

Equally, the planned establishment of the SIS was turning day by day more into a reality, despite disagreements as to its exact location (finally agreed as Strasbourg) and some searching questions about the nature of the information to be exchanged between member states' enforcement agencies.[37] In the United Kingdom there were even suggestions that the police authorities were anxious to be part of the SIS but these were brushed off by the Home Office.[38]

At the level of the EC-12, work on the conventions on asylum and the crossing of external frontiers proceeded in parallel with, but often a few steps behind, the deliberations of the Schengen states. As the context for dealing with immigration issues became more pressing and less confident in 1990 and 1991, so it became less clear that Schengen was serving as a model for the whole of the EC, since both sets of negotiations were becoming blocked by similar difficulties. The decision to call intergovernmental conferences on political union, and on economic monetary union, triggered by the Strasbourg European Council in 1989 provided an opportunity for the German government and several others (e.g., the Netherlands and Italy) to call for a commitment to an EC immigration policy to be added to the EC Treaty base. In Germany's case there was not only a particular urgency because this country was the recipient of numerous immigrants and asylum-seekers. Germany was also hoping that decisions and actions at EC level could overcome its own constitutional constraints in seeking to limit the numbers of new arrivals.

From 1990 to the present day there have also been repeated calls for burden-sharing among the 12 EC states in handling the large numbers of refugees and asylum-seekers arriving on the territory of a minority of the member states (see Table 2). These calls were resisted during the Maastricht Treaty negotiations, although they seem to have met with some response as the crisis in Yugoslavia deepened in 1992.[39] The outcome of the intergovernmental conference on political union was to make visa policy part of the competence of the EU institutions and to include co-operation at intergovernmental level on asylum, refugee and immigration issues in the so-called third pillar of the Maastricht Treaty.[40] Article K9 also provides for the EU member states to use the full EU institutional panoply to legislate in these areas if they agree to do so unanimously, although the subsequent decisions of the Edinburgh European Council with respect to Denmark's late objections on citizenship of the European Union would appear to rule this possibility out for the foreseeable future.[41] Interestingly, the EU will be able to take decisions on visa policy at first on the basis of unanimity only, but from 1996 on the basis of a qualified majority vote.[42] Maastricht, however, adds little that is new to the EU-12's activities in the field of immigration although it does place fully on public record the range and nature of the intergovernmental agendas for this subject. While the European Court of Justice is permitted to have jurisdiction over international conventions which the 12 EU states agree to, where this is expressly provided for, the Commission retains a very limited role in home affairs and justice issues.

Alongside the formalised negotiations of the Schengen states and the intergovernmental conference on political union, the EC institutions were themselves beginning to articulate ever more strongly their interest in immigration issues from 1989. The main effect in political terms of this development was to draw the Commission in Brussels into the debate despite the fact that it had legally limited competence in this policy field. The Council of Ministers and the European Council looked to the Commission to service many of their discussions on immigration matters and to keep a watching brief on other related international discussions. The Commission also had an interest in the subject arising from the clear overlap with border control issues. Thus the Commission established a study group at the request of the Council to report on the different state of national immigration laws within the EC and later brought together a group of experts to suggest which areas of immigration policy could benefit from some Community initiatives.[43] The

TABLE 2

ESTIMATED NUMBER OF ASYLUM-SEEKERS ARRIVING IN EC MEMBER STATES 1980–1991

	1980	1985	1986	1987	1988	1989	1990	1991
Belgium	2700	5300	7650	6000	5100	8100	12950	13750
Denmark	50	8700	9300	2750	4650	4600	5300	4600
Germany	107800	73850	99650	57400	103100	121300	193050	256100
France	13700	25800	23500	24900	31700	58750	49750	45900
Greece	1800	1400	4250	6950	8400	3000	6200	2650
Italy	7450	5400	6500	11050	1300	2250	4750	23300
Netherlands	3700	5650	5850	13450	7500	13900	21200	21600
Portugal	N.A.	100	250	450	350	150	100	250
Spain	N.A.	2350	2300	2500	3300	2850	6850	7250
U.K.	9950	5450	4800	5150	5250	15550	25250	44750
TOTAL	147150	134000	164050	130600	170650	230450	325400	420150

Source: UNHCR Regional Office for the European Institutions, October 1992.

negotiations to conclude a European Economic Area (EEA) Agreement between the EC and European Free Trade Area states also provided for the extension of free movement rights within the EEA to all EEA nationals along almost identical lines to the free movement rights enjoyed currently by EC nationals within the EC.[44]

The Commission communications on immigration and on the right of asylum issued in 1991 were seen as part of the preparation for discussions at the Maastricht intergovernmental conference.[45] The Commission argued that the EC needed to have a common right of asylum once internal border controls were removed. Although all 12 EC states were signatories to the 1951 Geneva Convention on refugees, some categories of asylum seeker were not covered by the Convention (e.g., those leaving their home country because of political disturbance). The Commission was anxious to ensure that the EC harmonised the procedures, even if on an intergovernmental basis, concerning the treatment of asylum-seekers at the EC's external frontiers, those asylum-seekers not covered by the Geneva convention, and all applicants for asylum in regard to rights of residence, access to the labour market and to social security, while their cases were under consideration. The Commission also called for a speeding-up of the handling of all asylum applications in the EC member states, and suggested that the Dublin Convention could be opened to non-EC states such as Sweden.

In its communication to the Council on immigration, the Commission noted that all EC member states, except the Republic of Ireland, were now affected by a rise in political concerns over immigration and by a change in the character of immigration. In place of the traditional search for work in host countries the trend in immigration had been towards family reunification and requests for asylum. High unemployment in the Community in the late 1980s had led to political demands for a halt to immigration. The Commission acknowledged that Community economic aid to third countries could have an indirect effect of reducing migration to Western Europe, and that hitherto the countries of southern Europe had been most concerned by the pressures of immigration upon their societies. The rapid turn of events in central and eastern Europe had however increased the scale and complexity of the problems. Once again, the Commission linked the right of free movement of persons within the Community to the need for member states to ensure that immigrants, of all nationalities, were well integrated into their host societies. The Commission was now persuaded that such integration could only occur if immigration was controlled. Accordingly there was now a case to be made for common policies on family reunification and illegal immigration (in some cases in the absence of any such policies at national level), and for uniform sanctions against illegal immigrants.

The Commission called *inter alia* for an exchange of immigration statistics between all member states; the encouragement of intellectual elites in countries from which immigrants originated to stay put so as to assist the development of their home states; a common policy on the deportation of illegal immigrants; and for measures to prevent discrimination against immigrants in a variety of areas (e.g., education and training, illiteracy, lack of local language knowledge, employment and housing). The Commission's initial interest in resolving issues that were the by-products of the drive to complete the single European market was by mid-1991 clearly becoming a more ambitious claim for some common immigration rules and policies.[46]

The most immediate problem facing policy-makers was the rising number of asylum-seekers and refugees reaching the EC states. In 1992 some 700,000 asylum-seekers arrived in Western Europe, around one quarter of the total number of immigrants to the region, the vast majority arriving in the EC member states. EC ministers responsible for immigration indicated from 1991 that they were very concerned about the multiplicity of applications, the number of 'bogus' applications being made, and the slowness in the procedures and processes for handling such applications. The costs to national and local governments, in terms of welfare payments and provision of accommodation while applications were pending (a period of several months, and often years) were also an unwelcome growing financial burden at a time of economic recession and enlarged government deficits. Governments in Western Europe accordingly have sought to cut down the numbers of applicants whom they regard as legitimate asylum-seekers, to stem the flow of refugees out of Yugoslavia in particular, and to speed up the processes for deciding upon asylum applications, even if at the cost of diminishing applicants' chances of adequate representation or appeal.

With EC governments unable to accept at Maastricht that EC Treaty-based institutions should lead on immigration matters (other than visa policy), it was left to individual states, acting separately but in concert, to put in place policy and administrative changes to find more resources and to secure changes in national law if needed. The German government and parliament, after much heart-searching, even amended Article 16 of the Basic Law to curb the almost unlimited right of asylum this offered, and a much more restrictive asylum regime was introduced on 1 July 1993.

In addition, all EC states combined from 1991 to contain the threat of a mass exodus of refugees from Yugoslavia by redefining the criteria they applied for accepting requests for asylum, insisting meanwhile that such refugees were kept as close to their original homes as possible and within the borders of the former Yugoslavia.

The predictable knock-on effect of a government-led curb on the granting of asylum in the absence of any change in the 'push' factors impelling people to seek asylum is to force a rise in illegal immigration. Some official estimates of this essentially unquantifiable phenomenon put the numbers of illegal immigrants in the EC states in the early 1990s as between four and five million people, but this figure probably understates the position significantly. What is clear is that concerns about illegal immigration are clearly at the core of the policy agenda of bodies such as the *ad hoc* Working Group on Immigration, and this is demonstrated by the detailed prescriptions of the External Frontiers Convention on border surveillance, the renewed drive on internal checks especially at the point of employment on employers' premises, and the EC-wide moves to facilitate deportation.[47]

It is clear that while the proposed European Economic Area, which is expected to be implemented early in 1994, does offer full free movement rights to EU and non-EU EEA nationals across the whole area, and signals mutual concerns about border controls without making any commitments other than to discuss, the association agreements between the EC and the four central and eastern European states of Poland, Hungary, the Czech Republic and Slovakia are far more modest in intent. Full free movement rights for persons are not on offer, although member states have removed visa requirements. Co-operation between the two groups of countries is already occurring on border and migration issues and bilateral deals between Germany and Poland, and Germany and the Czech Republic point to economic aid being made conditional upon such co-operation. Germany is offering financial and practical assistance to these countries, which are becoming immigration buffer states, as it attempts to seal its eastern frontiers and to toughen its rules on granting asylum. Journalistic accounts of the impact of the change of regime in Germany in July 1993 suggest a predictable increase in clandestine immigration from Poland to Germany.[48]

The London meeting of the WGI ministers and officials on 30 November and 1 December 1992 resulted in agreement between the EC-12 on several important subjects: further agreement was made on the handling of manifestly unfounded applications for asylum, and on refusing to entertain asylum applications from host third countries which asylum-seekers have left unlawfully. The WGI is also developing a 'no serious risk of persecution' test which would automatically prompt a refusal of any asylum application from individuals resident in a country considered safe by the EC. A common list of undesirable aliens is being prepared for circulation EC-wide to the relevant enforcement agencies. Common training of officials is being organised so as to improve the detection of forged documents, and a new centre for information, discussion and exchange on the crossing of borders and immigration (CIREFI) is to be established. Further work was promised on the harmonisation of immigration rules in regard to family reunification, where practice in the member states varies widely. There was general agreement that refugees from the conflict in the former Yugoslavia should wherever possible be confined to that territory, although temporary admissions on the basis of proposals made by agencies such as the UNHCR would be possible.[49] The next WGI meeting at Copenhagen on 1 June 1993 did agree a resolution on family reunion rules and recommended more frequent and systematic internal checks on non-EC nationals together with clear criteria for expulsion from EC states of those not eligible to stay.

There is clearly a long potential agenda for future WGI meetings as the details and anomalies in national immigration policy and practice in the EU are addressed. Some issues which can reasonably be expected to come to the fore in future are: short-term contracts for workers from third countries (especially from eastern Europe) as a means of containing migratory pressures; the different treatment of spouses marrying EU nationals in various member states; the protection of dependants of non-EU nationals based in the EU in the event of death, divorce or separation; the problems of unaccompanied minors arriving in the Community; and the position and rights of long stay immigrants in the EU who have not acquired the nationality of a member state.[50]

This last concern introduces a much broader policy discussion about the evolution of nationality policy in the member states. Not only does the grant of nationality by one EU state give EU-wide political and social rights to each individual, which thus impacts upon all member states, but the refusal of citizenship to long-term immigrants en bloc is increasingly perceived as a real barrier to their integration into the host country and to social cohesion at times of political uncertainty or difficulty. The German government's policy in this regard has been particularly restrictive compared with other states with large immigrant populations such as France and the United Kingdom. Even the German authorities are beginning to appreciate the difficulties of maintaining policy in this regard unchanged and staying out of line with practice in other EU states. As information about and experience of these matters is now spreading easily across the political frontiers, so the force of arguments for policy convergence are strengthened. Indeed, it would be logical for the EU states to address the issues raised by nationality policy jointly, perhaps agreeing broad ceilings on how many new citizens EU-wide should be created and to consult each other before offering large-scale repatriation from third countries (as clearly did not occur in regard to the rights of citizens of Hong Kong and Macao).[51] The development of EU-wide citizenship rights is given further impetus by the Maastricht Treaty which will offer voting rights across the EU and rights to consular facilities in third countries to all EU citizens.

CONCLUSIONS

Citizenship rights thus are being both developed and restricted by the process of European integration, but on an *ad hoc* rather than on any coherent basis. Despite the implications of the granting of nationality by individual member states for the exercise of free movement rights across the EU as a whole, there is no evidence of purposeful harmonisation or co-operation in this field. Some convergence is nevertheless occurring as instanced by the withdrawal of the right of Latin American nationals to opt for Spanish or Portuguese nationality, in conjunction with development on an EU visa policy.

The single market programme of 1985 has had a powerful effect in raising the significance of issues linked to the movement of persons as an essential element in delivering a frontier-free Community, even if the EC institutions found themselves lacking in legal competence to deal with many of these issues. Here there is evidence of a 'spillover' effect at work, both in the need for the Community to resolve issues usually well outside its reach in order to deliver the single market promise, and in the slow, albeit reluctant, association of the EC institutions with more and more issues (visa policy, family reunification and the primary purpose rule, migration policy) which national governments had previously dealt with separately or intergovernmentally. Despite widespread resistance to EC institutional involvement in immigration matters, national governments once again are finding the EC is being drawn into the evolution of policy for legitimate and practical reasons. Many aspects of immigration policy have an interface with EC competences which the renewed emphasis on free movement and other social rights in the wake of the single market programme has made clear.

By the late 1980s it had also become evident to policy-makers that the nature of future immigration to Western Europe was changing dramatically in scale, scope and cause, such that a collective and concerted response by national governments was required if some states were not to be overwhelmed by events, with potentially major repercussions for continued political stability and internal cohesion in some EC states. The coincidence of these two forces has driven the evolution of EC immigration at a relatively rapid rate, despite repeated denials by its authors.

It is still the case that there is no truly common EU immigration policy, nor yet a common citizenship policy. Equally clearly the EU is acquiring authority and competence in aspects of immigration policy, even if there is no coherent strategy to bring this about, and even if the institutional responsibility is shared and mainly intergovernmental. Intergovernmental co-operation may be the member states' chosen method for policy development, but it has shown itself already to be slow, messy, halting and untransparent in its progress. The legitimacy of its activities in fields where individual civil liberties are at stake has been challenged by lawyers and parliamentarians both because the process is not transparent and almost impossible to subject to democratic control, and because so much executive discretion is brought into play in these policy areas that it is often difficult to subject the implementation of policy to due process of law. The Maastricht Treaty offers one, among several, indications that immigration policy is set to become more and more of an EU affair as the consequence of greater economic interdependence and the shared perceptions of common threatening external pressures work themselves through. It is ironic that at a time when national governments are keen to stress the importance of subsidiarity as a bulwark against the centralising trends emanating from Brussels, national governments should find themselves agreeing to cede ground over immigration policy to the Community inch by inch out of strong practical necessity. While the public face of national governments in the EU suggests that each member state is still firmly in control of immigration issues, the reality is quite different. There is no appreciation that the EU states as a bloc have become countries of immigration, in contrast to the rhetoric of their political leaders. West European societies (in the EU and outside) are open in theory but not in practice when it comes to immigration from outside or within the EU. Perceptions and realities are still far apart, even though the gap appears to be closing.

NOTES

1. See Doreen Collins, *The European Communities: the social policy of the first phase* (London, 1975).
2. Council of Ministers [hereinafter COM] (85) 310 final, June 1985.
3. See reports on the implementation of EC law in the European Commission's annual General Report on the Activities of the European Communities.
4. See discussion on 'Geographical Mobility and its Social Implications' in Social Europe, 'The Social Aspects of the Internal Market', Vol.9, Suppl. 7/88.

5. See *Social Europe* 'Immigration of citizens from third countries into the Southern Member States of the European Community', Suppl. 1/91, p.29a.
6. COM (85) 310 final, paras. 24 to 56.
7. Ibid., paras. 88 to 94.
8. Article 8(a) of the Single European Act (SEA) reads:

   > The Community shall adopt measures with the aim of progressively establishing the internal market over a period expiring on 31 December 1992 . . . The internal market shall comprise an area without internal frontiers in which the free movement of goods, persons, services and capital is ensured in accordance with the provisions of this Treaty.

   A general declaration attached to the SEA, concerning Articles 13 to 19, states that:

   > Nothing in these provisions shall affect the right of member states to take such measures as they consider necessary for the purpose of controlling immigration from third countries, and to combat terrorism, crime, the traffic in drugs and illicit trading in works of art and antiques.

   The legal force of this general declaration in relation to the interpretation of Article 8(a) is contested.
9. For further discussion of the general questions raised by the abolition of EC internal border controls see Alan Butt Philip, 'European Border Controls: Who Needs Them?' in *Public Policy and Administration* 6/12 (1991), and Alan Butt Philip *Dismantling European Border Controls* (London: Royal Inst. of Int'l Affairs, Pinter, forthcoming).
10. Quoted in extenso in *The Times*, 21 Sept. 1988.
11. Communication of the Commission on the Abolition of Border Controls, SEC (92) 877, 6 May 1992.
12. E.g., see Richard Plender, 'Competence, EC Law and nationals of non-member states' in *International and Comparative Law Quarterly* No.39 (1990).
13. The Commission Decision of 85/381/EEC is published in the Official Journal for 1985, L217, p.25: the joined cases 281, 283–285 and 287/85 Germany and Others v. Commission are reported in [1987] ECR 3203. For an account of this see G. Callovi, 'Regulation of Immigration in 1993: Pieces of the European Community Jig-Saw Puzzle' in *International Migration Review* 26/2 (1993), pp.353–72.
14. Further explanation is given in E. Guild, *Protecting Migrants' Rights*, CCME Briefing Paper No.10, Brussels, undated (Churches Committee for Migrants in Europe).
15. SEC (92) 877 6 May 1992.
16. In 1985 the Commission had proposed a directive on the 'Easing of Controls at intra-Community Frontiers' (OJ C 47, 19 Feb. 1985 as amended by OJ C 131, 30 May 1985) which encountered considerable resistance in the Council of Ministers and was later dropped. The Commission also brought a case against the Belgian government to the ECJ regarding police checks at the Belgian border to see if Belgian nationals were carrying identity cards. The ECJ held that Belgium was not violating EC law but that the position would have been viewed differently if the checks had been carried out in a systematic or arbitrary or unnecessarily constricting way (Case 321/87).
17. Communication of the Commission on the abolition of controls of persons at intra-Community borders, COM (88) 640 final, 7 Dec. 1988.
18. The Palma Document is published in full in the House of Lords Select Committee on the European Communities, *1992: Border Control of People*, 22nd Report of Session 1988–89 (HL Paper 90), pp.55–64.
19. The definitive statement of the UK position was given by Douglas Hurd, as Home Secretary, in *Hansard*, HC Debates 4 May 1989, col. 395 et seq.
20. See, e.g., the Surinder Singh case (Case No. C 370/90) where the ECJ gave judgement on 7 July 1992 against the UK government. The case is reported in the EC Official Journal and in the law report of *The Times*, 31 Aug. 1992, as *R.*v. *Immigration*

Appeal Tribunal and Surinder Singh Ex Parte Secretary of State for the Home Department.

21. See Simon Bulmer and Wolfgang Wessels, *The European Council* (London: Macmillan, 1987).
22. The WGI usually meets formally twice a year.
23. For further discussion of the Schengen Agreement, see Michael Spencer, *1992 and All That: Civil Liberties in the Balance* (London: Civil Liberties Trust, 1990); Monica den Boer, 'Schengen: Intergovernmental Scenario for European Police Co-operation', Working Paper No5 in series 'A System of European Police Co-operation After 1992', (Dept. of Politics, Edinburgh Univ., 1991); H. Meijers *et al.* (eds.), *Schengen: Internationalisation of central chapters of the law on aliens, refugees, privacy, security and the police* (Deventer: Kluwer, 1991); and A Pauly (ed.), *Les Accords de Schengen: Abolition des frontières intérieures ou menace pour les libertés publiques?* (ELPA, Maastricht, 1993).
24. A parallel convention on asylum, linked to the Dublin Convention, is also under discussion with third countries such as Sweden.
25. The draft External Frontiers Convention is not officially a published document, a fact which caused Mr Kenneth Clarke, as UK Secretary of State for Home Affairs, considerable embarrassment in July 1992 (*Guardian*, 2 July 1992). The unpublished version of this draft Convention prepared by the WGI secretariat in Brussels is dated 24 June 1991 and referenced as SN 2528/91 WGI 822.
26. The complex dispute between the UK and Spain shows little sign of being resolved and may leave the External Frontiers Convention unsigned indefinitely. Compromise proposals from the Portuguese presidency (reported in the *Independent on Sunday*, 29 May 1992) appear not to have found favour. The Gibraltar government is meanwhile in dispute with the UK government over the terms of an EC air transport liberalisation measure and is threatening to restrict work permits given to UK, but not to other EC nationals (*The European*, 15–18 July 1993).
27. Antonio Cruz, 'Carrier sanctions in four Community states' in *Nederlands Turistenblad*, 31 Jan. 1991, Afl.5, pp179–88. See also Antonio Cruz, *Carrier Sanctions in Five Community States: Incompatibilities between International Civil Aviation and Human Rights Obligations*, CCME Briefing Paper No. 4, Brussels, 1991 (Churches Committee for Migrants in Europe).
28. Further discussion of the issue of intergovernmentalism in this context can be found in P. Boeles, 'Schengen and the rule of law' in Meijers *et al.* (note 23) 1991; Antonio Cruz, 'Schengen, ad hoc Immigration Group and other European Intergovernmental Bodies', CCME Briefing Paper 12, Brussels, 1993 (Churches Committee for Migrants in Europe); David O'Keeffe, 'The Schengen Convention: A Suitable Model for European Integration?', *Yearbook of European Law*, Vol.11, 1991, pp.185–219; and in the House of Lords Select Committee on the European Communities, *Community Policy on Migration*, 10th Report of Session 1992–93 (HL Paper 35) passim.
29. For a record of the communiqués issued after each meeting of the European Council see the *Bulletin of the European Communities*, usually for June and Dec. each year.
30. See Luise Drüke, 'Refugee Protection in the Post Cold War Europe. Asylum in the Schengen and EC Harmonization Process' in A. Pauly (ed.), *Les Accords de Schengen. Abolition des frontières intérieures ou menace pour les libertés publiques?* (Maastricht, 1993, pp.105–69).
31. OECD, *The Future of Migration,* (Paris, 1989). Also OECD, *Migration: the demographic aspects* (Paris, 1991).
32. See, e.g., Edward Mortimer, 'The immigrants we need' in the *Financial Times*, 16 Oct. 1991, and the report of the findings of the IFO institute for economic research in Munich on the economic effects of immigration into Germany given by Dominic Spencer in *The European*, 1 July 1993.
33. Remarks by Nafis Sadik, director of the UN Population Fund, accompanying publication of a UN population survey quoted in *The Times*, 7 July 1993.

34. See Philip (note 9, 1991).
35. John Carvel, 'EC Schengen Group to End Border Posts', *Guardian*, 6 Sept. 1993, and David Buchan, 'EC delay on ending passport checks', *Financial Times*, 19 Oct. 1993.
36. Italy joined the Schengen group in 1990, its membership application having been delayed while the five founder members sought guarantees about the robustness of Italy's external and internal controls. Spain and Portugal joined the Schengen group and Greece became an observer in 1991.
37. Martin Baldwin-Edwards and Bill Hebenton, 'Will SIS be Europe's 'Big Brother'?' in Malcolm Anderson and Monica den Boer (eds.), *Policing Across National Boundaries*, (London: Pinter, forthcoming).
38. See John Carvel, 'British Police Frozen out of EC Databank', in *Guardian*, 6 Sept. 1993, and official responses in the following day's editions.
39. See Colin Brown and Annika Savill, 'Britain to take 4000 Refugees' in *The Independent*, 1 Dec. 1992, and other press reports following the WGI meeting at Copenhagen.
40. *Treaty on European Union*, Title VI.
41. See Bulletin of the EC, 1992 No.12 for the full version of the Edinburgh Summit Communiqué, pp.7–40 (esp. pp.25–7). The first protocol of the *Treaty on European Union* enables in addition Denmark to maintain its existing legislation on the acquisition of second homes by non-Danish nationals in the Kingdom. The 31st declaration of the *Treaty on European Union* (on asylum) commits the Council to consider by the end of 1993 some EU-level harmonisation of member states' asylum policies using the full EU institutional procedures as provided for in Article K9.
42. *Treaty on European Union*, Article 100c.
43. The report on national immigration laws was submitted to the Commission in 1990. The expert group on future Community actions in the immigration field reported in 1991.
44. The EEA Agreement was signed on 2 May 1992 and was intended to come into force on 1 Jan. 1993. However the rejection of the Agreement by Swiss voters in a referendum in Dec. 1992 has caused further negotiations among the remaining six EFTA states (as well as with the EC) who wish to proceed with implementing the Agreement. Some of the preparations for the EEA are discussed in M. Baldwin-Edwards, 'The Context of 1992', *Runnymede Bulletin* No. 252 (Feb. 1992), pp.5–6.
45. Communication of the Commission on the Right of Asylum (EC Doc. 8810/91). Communication of the Commission on the possibility of developing a Common Immigration Policy (EC Doc. 8811/91).
46. It is notable that by summer 1993, before the final ratification and adoption of the Maastricht Treaty, the Commission already had four officials working on immigration and related issues full time.
47. For further discussion of illegal immigration, see W.R. Böhning, 'Immigration and Integration Pressures in Western Europe', in *International Labour Review* 130/4 (1991), pp.445–58.
48. See, e.g, press reports concerning the strengthening of the German eastern external frontiers (Anna Tomforde, 'Germans sign up to curb illegal immigration', The Guardian, 17 Feb. 1993) and in regard to the results of the implementation of the new German asylum laws (Tony Paterson, 'The refugees falling at the final frontier', The European, 8–11 July 1993).
49. See reports by Brown and Savill, (note 39), and by Andrew Marshall, 'EC set to fence out refugees', *The Independent*, 2 Dec. 1992.
50. For a fuller discussion of several of these issues, see the House of Lords Select Committee on the European Communities, 10th Report of Session 1992–93. One academic denotes the situation of immigrants having social rights without political rights as a condition of 'denizenship' – see T. Hammar, *Democracy and the Nation State* (Aldershot: Avebury, 1990).
51. For a fuller discussion on nationality issues in this context see Andrew Evans, 'Nationality Law and European Integration' in *European Law Review* (1991).

Briefing Paper: Naturalisation Policies in Western Europe

RAINER BAUBÖCK and DILEK ÇINAR

Naturalisation procedures have become a hotly debated political issue in several European countries. Frequently naturalisation is seen as the most important legal instrument to facilitate the integration of resident immigrants and of subsequent generations. Discussions and changes focus on the following issues: *ius sanguinis* regulations which turn children born in the country into alien citizens; dual citizenship; immigration rights and free admission to citizenship for *Aussiedler* (ethnic Germans from Central and Eastern Europe) and automatic acquisition for children born from alien parents in France at reaching majority. The new French government has changed legislation which abandoned this latter right. Before this recent change, acquisition of French citizenship at majority by those born in France was automatic unless it was explicitly rejected, whereas now a positive declaration of intent has to be made. At the same time, a broad political campaign is unfolding in Germany demanding some form of *ius soli* and acceptance of dual nationality. Switzerland has recently amended its citizenship law so as to allow the retaining of a previous citizenship in naturalisations. In the Netherlands, since January 1992 renunciation of former citizenship is no longer required and an amending bill is currently under discussion.[1] This brings these two countries in line with the traditional immigration states USA, Canada and Australia and with other Western European states such as the United Kingdom and France which have generally allowed the acquisition of several nationalities. Among Western European immigration states Germany, Austria and Luxemburg now remain as the major examples of a strict renunciation requirement, while Sweden has more or less quietly accepted dual nationalities in many cases. The Council of Europe Convention of 1963, aiming at the reduction of cases of multiple nationality, has been somewhat watered down by a second protocol issued for ratification recently and there may be further and more substantial revisions in the near future.

Citizenship rights and naturalisation of immigrants have also found more attention in political science. Both comparative research and theoretical reflection on this subject have flourished in recent years. Our own efforts take as a starting point the idea, proposed among others by

TABLE 1

NATURALISATIONS AND NATURALISATION RATES IN SOME EUROPEAN STATES

thousands

COUNTRY	residence requirement	dual nationality	1990	1991	1990 %	1991 %
Austria	10 years	no	9.2	11.4	2.2	2.2
Belgium[1]	5 years	yes	8.7	8.5	0.9	0.9
Switz.	12 years	yes	8.7	8.8	0.8	0.7
Germany[2]	10 years	no	20.2	27.3	0.4	0.5
"			101.4	141.6	(1.9)	(2.4)
France[3]	5 years	yes	88.5	95.7	2.5	2.7
"			65.0	72.2	(1.8)	(2.0)
Netherl	5 years	yes	13.6	30.1	2.0	4.1
Sweden[4]	5 years	(yes)	16.8	27.7	3.5	5.6
UK	5 years	yes	57.3	58.6	3.0	3.3

* Naturalisation rates are calculated as naturalisations per 100 resident aliens of the same year; for France, the 1991 rate is calculated as a percentage of resident aliens in 1990.

1 In 1992 46,485 foreigners acquired Belgian citizenship. This is due to the new law of 13.6.91 (in force since 1 January 1992). Since then, children born in the territory acquire citizenship either at birth or by declaration before the age of 12. Thus the rate of acquisitions has increased sixfold between 1991 and 1992.

2 The second row includes acquisition by Aussiedler.

3 The first row includes estimated automatic acquisition at majority to children born in France.

4 **Despite the formal requirement of renunciation of former nationality, toleration of dual nationality is emerging**

Source: SOPEMI 1992, national statistics.

Tomas Hammar[2] and Layton-Henry[3], that resident immigrants enjoy a new kind of 'denizen' status which is characterised by substantial rights of citizenship, with the major exception of national voting rights and access to public office. Elaborating these considerations one can understand that in naturalising immigrants really make two different choices: one is a change in their legal status as formal members of political communities, the other is a change in the bundle of rights which they enjoy with respect to two different states. Choices will be guided by individuals' attempts to maximise those rights which are specific to their particular social position. Given a basic level of residential citizenship (including free access to employment, relative security of residence and social welfare benefits), keeping their external citizenship (e.g., the right to return to, and to inherit or to buy property in, the country of origin) will be more important for many immigrants than acquiring the full internal citizenship of their host countries by naturalisation.

On the other hand, the change of legal status involved in naturalisation is often overcharged with symbolic meanings and requirements of abandoning not only rights tied to the previous citizenship but also cultural affiliations and political loyalties. Immigrants are frequently disinclined to improve their legal position by naturalisation when this involves a devaluation of their biographies and cultural affiliations and when naturalising will not eliminate ethnic and racial discrimination. This may lead to forms of constrained or bounded rationality in which ascribed identities have the effect of excluding certain options from the range of choices considered to be available.[4] It has to be borne in mind that it is first the receiving state's cultural interpretation of its own national identity which creates an obstacle for immigrants. Immigrants see their citizenship of origin as a symbol of their collective identity only where such an interpretation has already been established within the host society. While xenophobia may thus strengthen the immigrants' reluctance to abandon their existing citizenship, a tightening of alien laws especially with regard to security of residence will create a more instrumental attitude towards naturalisation. This is one result of our research among immigrant groups in Austria. Politicians who want to maintain a substantial distance between the rights enjoyed by aliens and by naturalised immigrants often claim that this will emphasise the importance of naturalisation as an act of voluntary commitment towards a receiving state. However, under current conditions the very opposite effect can be observed: for many immigrants naturalisation is simply a way of achieving more security of residence and access to social rights without involving a change in their collective identities and affiliations.

Choices are further influenced by what can be analysed as imposed transaction costs in naturalisation. These include often substantial payments both for renouncing a previous citizenship and for acquiring a new one, as well as other aspects of the procedure which function as deterrents, such as long waiting periods, language tests, the scrutiny of private lives, etc.

This approach raises the question whether stagnant or declining naturalisation rates should be taken as indicators for integration barriers. First, there are some problems of making statistics comparable. Naturalisation rates are calculated as percentages of the resident population of alien citizens. Official counts often cannot be compared across countries because they either include or exclude automatic acquisitions. (The same descendants of immigrants who gain citizenship automati-

TABLE 2

EFFECTS OF POLICY CHANGES ON NATURALISATIONS AND INCLUSION INDICATORS

POLICY CHANGES	Effect on:	
	naturalisation	inclusion
* permitting dual citizenship	+	+
* shorter residence requirements	+	+
* lowering transaction costs	+	+
* abandoning assimilation tests	+	+
* from discretion to entitlement	+	+
* introducing *ius soli*	0	+
*strengthening residential citizenship for aliens	-	+
* enhancing rights of external citizenship for aliens	-	+

cally or by declaration in France, for example, would have to apply for naturalisation in other countries.) Additionally, in *ius sanguinis* states, the number of alien citizens is inflated by adding those born in the country to immigrants in the proper sense of the word. Second, disinterest in naturalisation can also be a result of social and legal integration. A group that illustrates this well is citizens of EC member states living in other EC states or in EFTA countries which intend to join the EC. Their naturalisation rates have mostly declined because they have already obtained, or expect to obtain soon, a secure position of residential citizenship derived from their Union citizenship.

We would like to propose that more reliable and more sophisticated indicators for legal inclusion and exclusion could be developed in further research. These indicators should show how many immigrants and persons of immigrant descent are excluded from basic rights of citizenship at a certain point in time, for how long during their lives they remain excluded in this way, and what are the rates of transition into more secure, or more deprived, positions of citizenship. Policy changes could then be evaluated by assessing whether they contribute to improving these indicators. As suggested in Table 2, the same policy can have different effects on naturalisation rates and on inclusion indicators. On a normative level we would argue that democratic integration policies should optimise inclusion rather than merely focus on naturalisations. While easier naturalisation rules will increase both indicators, legal discrimination of resident alien citizens will increase the latter, but diminish the former. Inclusion should also not be defined only with regard to the receiving society, but must take into account social ties which connect migrants with the state from which they have come. Thus what we call external rights of citizenship such as the right to return to, to own property in, or to vote in one's country of origin should be seen as furthering inclusion within a wider transnational context. In this view, dual nationality is not only a way of facilitating naturalisation in receiving countries but also a way of achieving full citizenship in mobile societies whose boundaries no longer strictly correspond with those of territorial states.

NOTES

1. Ruud Van den Bedem, 'Towards a System of Plural Nationality in the Netherlands: Changes in Regulation and Perceptions', Paper presented at the conference 'From Aliens to Citizens' – redefining the Legal Status of Immigrants in Europe', Vienna, 5–6 Nov. 1993.
2. Tomas Hammar, *Democracy and the Nation-State, Aliens, Denizens and Citizens in a World of International Migration*, (Aldershot: Gower, 1990).
3. Layton-Henry, Zig (ed.) *The Political Rights of Migrant Workers in Western Europe*, (London: Sage, 1990).
4. Rainer Bauböck, 'Optional Citizenship; Articulation of Interests and Identities in Naturalisations', *Innovation* 5/2 (1992), pp.51–68.

Guide to Further Reading

DATA SOURCES

Council of Europe. *People on the Move: New Migration Flows in Europe*. Strasbourg: Council of Europe Press, 1992.

Commission of the European Communities. *Eurobarometer* 39, June 1993, survey of attitudes on immigration.

OECD *Continuous Reporting System on Migration (SOPEMI): Trends in International Migration*. Paris: 1992.

Salt, J., A. Singleton and J. Hogarth. *Europe's International Migrants: data sources, patterns and trends*. HMSO: 1994.

EUROPE

Brubaker, William Rogers, ed. *Immigration and the Politics of Citizenship in Europe and North America*. Lanham, MD: University Press of America, 1989.

Buechler, Hans Christian and Judith-Maria Buechler, eds. *Migrants in Europe: the role of family, labor and politics*. New York: Greenwood Press, 1987.

Collinson, Sarah. *Europe and International Migration*. London: Pinter, 1993.

Council of Europe. *People on the Move: New Migration Flows in Europe*. Strasbourg: Council of Europe Press, 1992.

Hamilton, Kimberly, A., ed. *International Migration and Europe*. Washington, DC: CSIS Books, 1993.

Hammar, Tomas, ed. *European Immigration Policy: A Comparative Study*. Cambridge: Cambridge University Press, 1985.

—— *Democracy and the Nation State: Aliens, Denizens and Citizens in a World of International Migration*. Brookfield, VT: Avebury, 1990.

Hollifield, James Frank. *Immigrants, Markets and States: the Political Economy of Postwar Europe*. Cambridge, MA: Harvard University Press, 1992.

King, Russell, ed. *Mass Migrations in Europe: the Legacy and the Future*. London: Belhaven Press, 1993.

Kritz, M. and Zlotnik, H., eds. *International Migration Systems*. Oxford: Clarendon Press, 1992.

Layton-Henry, Zig, ed. *The Political Rights of Migrant Workers in Western Europe*. London: Sage, 1990.

Martin, Philip L. *The Unfinished Story: Turkish Labour Migration to Western Europe*. Geneva: ILO, 1991.

Messina, Anthony M., Luis R. Fraga, Laurie A. Rhodebeck and Fréderick D. Wright, eds. *Ethnic and Racial Minorities in Advanced Industrial Democracies*. New York: Greenwood Press, 1993.

Papademetriou, Demetrios G. *Europe and Migration*. Washington, DC: Brookings, 1994.

Schnapper, Dominique. *L'Europe des immigrés: essai sur les politiques d'immigration*, Paris, François Bourin, 1992.

— and H. Mendras, eds. *Six Manières d'être européen*. Paris: Gallimard, 1990.

Soysal, Yasemin Nuhoglu. *Limits of Citizenship: Post-national Citizenship in the Contemporary Nation-state System*. Chicago: University of Chicago Press, 1994.

Thranhardt, Dietrich, ed. *Europe – A New Immigration Continent. Policies and Politics in Comparative Perspective*. Munster/Hamburg: Studiem zu Migration un Minderheiten, Bd. 1, Lit Verlag/Westview 1992 and Lit Verlag/Westview, 1994.

COUNTRY STUDIES

FRANCE:

Brubaker, William Rogers, *Citizenship and Nationhood in France and Germany*, Cambridge, MA: Harvard University Press, 1992.

Costa-Lascoux, Jacqueline. *De l'immigré au citoyen*. Paris: La Documentation française, 1990.

Horowitz, Donald and Gérard Noiriel, eds. *Immigrants in Two Democracies: French and American Experience*. New York, New York University Press, 1992.

Ireland, Patrick. *The Policy Challenge of Ethnic Diversity*. Cambridge, MA: Harvard University Press, 1994.

Schnapper, Dominique. *La France de l'integration, sociologie de la nation en 1990*. Paris: Gallimard, 1990.

Silverman, Maxim. *Deconstructing the nation: Immigration, Racism and Citizenship in Modern France*. New York: Routledge, 1992.

Weil, Patrick. *La France et ses étrangers: l'aventure d'une politique de l'immigration, 1938–1991*. Paris: Calmann-Levy, 1991.

Wihtol de Wenden, Catherine. *Les immigrés et la politique: cent cinquante ans d'evolution*. Paris: Presses de la Fondation nationale des sciences politiques, 1988.

GERMANY:

Booth, Heather. *Guestworkers or immigrants? A demographic analysis of the status of migrants in West Germany*. Coventry: Centre for Research in Ethnic Relations, University of Warwick, 1985.

Brubaker, William Rogers, *Citizenship and Nationhood in France and Germany*. Cambridge, MA: Harvard University Press, 1992.

Cohn-Bendit, Daniel and Thomas Schmid. *Heimat Babylon. Das Wagnis deer mulikulturellen Demokratie*. Hamburg: Hoffman und Campe, 1992.

Lee, W.R. and Eve Rosenhaft, eds. *The State and Social Change in Germany, 1880–1980*. New York: St Martin's Press, 1990.

Meier-Braun, Karl-Heinz. *"Gastarbeiter" oder Einwanderer? Anmerkungen zur Auslanderpolitik in der Bundesrepublik Deutschland*. Frankfurt am Main: Ullstein, 1980.

ITALY:

Balbo, Lasura, and Luigi Manconi, eds. *I razzismi reali*. Milan: Feltrinelli, 1992.

Iraci Fedeli, Leone. *Razzismo e immigrazione – il caso Italia*. Rome: Edizioni Acropoli, 1990.

Sergi, Nino and Francesco Carchedi, eds. *Immigrazione straniera a Italia – il tempo dell'integration*. Rome: Edizioni Lavoro, 1991.

UNITED KINGDOM:

Dummett, A. and Andrew Nicol, *Subjects, Citizens, Aliens and Others: Nationality and Immigration Law*. London: Weidenfeld and Nicolson, 1990.
Holmes, Colin. *A Tolerant Country? Immigrants, Refugees and Minorities in Britain*. London: Faber and Faber, 1991.
Katznelson, Ira. *Black Men, White Cities*. New York and Oxford: Oxford University Press, 1973.
Layton-Henry, Zig. *The Politics of Immigration*. Oxford: Blackwell, 1992.
Messina, Anthony. *Race and Party Competition in Britain*. Oxford: Clarendon Press, 1989.
Miles, Robert, *Racism After 'Race Relations'*. London: Routledge, 1993.
Saggar, Shamit. *Race and Politics in Britain*. Hemel Hempstead: Harvester Wheatsheaf, 1992.

AUSTRIA:

Prader, Thomas, ed. *Moderne Sklaven: Asyl- und Migrationspolitik in Osterreich*. Vienna: Promedia, 1992.

UNDOCUMENTED MIGRANTS AND REFUGEES

Castles, Stephen and Mark Miller. *The Age of Migration*. London: Macmillan, 1993.
Joly, Danièle, C. Nettleton and H. Poulton. *Refugees: Asylum in Europe?* London: Minority Rights Group, 1992.
The UN High Commissioner for Refugees. *The State of the World's Refugees: The Challenge of Protection*. New York and London: Penguin, 1993.
US Committee for Refugees. *World Refugee Summary, 1993*. Washington, DC: 1993.
Zolberg, Aristide, A. Sergio and S. Astri, *Escape From Violence: Conflict and the Refugee Crisis in the Developing World*. New York and Oxford: Oxford University Press, 1989.

Notes on Contributors

Martin Baldwin-Edwards is a Research Fellow in the Institute of European Studies, The Queen's University of Belfast and formerly Lecturer in European Social Policy, University of Manchester. He has lectured in both European Economics and European Politics at the Manchester Metropolitan University and the University of Hull. Since 1990 he has been a member of, and contributor to, the Europe-12 Consortium organised by the University of Bonn, whose assessment of the impact of EC membership on member states is published by Frances Pinter in the series *European Community Membership Evaluated*. His publications cover European immigration (both comparative and transnational), the social policies of the EC, and data protection provisions of the Schengen Treaties; currently he is preparing a book analysing the development of European immigration.

Martin A. Schain is Professor of Politics and Chair of the Center for European Studies at New York University. He is the author of *French Communism and Local Power* (1985), co-author of *Politics in France* (1992), *The State, Socialism and Public Policy in France* (1985), *French Politics and Public Policy* (1980) and *European Society and Politics* (1976). He has also published numerous scholarly articles and book chapters on politics and immigration in France and Europe, the politics of the extreme Right in France, political parties in France, and trade unions in France. He has taught and lectured in both France and England.

Rainer Bauböck, Dr.Phil., born 1953 in Austria, is Assistant Professor at the Department of Politics, Institute for Advanced Studies, Vienna and lecturer in political science at the University of Innsbruck. His main research interests are migration policies and theories of citizenship, nationalism and ethnicity. He has earlier publications on social and housing policies, and domestic labour exploitation.

Alan Butt Philip is Reader in European Integration at the School of Management, Bath University. His research interests include EC regional policy, EC social and environmental regulation, the implementation of EC law, and the evolution of the single European market. As Associate Fellow of the Royal Institute of International Affairs in

London he has recently researched the problems raised by the removal of internal border controls within the EC. His book *Dismantling European Border Controls* (London: RIIA/Pinter) will appear shortly.

Dilek Çinar, MA, born 1960 in Turkey, was a postgraduate student at the Institute for Advanced Studies (IAS), Vienna from 1988 to 1990. Since 1991 she has been involved in migration research at the Department of Politics at the IAS. Current research interests include naturalisation policies in Western Europe; immigration, multiculturalism and racism; Islam, Fundamentalism and Orientalism.

John Crowley is a Lecturer in Politics at the Institut d'Etudes Politiques in Paris. His current research centres on the political theoretical implications of the 'immigration' issue, specifically in the UK and France. Recent publications include contributions to *Théories du nationalisme: nation, nationalité, ethnicité*, edited by G. Delannoi and P. Taguieff, to *Logiques d'Etats et immigrations*, edited by J. Costa-Lascoux and P. Weil, and to *New Community*.

Thomas Faist is a researcher at the Centre for Social Policy Research at the University of Bremen, Germany. He received his PhD from the New School for Social Research, New York. Currently he is engaged on a comparative study of immigration and welfare states in Western Europe and North America.

Diana Kay is a sociologist, currently living in The Netherlands. She is co-author with Robert Miles of *Refugees or Migrant Workers? European Volunteer Workers in Britain 1945–1951*, (London: Routledge 1992) and of *Chileans in Exile* (Basingstoke: Macmillan 1987).

Robert Miles is Head of Department and Reader in Sociology at the University of Glasgow. He is also Visiting Professor of Sociology at Glasgow Caledonian University. In addition to his books co-authored with Diana Kay and Annie Phizacklea, he has also published *Racism and Migrant Labour* (London: Routledge and Kegan Paul 1982), *Capitalism and Unfree Labour: Anomaly or Necessity?* London: Tavistock 1987), *Racism* (London: Routledge 1989) and *Racism After 'Race Relations'* (London: Routledge 1993).

Mark J. Miller is a Professor of Political Science and International Relations at the University of Delaware. He has served as the assistant editor of the *International Migration Review* since 1984. From 1983 to 1989 he served as the US correspondent to the OECD's committee of migration specialists – SOPEMI – and drafted the *SOPEMI Reports* 1985–1987. Most recently he has co-authored *The Age of Migration* published in 1993 by Macmillan and, in North America, Guilford Publications. He is a graduate of the University of Wisconsin and presently is working on a book entitled *The Quest for Control* looking at efforts to prevent unwanted migration.

Dominique Schnapper is Director of Studies at the Ecole des Hautes Etudes en Sciences Sociales, Paris. She has worked for many years on collective identity, immigration and nationalism. Her publications include *Jewish Identities in Contemporary France* (Chicago, 1983), *Six manières d'être europeén* (edited with H. Mendras, Paris, 1990), *La France de l'integration, sociologie de la nation en 1990* (Paris, 1991) and *L'Europe des immigrés, essai sur les politiques d'immigration* (Paris, 1992).

John W.P. Veugelers is currently a PhD candidate in sociology at Princeton University. His dissertation provides an historical-comparative analysis of the rise of France's *Front National.*

Patrick Weil is a professor at the Institut d'Etudes Politiques de Paris and at the University of Paris IX. His PhD, from the Institut d'Etudes Politiques de Paris examined French immigration policy in 1974–88. Publications include *La France et ses Etrangers* (Paris: Calman-Lévy, 1991) and co-edited with Jacqueline Costa-Lascoux, *Logiques d'État et Immigrations* (Paris: KIME, 1992).

Catherine Wihtol de Wenden is Director of Research with the CNRS at the Centre d'Etudes et de Recherches Internationales, Paris. She is the author of *Les Immigrés et la politique* (Paris: Presses de la FNSP, 1988) and has edited *La citoyenneté* (1988) and *Les Immigrés et la cité: expériences européennes* (1993). She has published extensively on immigration and politics in France, and also has conducted several pieces of field research.

Rudiger Wischenbart was born in 1956 in Austria and studied German and French literature at Graz University, from which he obtained a PhD in 1983. Currently he is a journalist working for the Austrian Broadcasting Corporation and also works as a documentary journalist for several Austrian and German newspapers, focusing on central and southeastern Europe. Publications include *Literarischer Wiederaufbau in Österreich 1945–1949* (1983) and *Karpaten. Die dunkle Seite Europas* (1992). A new book on European frontiers to the southeast, *Europe's Ende*, will appear in 1994.

Index

QM LIBRARY
(MILE END)

- focusing on
illegal immigration / asylum seeker /

- other factors on the flow of ~~[illegible]~~ movement of people